P9-BYQ-640

COACHING HOCKEY SUCCESSFULLY

SPECIAL USA HOCKEY EDITION

Dennis "Red" Gendron
with
Vern Stenlund

Human Kinetics

ISBN: 0-7360-4636-4

Copyright © 2003 Dennis Gendron

All rights reserved. Except for use in a review, the reproduction or utilization of this work in any form or by any electronic, mechanical, or other means, now known or hereafter invented, including xerography, photocopying, and recording, and in any information storage and retrieval system, is forbidden without the written permission of the publisher.

Managing Editor: Wendy McLaughlin; **Assistant Editors:** Dan Brachtesende and Kim Thoren; **Copyeditor:** Barb Field; **Proofreader:** Coree Clark; **Graphic Designer:** Nancy Rasmus; **Graphic Artists:** Kim McFarland and Brian McElwain; **Cover Designer**: Jack W. Davis; **Photographer (cover):** © Monty Rand; **Photographer (interior):** Tom Roberts; **Illustrator:** Craig Newsom; **Indexer:** Sharon Duffy; **Printer:** Versa Press

Quote on page 79 comes from Ken Dryden's *The Game,* published by NY Times Co.: New York

Special USA Hockey Edition

Printed in the United States of America

10 9 8 7 6 5 4 3 2

Human Kinetics
Web site: www.HumanKinetics.com

United States: Human Kinetics
P.O. Box 5076
Champaign, IL 61825-5076
800-747-4457
e-mail: humank@hkusa.com

Canada: Human Kinetics
475 Devonshire Road, Unit 100
Windsor, ON N8Y 2L5
800-465-7301 (in Canada only)
e-mail: orders@hkcanada.com

Europe: Human Kinetics
107 Bradford Road
Stanningley
Leeds LS28 6AT, United Kingdom
+44 (0)113 255 5665
e-mail: hk@hkeurope.com

Australia: Human Kinetics
57A Price Avenue
Lower Mitcham, South Australia 5062
08 8277 1555
e-mail: liaw@hkaustralia.com

New Zealand: Human Kinetics
Division of Sports Distributors NZ Ltd.
P.O. Box 300 226 Albany
North Shore City, Auckland
0064 9 448 1207
e-mail: blairc@hknewz.com

CONTENTS

Acknowledgments v

Introduction ix

Key to Diagrams x

Part 1   Coaching Foundations

Chapter 1   Characteristics of an Effective Coach 2

Chapter 2   Purpose and Philosophy 9

Chapter 3   Communication and Motivation 15

Part 2   Planning for Success

Chapter 4   Season Plans 24

Chapter 5   Practice Preparation 29

Chapter 6   Building a Feeder System 35

Chapter 7   Two Principles for Better Team Play 39

Part 3   Teaching Play in the Defensive Zone

Chapter 8   Defensive Zone Play 43

Chapter 9   Defensive Zone Drilling 56

Part 4 Teaching Play in the Neutral Zone

Chapter 10   The Neutral Zone and Transition 78

Chapter 11   Neutral Zone and Transition Drilling 83

Part 5 Teaching Play in the Offensive Zone

Chapter 12   Offensive Zone Skills and Strategies................ 111

Chapter 13   Offensive Zone Drilling...................................... 131

Part 6 Coaching in Games

Chapter 14   Special Teams Play 160

Chapter 15   Bench Coaching, Analysis, and Scouting 212

Resources 221

Index.. 223

About the Authors 227

ACKNOWLEDGMENTS

The contents of this book are attributable to a lifetime of experiences in the game of hockey and sports in general. All of the people acknowledged contributed in one way or another to some aspect of this book directly or indirectly.

First and foremost, I must acknowledge the most important people in my life: my loving and completely supportive wife, Janet, and our two daughters, Katelyn and Allison. Without their patience and support, this project and all my adventures in the hockey world over the last 20 years would have been impossible. My parents, Frank and especially my late mother, Amy Gendron, also deserve credit, for it was they who afforded me opportunity to play hockey as a child and supported me through my college years.

Many players, coaches, and peers have given me the opportunity to develop and achieve as a player and coach. Back in Berlin, New Hampshire (once called Hockey Town USA), coaches like Husky Poirier and Albie Brodeur had a profound impact on me. Some of the coaches in other sports—Mark Tilton, Mike Walsh, Dan Brigham and Rusty Ross—influenced my thinking in coaching and elements of many of their philosophies reside within these pages.

The two college hockey coaches I had the good fortune to play for Mickey Goulet and Bill Beaney—both who gave me my first truly keen insights into the game.

While we lived in St. Albans, Vermont, much of what I learned firsthand as a coach and the success our teams had can be attributed to many of the fine players, coaches, and teachers found in that community. Bob Ashton, Chet Massa, and Marty Wennar had the faith to give me a chance as a high school head coach. Mr. Ashton's support as director of athletics, in my early years, was vital. The players I worked with did more for my development and career than anyone. As a coach you develop credibility through winning and many of the players who found a way to get the big wins in the big games pushed my career along. I can't name them all but there are a few I would like to mention: Mike Hodet, the late Jamie Jackson, Tim Vallee, Brian Bliss, Jeff Roberts, Tim Trombley, Toby Ducolon, John LeClair, Mark Toof, Jeremy Benoit, the late Gary Larose, Sami Lehtinen, Gary Smith, the Cioffi boys (Luke and John), the Dukas twins (Jerry and Gary), and many more. My teaching and coaching colleagues at St. Albans were of enormous value to me: Tom McDonald, Paul Bilodeau, Dr. Henry Tulip, the late Jim Bashaw, John Beerworth, Dave Peterson, Ken Fairchild, and Dan Marlow.

During those years in St. Albans I also had the good fortune to become involved in USA Hockey, where I was given an opportunity to coach international hockey and administer the Coaching Achievement Program in New England. Armand Desrosiers, Larry Reid, the late Dave Peterson, Bob O'Connor, Keith Allain, Dick Emahiser, Keith

v

Blase, the late Bob Johnson, Art Berglund, Lou Vairo, Walt Kyle, Al Globensky, Gary Firco, Jimmy Dunn, John Hamre, and the late Kevin Kodalen all had a hand in shaping my career.

I also had the good fortune of working with and learning from some of the great college hockey coaches in our country: Tim Taylor, Terry Meagher, Bob Gaudet, Jim Torterella, Ben Smith, Doug Woog, Jay Leach, Mike Sertich, and Mike Gilligan to name a few.

The people at the University of Maine gave me an enormous opportunity to coach at the highest level of college hockey and learn from two of the greatest college coaches of all time, Shawn Walsh and Grant Standbrook. While there I had the additional good fortune of working with other great coaches like Tim Whitehead, Campbell Blair, Bruce Major, and Guy Perron. As was the case in St. Albans, Vermont great players make great coaches, and the success those players created had a profound impact on my ability to move up the ladder in the coaching ranks.

While at the University of Maine I began working for Huron Hockey Schools during the summer months. I was fortunate enough to meet and learn from a whole new set of terrific hockey men: Paul O'Dacre, Ted Sator, Rick Comley, Casey Jones, Gene Riley, John Markell, and Newell Brown, among countless others.

The New Jersey Devils, its management team, the fine coaches, players, and staff were perhaps the greatest teachers of the game in my entire career. Just having the opportunity to work for one of the premier professional hockey organizations is the equivalent of studying for a PhD in hockey. Lou Lamoriello, Dr. John McMullen, Jacques Lemaire, Larry Robinson, Jacques Caron, Viacheslav Fetisov, Robbie Ftorek, Dave Conte, Bob Hoffmeyer, and John Cunniff contributed immensely to my development and very directly to the pages of this work. I cannot thank them enough.

The photo session for this book was conducted in Ann Arbor, Michigan, home of USA Hockey's National Team Development Program. Without the efforts of Doug Palazzari, Scott Monaghan, coaches Mike Eaves, Moe Mantha, and the players of our National Team Development Program, the book would look much different and be far less enjoyable to peruse.

Finally, I must acknowledge the fine people of Human Kinetics whose professionalism and support made this text possible. In particular, the work of Dr. Vern Stenlund, whose keen understanding of the game, coaching, and outstanding ability in the field of scholarly works is acknowledged with utmost gratitude.

—*Red Gendron*

It was a great pleasure and thrill for me to be invited into this project for a number of reasons. Allow me to acknowledge some of those reasons, in the form of people, at this time.

First, to Red Gendron, let me say that helping you with this book has been a tremendous learning experience for me. As I read through the various drafts of component chapters, I realized just how little I really knew about the game. For my money, this is the most comprehensive hockey book I have ever come across, and it is a credit to Red and his expertise. Old friend, it has been an honor!

To Wendy McLaughlin at Human Kinetics, let me say this: Your humor and understanding, combined with your great professionalism, were truly inspirational. Certainly, you have been transformed into a "hockey person" after our years in the trenches together. Wendy, this project would not have happened without you.

To Tom Roberts, our photographer. Tom, by now you must be considered a leader in hockey photography. As with all the books we've done, great job.

And finally, to my old nemesis, Ted Miller, the man who makes things happen at Human Kinetics. Without his vision, this book would have never happened. Without his patience, we would have outlived numerous deadlines! And without his friendship, the world would be a gloomier place. Thanks Ted...you're the man!

—*Vern Stenlund*

INTRODUCTION

Welcome to *Coaching Hockey Successfully*. This book is written primarily for hockey coaches who work with players aged 16 to 20. Coaches who are developing players in younger age groups will also find this text useful; however, be aware that some of the materials in this book may be too advanced for younger age levels. Therefore, as you read through these pages, you should be gleaning information that is meaningful and age/skill-level-appropriate to your own coaching situation.

Over the past 20 years, I've coached at a variety of levels, including high school, national teams in international competition, U.S. college hockey, minor professional hockey, and in the NHL. In addition, most of the past 20 summers have been filled by working at hockey schools with players from the earliest stages of their development right through to those competing at the most accomplished levels of the game. Through the years, I have attended countless hockey symposiums as both participant and presenter at venues all over North America and Europe. During this time, I have had the good fortune to work with and learn from some of the finest coaches in North America. This broad spectrum of coaching experiences and relationships is the foundation on which this book has been written.

No coach should ever presume that his way is the "right way" or the only way to go about the process of coaching, irrespective of the sport. Certainly, great coaches have greatly influenced my own coaching philosophy, even as my personal views have continued to evolve. After all, there are few absolutes in coaching, and where absolutes do exist, multiple methods are often available to arrive at successful outcomes.

Within these pages you will find information that covers a wide spectrum of coaching topics, including organization, philosophy, communication, motivation, advanced skills and tactics, systems, special teams, bench coaching, scouting, analysis, and evaluation. In areas where gaps exist, the reader is provided with supplemental reading suggestions through the resource section at the back of the book. In some cases, these suggestions include videotapes rather than written text. Successful coaches will tell you that text alone is no substitute for the power of videotape, particularly when it applies to teaching and learning technical skills.

Here's hoping you will enjoy the read.

KEY TO DIAGRAMS

X or O	Player/opposing player/pair of players
(C/L)	Coach or leader
D	Defenseman
F	Forward
R	Receiver
F^1 F^2	Designated forward
(G)	Goaltender
→————→	Forward skating
∿∿∿∿→	Forward skating with puck
∞∞∞∞	Backward skating
⊙⊙⊙⊙	Backward skating with puck
= ‖	Stopping
♇	Turns
♇	Tight turns
⌒	Pivots (forward to backward, backward to forward)
- - - -→	Passing
⇒	Shooting
∴∙	Pucks
△	Pylons or cones
⌐	Hockey stick

Part 1

COACHING FOUNDATIONS

Chapter
1

CHARACTERISTICS OF AN EFFECTIVE COACH

From time to time, coaches find themselves confronted with any of a number of dilemmas that must be addressed and resolved quickly and efficiently. For example, how often have you heard stories about coaches who appeared willing to sacrifice everything for the sake of the win. Unfortunately, sometimes we are talking about mite-level coaches who are more inclined to look at the scoreboard than at the development track their players are on. This kind of coaching dilemma calls for some initial soul searching as to what your principles are with respect to your coaching duties. Perhaps the best way to begin this process is by first defining the key attributes we might identify with any effective coach.

Specifically, what are the characteristics of an effective coach? For starters, it's safe to say that an effective coach must be the team's main teacher and its top leader. Like the conductor of an orchestra, coaches must see "the big picture," so that all the members of the group perform their roles at the proper time and with skill. A coach is like an architect who designs and builds a safe, positive, productive environment. A coach must be a key visionary for the team and should become a communicator of ideas, both great and small. Coaches should be fierce competitors, yet at the same time possess the empathy and understanding of a parent. An effective coach should become an authority in the areas of skills, tactics, and strategy, all the while serving as a guardian of the integrity of the game. Certainly, a coach is all this and probably much, much more.

Coaches must be able to see the big picture and communicate clearly to players.

How do you become an effective hockey coach? In concept, it all sounds so simple. It means working hard every day. It means a relentless commitment to learning from other coaches, daily situations, players, books, videotapes, clinic work, and other sources of information. Simply put, it means a perpetual commitment to self-improvement. As the great football coach Lou Holtz once said, "No one ever stays the same . . . you either get better or you get worse."

If the concept of how to become an effective coach is simple, the realities of execution are far more difficult. It is a process and not an event—a journey and not merely a destination. It is humility following success and persistence following failure. It is passion and emotion properly mixed with patience and logic. The work involved requires a massive commitment that borders on total immersion. Those who become successful hockey coaches put in the necessary time and effort relentlessly.

Is coaching an art, or is it science? Are some born with the skills needed to achieve as coaches, or are these skills developed over time? In reality, it is probably a bit of both. For example, some coaches are naturally gifted as public speakers, while others have to work at their oratory skills. One coach may be strong in organizational skills but weaker in the skills associ-

ated with successful bench coaching. Some coaches appear to possess an intuitive understanding of what to say or do in difficult situations, while others must develop this ability through experience and analysis. It's important for coaches to learn where their strengths and weaknesses lie. It is equally important to understand that an area of weakness can be turned into a strength if the coach is willing to expend the effort required to improve. Either way, coaching skills can be learned, refined, and improved through the prerequisite of hard work!

In the following pages, I describe three component areas that any coach at either end of the experience spectrum might wish to review and consider as a means of establishing solid coaching practices. These components and their associated subthemes each represent the thoughts of many of the finest coaches in the game as they relate to developing a foundation for your role as coach.

COMPONENT 1:
THE COACH AS TEACHER

Coaching and teaching are synonymous. A coach must have a solid fundamental repertoire of teaching skills and know how and when to apply each. The purpose of teaching is to promote learning, and in hockey, learning can be defined as a change in behavior on the part of individual players that affects the culture of the team. An effective coach is someone who can motivate players to exhibit desired behaviors, with the team becoming the ultimate beneficiary. However, we all know that some teachers are more successful than others at achieving these outcomes. How can we as coaches give ourselves the greatest possible opportunity to become effective teachers? The answer can be traced to any coach's understanding and abilities within the broad areas of preparation, delivery, and assessment. Let's take a look at some "tricks of the trade" that will greatly affect these three areas in a positive way.

Preparation

As with successful teaching, successful coaching requires thoughtful preparation. The concept of preparation consists of many detailed areas including: time spent thinking about desired outcomes; what will be presented to your players; how this content will be presented; how it should be drilled; how the eventual outcomes will be analyzed; and most important, how the coach believes it will be received. Sometimes the best lesson plans fail to achieve the desired results because the players' ability to receive the information and execute efficiently is not accurately evaluated.

Careful planning and consideration of probable player reactions do not guarantee that a lesson will succeed. Unforeseen circumstances may result in failed teaching/learning situations. You should not be embarrassed about a lesson gone awry. Coaches are allowed to make mistakes too. Mistakes can be minimized, however, and are less likely to reoccur when you have carefully attended to your preparation.

Delivery

Preparation and delivery are equally affected through this first example. As with many coaches, after you have designed your practice for the day, you probably look at your piece of paper and think to yourself, "There it is . . . the Rembrandt of all practice sessions!" It is, in your humble opinion, the ultimate practice plan, something that you have diligently sculpted for the satisfaction of your coaching staff and players alike. Now is the time to "set the table," as you attempt to provide clear information for the work that follows. Before attempting to instruct, you must be certain that you have the complete attention of all your players. This simple, commonsense principle is often lost to the less experienced coach. When you have the full attention of the group or individual, the teaching/learning dynamic can begin. A key point here is to never allow players or assistant coaches to continue conversations once you've demanded attention. Understand that this is vital to your ability to teach effectively. At practice, a simple gimmick that can be used to ensure your players are attentive is to make them take a knee. Demand that they look you in the eye whether you are on the ice, in a dressing room, or at a meeting area. This teaching concept is an absolute must if you intend to create a learning environment within your team.

Learning Over Time

A difficult lesson for many teachers and coaches to grasp and accept is that learning takes time—often more time than you might care to take. We understand the skill sets, concepts, and tactics we teach. It can be difficult to accept that a concept or skill, which seems so simple for us to understand and execute can be so difficult for players to comprehend. As coaches, we want our players to understand and execute immediately. Unfortunately, sometimes learning is simply "lost in time," and a coach must learn to be patient. If the players don't learn immediately, it does not mean you are an ineffective coach, nor are you an unsuccessful coach if you don't immediately learn the multitude of skills required to coach successfully.

Learning Through Different Styles

Each individual on your team has a unique learning style and learning curve. Some players

Coach O'Connor explains tactics as players take a knee.

may be able to learn by simply listening to an explanation. My experience has been that most successful coaches eventually become skilled auditory learners. This means that you can listen to a verbal explanation of a drill, for example, and then visualize how it is supposed to look upon execution. Many of the individuals on your team may lack this ability. Some may require a chalkboard session. As with auditory learning, a degree of visualization skill is required to transform the lines, letters, and arrows into a clear mental picture of how it will occur on the ice.

Other players may require a physical demonstration to understand a teaching point. This could be a walk-through of your team's system of play in selected situations or a demonstration of a skill technique. For example, assume you have to demonstrate how a defenseman walks toward the middle of the ice along the offensive blue line with the puck during a power play situation. The easiest way for your players to understand this skill is to watch you perform it accompanied by an explanation of why the skill is important. If you or your assistant coach cannot demonstrate this because your own skill level is inadequate, utilize a skilled player or an instructional videotape. If you cannot find the desired skill properly demonstrated on an instructional tape, try taping a college or professional game from television and finding the desired skill to show your players.

In 1986, our coaching staff at Bellows Free Academy wanted to introduce a new power play alignment and associated play options to our players. We had a copy of a power play tape that coach Bob Johnson had used as part of a symposium presentation he made on the same topic. Coach Johnson's tape of his Calgary Flames team on the power play best illustrated what we as a staff wanted to accomplish with our own team. We implemented the alignment rather quickly and with great success and remain convinced that Coach Johnson's tape accelerated the learning process significantly.

To accommodate the many different learning styles, you as coach must be prepared to incorporate various teaching styles. This way, you will discover what works best for developing each topic and what works best for each individual. Depending on the complexity of what is being taught, it is possible that any approach will work for almost any player. If you vary your style of presentation, you reduce the likelihood of creating a boring environment. How do you vary your presentation methods? At times, the coach simply talks to the team about desired outcomes. Sometimes it means an on-ice demonstration. At other times, it may mean a chalkboard session or a review of performance using videotape. It might include bringing in a famous athlete to speak to the team or having a sport psychologist make a presentation to drive home important mental aspects of playing the game well.

Lastly, remember that all questions are valid questions! The only dumb question is the one that goes unasked. Model this attitude for your players so that, over time, they will become comfortable with asking you for advice or general information. If you ridicule players for seeking understanding, they will shut off the two-way dynamic that is critical for effective learning. This is a form of respect the teacher/coach must have with all students/athletes. Although some questions may appear to be a waste of time because the answers seem obvious, realize that it may be obvious to everyone except the person asking the question and that their self-esteem may be on the line.

Assessment

Another important concept for successful teaching is recognizing when unpredictable opportunities arise for the teaching/learning dynamic. These opportunities represent what is often referred to as a teaching or coaching "moment." For example, you may have been talking to your team about the importance of not retaliating when opponents use their sticks on your players. During a game, right in front of your bench where all your players have a clear view, an opponent slashes one of your players. Your player doesn't retaliate. At that precise moment, you would be wise to point this out to the team while praising the individual who did not retaliate. Make the player a hero in the eyes of the other team members. Reinforcement through teachable moments has the potential to be a very powerful teaching tool as you attempt to mold attitudes on your bench! Emerson once wrote, "Nothing great was ever achieved without enthusiasm," and I tend to agree, at least within the context of sport. No matter what you are teaching, you had better show your players that you are interested and excited about what you are preaching and delivering. If you are enthusiastic about the material, your players are more likely to be enthusiastic about learning it. In addition, you should be the number-one believer in the material you present. If you appear uncertain about the value of your lesson plan, this will surely be evident to your players, and the results probably won't be positive.

This section of the chapter has reflected on the coach as a teacher. Remember that teaching is the single most important coaching skill and represents the true essence of coaching. If your teaching skills are solid, it will compensate for inefficiencies in other areas of your coaching repertoire. Without solid teaching mechanics, your potential for becoming an effective and successful coach is greatly diminished.

COMPONENT 2: THE COACH AS LEADER

Let's begin with a simple yet extremely difficult question to answer: What is leadership? Yes, there is a dictionary definition, and I've no doubt that a hundred different people would provide a hundred different responses to this question. For our purposes, and given my own experiences within the coaching profession, I choose to define *leadership* as "having the ability to guide and motivate a group toward a common goal or goals." When you assume a position of leadership, you assume the ultimate responsibility for the well-being of the individuals in your group and the overall responsibility for the group achieving its goals.

You can gain insight into leadership by reading books written by and about the great business, political, and military leaders of history. You can gain insight by reading books written by and about successful coaches. You should read as much as possible about successful leaders, past and present, as this will provide information that will assist in your effort to become a better coach. This type of reading

Every coach has a unique coaching style.

must remain properly grounded with the notion that, first and foremost, you must be yourself. Never apply principles and tactics used by other leaders that don't fit your own personality and leadership style. Players will recognize this, and you will appear insincere. It could become a case of good intentions leading you down the path to disaster.

Every coach has his or her own leadership style. Some coaches lead in a very direct and dictatorial manner. Some are demagogues, appealing to the emotions of their athletes. Others lead by developing a respect from athletes through their knowledge of the game and superior intellect. Still others use a cooperative and democratic approach, involving the athletes in the decision-making process and subsequently allowing players to feel a greater sense of ownership in the team. The key is to find your own style, then develop it to its full potential.

One popular theory on leadership is called "Contingency Theory" or "Situational Leadership Theory." Subscribers to the principles of Contingency Theory would suggest that

those who have risen to lead armies to victory, nations to greatness, and teams to championships did so because they had the right leadership style and skills for the given circumstances. They also believe that under different circumstances, those same individuals might have failed, or that others without similar skills would have failed in the same situation.

Contingency Theory has some relevance to modern professional sports. Why is it that a team can have basically the same athletes in successive years, change coaches, and have very different results? The answer may be that if you have the right coach for the right players at the right time, the team is more likely to succeed.

Again, the most important thing in coaching is to be true to yourself. You should not try to lead like Franklin Roosevelt, George Patton, Bobby Knight, Vince Lombardi, Scotty Bowman, or anyone else. However, you should constantly work at developing new leadership skills, something that is consistent with Contingency Theory. Otherwise, the likelihood of becoming a victim of "wrong coach, wrong time, wrong place" is increased. Coaches must try to learn from others without compromising their own style. Incorporate what you can and discard what cannot or does not work for you. The more you know about leadership, about its varying styles and techniques, the better prepared you will be to meet the challenges of the dynamic environment that is modern coaching. The resource section of this book contains a list of readings specific to leadership and coaching leadership that are highly recommended.

Another important principle of leadership is to lead by example, sometimes called role modeling. If you exhibit solid behaviors and deportment, it will be easier for your players to do the same. If you ask for good work habits from your players, you had better work hard yourself. If you ask for discipline regarding referees' calls, you had better be in control of your own emotions on the bench. When players see that a coach is committed to following his or her own principles, they are more likely to do the same. That, in part, constitutes effective leadership!

To summarize our discussion on leadership, consider this simple yet classic thought: "Without a gardener, there is no garden." Coaches must be prepared to demonstrate leadership qualities so that their own "garden" will flourish over time. If not you, then who will lead your team?

COMPONENT 3: THE COACH AS TECHNICIAN

The third component associated with becoming an effective coach relates to your becoming an expert technician with respect to the game. You have to be knowledgeable in the areas of skill development, tactics and concepts, and systems and strategy. You must know not only how your team's system works, but also how other systems of play work. You should know how the human body functions specific to the rigors of hockey. Therefore, you need to understand the principles of conditioning and nutrition. You should understand how collections of individuals become a team—how the whole becomes far greater than the sum of the parts. As you read deeper into this book, you will notice that much of the content increasingly focuses on the technical aspects of coaching hockey. With that in mind, we will leave this aspect of coaching for deeper analysis in later chapters.

In summary, this portion of the book examined the three vital components of coaching: the coach as *teacher,* the coach as *leader,* and the coach as *technician.* Developing strengths within each of these areas will assist you greatly in becoming an effective coach and role model for all your players, now and into the future.

Chapter 2

PURPOSE AND PHILOSOPHY

Coaching at the high school level has traditionally been a relatively secure job. A team's win/loss record has seldom been the deciding factor in school administrators determining whether or not a coach is to be retained. In contrast, many junior-level teams in Canada have historically held their coaches accountable for won/lost records, often with disastrous outcomes for the coach! For high school coaches, things are beginning to change. Coaches must understand that more pressure to win is being applied at all levels. To achieve longevity at a school or with a junior team, coaches have to be adaptable. Flexibility in both leadership and coaching styles has become essential for coaches who want to improve their chances of retaining their positions. With this as a backdrop, let's examine your own unique purposes and philosophy with respect to coaching. By first understanding why and where you are headed, you can dramatically increase your chances of getting there in a productive way. Otherwise, as the famous quote suggests, "Any road will do if you've no idea where you're headed."

PURPOSE

Why does your team exist, and what purposes does the team serve? Answering these questions is an important first step toward developing a philosophy of coaching that will guide you through good times and bad. Most teams exist for multiple purposes. For example, from my experience at the pro level with the Albany River Rats, I can see three main purposes for the team to exist:

1. To have players ready to join the New Jersey Devils on a "just-in-time" basis
2. To develop players who will be useful to the Devils in future seasons
3. To win, developing winning attitudes and the expectation of winning performance among players

Are there other reasons for this team to exist? Certainly there are, including such things as providing entertainment for the community and region in and around Albany, providing employment opportunities for those positions associated with the operation of a professional team, and so on. However, from our organizational perspective, the first three purposes remain the key to our existence.

Other situations and levels of play might dictate quite separate purposes for continuing to operate. For instance, a major junior hockey team may exist for the purposes of making money, developing players for professional hockey careers, and providing entertainment for the community. If the team doesn't win enough—if they don't do well enough at the box office—the coach is in great danger of being replaced. From the coach's perspective, the fundamental purpose of the team may be development of players for careers at higher levels. However, this may not be the most important element for the ownership. It is vital that junior coaches understand just how important the bottom line is to the team's owners before accepting any coaching position.

A team in the United States Junior Hockey League may exist to generate income and provide athletes with the opportunity to earn college scholarships. A local Junior B team may exist simply to provide competitive opportunities and a chance to enjoy the game. A high school team may exist to extend societal and individual values such as teamwork, community responsibility, respect, discipline, hard work, and commitment. High school teams may also exist in part to develop players for college or junior hockey but at the same time provide entertainment for the community and improved school spirit. As the coach and person in charge, it is your duty to think first about the main purposes for your team's

existence. Once you do so, developing your philosophy within the framework or context of your own situation will be much easier.

As noted in chapter 1, coaches are often faced with the fundamental dilemma of "winning vs. development." The best coaches are those who find a way to win consistently while meeting the individual developmental needs of their players, a difficult task indeed! Remember this piece of wisdom from an old mentor of mine: Almost all the lessons you choose to teach will have greater impact on players if the team wins! Why? Because winning is important, and winning gives credibility to a coach's teachings. Two teams take the ice for each game, and usually one team will win. It might as well be your team. Like it or not, we live in a highly competitive society, and it is important for our youngsters to learn how to work together and find a way to win. Hockey, like other team sports, is a great environment in which to learn these lessons.

PHILOSOPHY

Philosophy, in this case, refers to a fundamental set of principles and beliefs that guide us in the day-to-day operation of our teams. A total philosophy for coaching hockey has three main areas

1. The framework or philosophy of the overall organization
2. Your philosophy about the game itself
3. The philosophy of how to deal with players and how players deal with each other

This third area will be covered in detail in chapter 3, so we will turn our attention to the first two areas described.

Philosophy of the Organization

If you coach a high school hockey team, that team is a part of an overall educational organization that extends far beyond the sporting context. Chances are, certain principles such as "win at all cost" will be incompatible with the larger organization's philosophy. Values like going to class, being a well-behaved student, and maintaining a respectable grade point average are more important than winning hockey games. It may be that some schools will compromise the larger principles in the interest of winning, a situation I will discuss later in this chapter through a personal reflection. This situation probably should not be allowed to occur, but it does. Conversely, if you coach a junior team, selling enough tickets to earn a profit may be a key organizational issue, and therefore winning takes on more importance. Usually, winning teams do better at the turnstiles. In this regard, some coaches and fans argue that fighting helps increase attendance figures. The reality might be that you are philosophically opposed to fighting, but if you intend to coach a junior hockey team in some leagues, you may have to modify your philosophy or seek a different coaching position.

Ideally, the organizational philosophy has already been clearly articulated for all involved. It becomes the cornerstone of all that you do. In difficult times, it is the guiding light showing you the way out of darkness. As alluded to previously, coaching high school hockey usually means being an extension of the school itself. It also means that certain philosophical principles are already in place for you.

The fundamental mission of a school is to prepare students for life after high school. The hope is that students leaving the school are better prepared to be good citizens, to be productive within the community, or perhaps move on to a higher level of schooling. It may mean that they are prepared to succeed in college. Your hockey team is another classroom, another part of the school's curriculum whose purpose is to prepare young people for life after high school. Remember that even at the finest hockey-playing high schools, the vast majority of players never play at a higher level. Besides helping your athletes to be better players, to win games, what else are you providing them with to assist them in life?

Here is a real-life example in answer to that question.

Several years ago I had the pleasure of coaching a player who is now an all-star in the National Hockey League—John LeClair of the Philadelphia Flyers. He was trying out for the Bellows Free Academy hockey team as a freshman. The media is fond of reporting the fact that he was cut from our high school hockey team his freshman year. The implication was that he wasn't good enough, or perhaps that his coach was a poor judge of talent and potential. The reason John was cut as a freshman had nothing to do with his ability as a hockey player. The decision was based on what we thought was best for John as a person at that time. Within the framework of our organizational philosophy, we believed that ninth-graders are not always best served socially by being associated with juniors and seniors in high school.

Whether we like it or not, high school juniors and seniors are often involved in social activities that ninth-graders don't need to be exposed to on a regular basis. John LeClair was ready athletically to play on one of the top two forward lines of our hockey team that season. Without question, he would have helped our team win. He might also have been ready to handle the social pressures that would have come with making the team that year. We simply decided, right or wrong, that it was in John's best interests as a person to play with the town's bantam travel team, to remain with the eighth- and ninth-graders. Looking back, the decision was made easier because of our overall philosophy, and no newspaper article could change our beliefs. In the long run, John probably benefited more . . . but I'll tell you, we sure could have used him that year!

Most schools have formal policies dictated by the high school's administration and the athletic department. Many high school athletic programs require the athlete to sign a contract with respect to appropriate behaviors both on and off the ice. As the coach, you must be aware of all school and athletic department policies and be prepared to enforce them. You may not agree with these policies, but because you and your team are part of a greater educational organization, you must be prepared to live by them. If not, you should consider trying to change such policies using appropriate channels, or you should resign.

When it comes to the philosophy of the school or the hockey program, the coach must be prepared to live up to the standards that have been set, and that is not always easy. The following story highlights an incident that illustrates this point.

We were preparing to play our biggest rival, Misissquoi High, in the final regular season game. Our philosophy was always that players had to be successful students first. If they misbehaved as students, the consequence would be loss of ice time. Misissquoi had planned a pep rally that day. We found out that some of our players were planning to skip classes, drive to our rival school, and raid the pep rally. As it happened, I personally witnessed the players rumored to be heading for Misissquoi in the hallway and warned them against skipping classes for any reason. At practice that afternoon, our athletic director informed me that three of our players had indeed missed classes and had driven to Misissquoi. We had little choice in the matter, so subsequently each of the guilty players was suspended for one game. Unfortunately, all of these kids were seniors.

As is the tradition at most schools and colleges, the seniors are honored before or after the final regular season home game. This meant that the guilty players would be introduced in street clothes and would be somewhat embarrassed before the community. We were under enormous pressure from the parents of those players to allow them to play. Lawsuits were threatened and negative comments were made, but we did not break our own organizational rules and philosophy. What was the outcome, you ask? Well, we lost the game, and a week later we also lost the playoff game. To this day, however, I believe we did the right thing. We were teaching our athletes how to be good citizens. The principle of appropriate behavior was more important than winning. Ironically, one of the players involved in the incident is now an assistant principal in charge of school discipline.

You might wonder how our other players viewed the decision to suspend the three players that day. Rather than bemoan the fact that their chances for success had been diminished, the rest of the team members decided to make the night of the last regular season game very special for all of us. When our seniors were introduced that night, they started a tradition that has remained part of Bellows Free Academy hockey ever since. As their names were called, they skated to the bench area to shake my hand in front of the entire community. When I looked into each of their eyes, I understood that the players respected the decision, that they respected the fact that I was willing to live up to the principle even when it hurt. Did that ruling hurt the team's chances of winning in the state tournament? The answer is a resounding yes. It certainly would have been easier to win the first playoff game at home rather than having to win it on the road. On the other hand, I believe that no team wins unless it is together, unless all its members believe in and adhere to the principles of the program. It's easy to declare the importance of high-minded principles, but it's far more difficult to adhere to them when you know it may mean losing.

What follows is an outline of our hockey team's philosophy at Bellows Free Academy and is included as an example of an organizational framework and set of beliefs. It is provided only as a guideline for coaches within the high school/junior age group. If you have not yet outlined a philosophy for your organization, please consider doing so as a future project for your leadership team. Developing your own unique philosophy is an extremely important exercise.

✓ Students first, hockey players second.

✓ Appropriate behavior and following of the school and team rules are a must.

✓ Punctuality is a must.

✓ We will always be attired as gentlemen on the road and when coming to and from the arena for home games, complete with shirt, tie, and sport coat.

✓ We will attire our team in the finest equipment and uniforms available, always exuding class.

✓ Respect for the authority of the coaches and referees must be maintained.

✓ Respect for and support of teammates is expected at all times.

✓ Hard work and commitment to improvement are expected at all times.

✓ Adherence to the team's system of play is a must at all times.

✓ Discipline in on-ice confrontations is expected at all times.

✓ We will commit to achieving the highest possible speed of execution of play patterns in both practice and games.

✓ We will play with intensity and determination to win in every game.

Develop your own coaching philosophy and stick to it.

Your Own Philosophy About the Game

You as coach need to develop a philosophy about the game itself and how you intend to run your team. Specifically, this refers to how you think the game should be played. For example, do you believe that a patient, controlled style of play is best, or do you want your players to be fast-paced "racehorses" geared toward an "in your face" style of play? While coaching at the high school level, my philosophy regarding playing style emphasized speed and puck pressure—in other words, the racehorse style. Later, while coaching at the University of Maine, we played a similar style. After joining the New Jersey Devils organization, I soon came to appreciate that our playing style philosophy emphasized patience and positioning, a relatively safe, defense-first approach. Different approaches to various aspects of play will be introduced later in the book. Armed with this information, you can decide for yourself, based on your current coaching situation, the best philosophical approach to the game for your team.

Remember that your philosophy, or that of the organization, may need to change over time. Change is often necessary for growth and can be very healthy for an organization if implemented properly. However, you should develop certain principles you believe to be true and of such importance that they will never change. One irrefutable principle that I follow is that a coach must always demand hard work and total commitment to the group from all players and assistant coaches. This principle never changes, is never compromised, and is never negotiable, regardless of the level you find yourself coaching at.

Chapter
3

COMMUNICATION AND MOTIVATION

Any coach who has even the slightest interest in achieving success must become a student of both communication skills and motivational techniques. These two areas combined will greatly influence your effectiveness as a teacher, as well as your ability to say or do the right thing at the right time. In this chapter, we will briefly examine these two key concepts, understanding that volumes have been written on both. We could never begin to illuminate all of the variables associated with each concept, yet within the context of coaching in hockey, you must become aware of certain aspects of both.

COMMUNICATION

The previous chapter was devoted in part to coaching philosophy, and nowhere is this concept more important than with respect to coaching and communication skills. Everything you say as a coach, how you stand, your facial expressions, your body language, are all being interpreted constantly by your players. Your players are always inferring meaning from all that you say and do. An important communication concept to understand is that *what you intend to convey is not always what your athletes have interpreted.*

Some coaches communicate in a dictatorial fashion, while others are kindlier and more cooperative in their approach to communication. Every coach falls somewhere at or between these two extremes. Sometimes coaches who are more cooperative in their approach to communication are criticized for lacking discipline with their teams. This is not necessarily true. Your individual style of communication has little to do with what is demanded of players. A cooperative style is simply a more humane way of communicating to get players to work toward a desired goal. The beauty of this style is that players tend to assume greater ownership of both their personal and team performance. Regardless of their approach, coaches must constantly demand effort and commitment to improvement.

When I began coaching at Bellows Free Academy, my communication style was decidedly dictatorial. There was only one right way, and that was my way. The players responded well to this because we had success immediately. Had we not been successful, I'm certain I would have had to modify my approach. The year was 1981, and most people, including the players, still believed in an ironhanded coaching style. I adopted this style of communication in part because the successful coaches I had played for had been dictators. It was what I knew, and my personality fit this approach nicely. This style was personally preferable as well, because I didn't respect what young players might know about the game and because I lacked the confidence in my own knowledge that would have allowed me to accept challenges to my methods. Finally, I knew that the previous coach had been forced to resign, in part due to a perception that his teams lacked discipline. The best way I knew to instill discipline at that time was to be a harsh and demanding coach. I knew that even if we didn't win, I would be respected using this style.

As the years passed, my respect for players increased, my personal confidence improved, and my overall understanding of communication techniques became more refined. The way players responded to coaching styles also changed. Perhaps the biggest revelation for me was understanding that even though everyone on a team has to be accountable to the same standards, each individual has a preferred way of being treated. To paraphrase the golden rule, we should "treat others as we would like to be treated." Perhaps a more appropriate version specific to communication skills might be to "treat others the way *they* would like to be treated." An effective coach understands the principles of positive and negative reinforcement. Most players want to be recognized positively when they perform well. Another reason they seek to do well is to avoid negative feedback or punishment from the coach. Certainly, communicating satisfaction with a player or the team's performance is very important. At the same time, however, mistakes have to be acknowledged and corrected. If they are not, the team cannot reach its potential. How the coach corrects mistakes is the central issue. Generally, the better approach is to focus on positively reinforcing good play as opposed to constantly providing negative feedback for poor play.

When a player makes a mistake during a game, a coach can handle it in several ways depending on the circumstances of the mistake and the player involved. If the mistake was obvious and the player knows what should have happened, I might choose to say nothing. If the mistake was obvious and is one that the individual has made several times in the past, I may choose to speak more harshly. If the mistake was less obvious, I might quietly ask the player how the situation could have been played out differently. I might choose to whisper a correction in the player's ear, avoiding an embarrassing moment in front of teammates, or I might choose to ignore the moment and sit down with the player after the game and review the play on videotape. There are many ways to communicate criticism without being unduly harsh or negative.

If players are mentally strong and self-confident, they can more easily deal with harsh communication techniques used by the coach. For the more sensitive player, this approach can be destructive. Knowing which approach each of your players responds to best is a key communication strategy. If you choose to deal harshly with a player, never attack personally. You can attack a player's performance, but never their humanity. For example, it's not a bad thing to say something like "That was a terrible play you just made." Never say "You're terrible. How could you make such a bad

Positive feedback is important when working with players on correcting mistakes.

play?" In the first example, the coach is being critical of performance. In the second instance, the criticism is leveled directly at the athlete's humanity. Remember that regardless of the technique you use to correct a player, *the player is ultimately responsible for interpreting your criticism*. You may think that you have been fair, perhaps even gentle, but the player may perceive it as a harsh attack. An effective coach always checks for understanding, making certain that the message delivered was the message received.

We all seek recognition, and each of your players has a different level of need in this regard. Remember that it is important for you to talk with all of your players, not just those who play significant roles. No matter how effective they are or how important their role is on the team, every player must be treated with respect. Having a special meeting with

the lower echelon players from time to time is helpful to them and to the team. When you don't have time to meet with them formally, a pleasant greeting at practice, or perhaps asking how things are going away from the rink, goes a long way for many players. Be aware that if you don't deal positively with these individuals, they can cause disruptions within the team, and that is the last thing any coach wants.

You never know when you will need a player to perform an important role. If you have ignored or mistreated specific players, either intentionally or unintentionally, they may not be able or willing to perform when the team needs them. In a perfect world, an individual acts as a good soldier would, patiently waiting for the commander's orders, always selfless, waiting to do their part for the good of the group.

Unfortunately, Coach, We Do Not Live in a Perfect World!

When speaking to your team before, during, or after a game or practice, you must know when they need a tongue-lashing and when a softer approach is appropriate. Generally, the best time to be harsher and more demanding is when things are going well. Conversely, the best time to soften up is when things are going poorly. As Lou Holtz so poignantly said in his video titled *Do Right,* "When you need love and understanding the most is usually when you deserve it the least."

When talking to the entire team, be prepared. By planning your comments, you seek to create or foster a certain mindset in your players while enhancing the possibility that they will receive the proper message.

A coach communicates with nonverbal signals as well. A simple pat on the back or a smile communicates a positive feeling from the coach. Facial expressions and sighs of disgust can communicate negative feelings. If a coach appears nervous or fearful of failure, such feelings can be communicated to the team, and the players may also become anxious. In the 1989-90, season we played three playoff games en route to winning the state championship. Each of these games went into overtime. After regulation time had expired in each of the games and the players assembled in front of the bench, I said very little. Basically, I stood tall, smiling calmly, thereby conveying to the players that I knew we would win. Just before our goalie went back to the net, I smiled and winked at him. I knew he would be feeling the greatest pressure.

That kind of communication didn't win us those games. The players won the games by making key plays when it mattered most. What I tried to do was remove the anxiety and fear of losing by showing them that I believed the only possible outcome was victory. By doing my part in lessening their anxiety, I hoped that our players would be relaxed enough to make the right play at the right time.

MOTIVATION

Motivation for individuals and for an entire team is integral to everything that is done by coaches and players daily. Every meeting, practice, bus ride, team meal, game, or video session is interconnected within the realm of motivation. It starts with the coach's own work habits, organization, leadership, and teaching behaviors. Everything that happens during the season is connected to something else and has influenced someone in some way.

How do you motivate players? Well, that certainly is the million-dollar question, isn't it! How many books have been authored claiming to possess at least some of the answers to this important question? In reality, the topic is a very complex one. It varies from player to player and from team to team. Players have their own reasons for playing. All players have a threshold regarding what price they are willing to pay to achieve a certain level of success. One thing I know for sure, only a very small part of the total motivation involves the emotional pregame speech.

Based on the work I have done with some of the greatest motivators in the game, it has become evident that one important key to understanding motivation for individuals is to understand each player's view of him- or herself. Each individual has a perception of how good they currently are as a hockey player and how good they can become. This perception is not always grounded in reality. We, as coaches, have the same types of feelings. How we see ourselves now versus how we see ourselves in the future is critical to understanding our own levels of motivation.

Motivation is associated with aspiration. What do the individuals on your team aspire to? Do they aspire to winning a championship? Do they aspire to a playing career at a higher level? As coaches, we must begin by helping our players develop a clear and accurate view of their present status as players and as a team. Once a player has an accurate view of the present, the coach can assist in the development of any aspiration. The key word is *assist,* because an aspiration is a very personal concept. *You can't make someone into something they don't want to become, and you can't make a great player out of someone who isn't potentially great!*

At times, individual players have aspirations beyond what is realistic. Players should be allowed to dream, even though we as coaches don't feel the dreams have basis in reality. One never knows how far the human spirit can take an individual. The only time a coach needs to get involved is if an unrealistic aspiration begins to hurt the individual or the performance of the team.

Some players aspire to being good players at their present level. They don't have aspirations beyond that point, and there is absolutely nothing wrong with that. Perhaps they aspire to winning a championship or having a successful season. Others aspire only to having fun playing at their current level. A player just out to have fun can be difficult for a coach to accept, especially the type of coach who is taking the time to read this book! I know that it is often difficult to accept people who do not share your passion for improvement and for the game itself.

You have two choices when this situation occurs. First, you can ignore the issue and allow the individual to give what they can, making certain that their relative lack of commitment does not adversely affect the team. Second, you can try to guide the individual toward a higher level of aspiration. Remember that if you choose the latter approach, you must be aware that you cannot force a person to be something or want something that is not important to them.

An important key to motivation is to somehow create a mindset within the players that what the team does and what they do as individuals is very special, even uncommon. The creation of this mindset must be attended to by the coach on a daily basis. It is not something that is said the first day of training camp and then forgotten, but rather it is worked at diligently each day. It is achieved through careful outlining and nurturing of your coaching philosophy. It is achieved by constantly adhering to the principle of doing everything right to the best of your ability. It is achieved by being thorough and precise when planning practices, by creating sound game plans, by planning travel effectively, and so on.

I learned this lesson when I was in high school playing baseball for a man named Rusty Ross. Coach Ross believed that we had to do all the little things well. He ran great practices that stressed fundamentals, made sure our uniforms were major league quality, and insisted that we wear those uniforms properly. He believed that long hair looked sloppy under a baseball cap. In the early '70s, short hair for high school students was uncommon, yet he succeeded in getting his players to believe as he did. In doing so, he made us believe that our team was uncommon—and uncommonly superior! He achieved this through constant attention to the little details on a daily basis.

Although the following story might not be hockey-specific, it nevertheless illustrates the notion of attention to detail. During my senior year in high school, our baseball team finished the regular season seventh in the state of New Hampshire. Our first playoff game was in Somersworth, near the seacoast. When we arrived at the field, we noticed that the fences were somewhat short. Our opponent was taking batting practice in a sloppy, matter-of-fact manner. When our turn came to take batting practice, Coach Ross broke out two dozen new baseballs. While our opponent watched, we hammered pitch after pitch over the fence. Even the smaller players were smashing balls out of the park. When we took infield practice, we executed with unparalleled precision and enthusiasm. We played a more talented team that day and won easily. And you know what? To this day *I still believe we won the game before it started*. We were motivated by the fact that we believed we were better, we believed we showed more class—that we looked more like a real ball club than our opponent. The cynical reader will say that we were motivated by the knowledge that if we could win that game and the next three, we would be

The level of confidence and enthusiasm you have prior to the game can make the difference between a win or a loss.

state champions. The cynic may not be entirely wrong! However, Coach Ross gave us that little extra advantage on that day while taking something away from our opponent, and I believe it made a difference.

Individual and Team Goals

You have done your homework and now know how your players perceive themselves. You know what they aspire to individually and collectively. How do you motivate them to achieve or reach beyond their aspirations? The first step is to help individuals and the group establish goals. Any goal that an individual or the team sets has to be attainable. It's nice to say that your goal is to win a championship, but if you have limited talent, it may not be realistic.

There are two basic types of goals. The first type is often referred to as performance-based. For an individual, it may mean setting a goal of scoring 50 points during the season or having a plus/minus ratio of plus 20 or better. For a team, it may mean winning more than half of its games, finishing the season high enough in the standings to have home ice advantage during the playoffs, or perhaps winning a championship. The second type of goal is effort-based. For an individual, it may mean committing to work hard each day in practice, to do extra conditioning such as push-ups and sit-ups each day, or to play every shift in every game with maximum intensity and determination.

The problem with performance-based goals is that they don't take into consideration the performance of your own teammates or opponents. For example, if a player has set a goal of scoring 50 points in a season but has linemates who can't finish off scoring chances, the goal probably will not be realized. Also, the goal does not take into consideration the play of opponents. The same player may have trouble reaching a goal of scoring 50 points in a season if playing against extremely talented goalies and/or excellent defensive teams.

It is easy to determine whether or not performance-based goals are achieved. This type of goal is very specific and objective and usually has a number attached to it. Determining whether or not effort-based goals are reached is usually far more subjective. A goal of working hard every day, every shift, every game is difficult to evaluate because each player and the coaches have differing views on what constitutes hard work. The beauty of effort goals for individuals is that they can be achieved regardless of what happens with teammates or opponents.

Let's assume for a moment that your team has a goal of trying to win every game. A game at the high school level usually involves 45 minutes of playing time (60 minutes at the junior hockey level) and thousands of situations blending together to form the final outcome. The thought of winning a game can be overwhelming.

The key to winning may be in establishing smaller goals for performance criteria within the game. For example, you might establish a list of objectives for each game in the following areas:

1. Score four goals or more
2. Allow two goals or less
3. Generate more scoring chances than the opponent
4. Have more attempted shots on goal from the primary scoring area than the opponent
5. Take no retaliation penalties
6. Have more power plays than the opponent
7. Score a power play goal
8. Do not allow a power play goal
9. Score a shorthanded goal
10. Win 60 percent or more of the face-offs
11. Deliver 75 or more hits

By establishing performance criteria such as these for your team, you take away the pressure that comes from thinking about winning the game. Players become aware of situations in which they must perform that will lead to a win. Heightened awareness is an important step toward improving your team's motivation.

At Bellows Free Academy we had a large poster on the wall listing each of our games,

Work closely with your assistants to develop clear goals and good rapport.

along with our game-by-game performance objectives. After each game, the players would gather around to watch as I checked off the objectives met by the team. They took great pride in trying to play a game where they had achieved all the objectives. I can't remember our team ever meeting all the objectives, but we did come close on several occasions. We found that when we were able to check off at least 67 percent of the objectives in a game, the outcome was always a victory.

Every player's goal for a specific game should be to play well and help the team win, but this is vague and can be daunting for certain players. By using a modified version of a team goal-setting model, you can help players create written goals for their individual performances.

I like to use a tool called a performance wheel. Developing a performance wheel for an individual is done by meeting with them and deciding what it is they must do to play well. The wheel is then divided by an appropriate number of spokes and circles (four) placed at equidistant intervals inside the wheel. Following each game, the individual rates their performance on a scale of one to five, shading the wheel in each performance area.

Performance wheels help individual players focus their efforts during games. Performance criteria for each of the wheel's sections can represent either tangible criteria such as goals and assists or subjective criteria such as defensive positioning, hustle, or physical play.

Once a player has elected to use a performance wheel, the performance assessment can be done privately without sharing with the coach, or it can be something the player and coach review together following games. Either way, it provides the player with a tool for review of performance on a game-by-game basis as well as a pictorial record of the review. By comparing wheels from game to game, a clear picture of the individual's performance over time appears. Figure 3.1 shows an example of a performance wheel.

In 1993, we had a freshman center at the University of Maine who was struggling to meet the expectations of the head coach. He was extremely talented and accustomed to being the best player on his team throughout his career prior to attending Maine. The head coach's demands were beginning to frustrate him because he was being asked to do things he had never been required to do before.

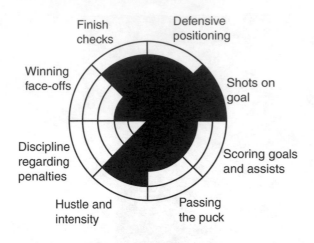

Finish checks

Defensive positioning

Winning face-offs

Shots on goal

Discipline regarding penalties

Scoring goals and assists

Hustle and intensity

Passing the puck

Figure 3.1   The performance wheel.

Prior to his arrival at Maine, his job was to score, and he had not been held accountable for such things as taking silly penalties, playing well defensively, or finishing his body checks. I worked with him to design a personal performance wheel that helped him improve his focus on the things the head coach wanted, as well as on the things he thought were important in his game. It helped reduce his anxiety level, and in the end, he played better with a performance wheel. The coach's satisfaction with this player increased, and thereafter we saw fewer instances when he received negative feedback from the coach.

Pregame Speeches

Prior to a game, it is customary for the coach to speak to the team. The main objective is to convey a game plan—what the team must do to be successful. The players are primarily responsible for getting themselves to the appropriate level of arousal required to play well and to execute the game plan. As coaches, we know that players have to be "ready" if they are to play well.

What is involved for a player to become ready prior to a game? To be truly prepared, players must be aroused to the point where they are excited to play, confident, yet calm. Excited yet calm sounds dichotomous. Being excited is natural for most players, as hockey is a game requiring emotion, speed, skill, courage, and quick decision making. If players are too excited and lack enough calmness, they will likely be able to perform with speed and perhaps courage but will be less likely to execute in terms of skill and decision making.

Understand that not all players show emotion before a game, whereas others appear to be too excited. The appropriate degree of arousal is an individual thing, and no two players are exactly alike. The calmness portion comes from a belief that they can succeed personally and as a team. If players lack confidence, if they fear a negative outcome, or if they physically fear the opponent, they can become too excited. The usual result of being too excited is that players can't execute the right play at the right time.

As the coach, when you perceive that your team is too tense or too excited, your pregame comments must be geared to establishing confidence and the subsequent inner calm that accompanies it. When a coach sees that the team lacks energy, that they don't appear to have the necessary excitement, that is the time to appeal to their emotions. That is when the fiery pregame speech might be appropriate.

In general, "rah-rah" speeches are most often used when the team is about to play an opponent that they do not respect or in a game that is considered to be of little importance. When the opponent is of high quality or when the game is important, that is when the coach should seek to create confidence and calmness within players.

This section of the book has looked at communication and motivation, two aspects of effective coaching that are inextricably linked. I could write enough stories and anecdotes to fill an entire book on these two subjects alone and never cover all the information that might come in handy during your journey as a coach. However, I hope the information provided has given you a framework for expanding your abilities and effectiveness as both a communicator and a motivator.

Part 2
PLANNING FOR SUCCESS

Chapter 4

SEASON PLANS

Coaches, you must hear this loud and clear. Organization and planning are your blueprints for success. I know of no successful group endeavor that was not preceded by careful planning and organization. This process begins with an analysis of the returning players. The second phase of planning involves a review of the previous season and some careful thought about where you want the team to be at the end of the upcoming season. Next, you must map out the season's schedule, including practices. As part of this phase, you will develop goals for various segments of the season. How many segments you create is up to you, and these are based on the length of the season and the demands of your schedule. Let's look at these three parameters of planning individually.

ASSESSING YOUR ATHLETES

A hockey coach should first create a depth chart by looking at which athletes are available for the upcoming season. Having done this, you can then begin to formulate a vision for how the season will progress. The depth chart begins with the athletes who are returning from the previous season. If you are coaching a high school team, the remaining positions on the chart are filled from the junior varsity squad or the local youth hockey program. If you are coaching a prep school or junior team, you will probably have to recruit or draft the athletes to fill those slots. When you are coaching a junior team, draft picks, recruits, and trades are the most likely methods for filling out your depth chart (see table 4.1).

Table 4.1   Sample Depth Chart

Returning players		
LW	**C**	**RW**
J. Cioffi	LeClair	L. Cioffi
Langevin	Toof	Rath
Stringer	Boucher	
LD	**RD**	**G**
Benoit	Smith	Johnson
G. Dukas	J. Dukas	
Tazolino	Gilmore	
Players available from bantams		
LW	**C**	**RW**
Charbonneau	Wood	
Villeneuve		
Camisa		
LD	**RD**	**G**
Larose	Ovitt	Puro

Once the depth chart has been completed, analyze the individual athletes' strengths and weaknesses. This will tell you whether your team will be fast, slow, small, big, skilled, or physical. Use the statistics from the previous season to support any conclusions you infer from this analysis. Make notations beneath each name on your depth chart describing the player's strengths, weaknesses, and perhaps how you see them helping your team in the upcoming season.

At the high school level, not much can be done about the type of team you will have, as recruiting is probably illegal. In a prep school or junior team scenario, you can possibly create the type of team you want by recruiting and drafting players who possess the attributes you need to play a certain style of game.

This analysis of your available personnel will tell you if your team is likely to be skilled offensively, solid defensively, and so on. It may indicate whether or not you have a chance to be effective on the power play or during penalty-killing situations. It can tell you what to expect in the areas of offensive production or defensive performance from specific players on the team. Once completed, you can begin to envision how your players might progress individually and collectively by the end of the season. Further, you can begin to outline possible line combinations and defense pairs, formations and patterns of play suitable to the personnel, power play alignments, and penalty-killing style. You will begin to see what your chances might be of making the playoffs or of winning a championship. The coach must be able to envision the final outcome of the season for the team and for individual players.

CREATING THE SCHEDULE

The next step in the planning process is to review the schedule of games for the upcom-

Recruit the players you need then envision how they'll progress individually and as a team.

ing season. It is important to note breaks in the schedule where you may be able to practice for several days without playing a game or periods when players may need time off due to too many games being played over a short time span. Take note of the travel requirements based on the schedule of games and be sure to plan accordingly. Keep in mind that long bus trips can have an effect on players. If a trip exceeds three hours on the bus, consider going to the site the night before the game, or perhaps plan for a coach bus rather than a school bus. Of course, financial constraints or classroom commitments may preclude you from making these types of arrangements.

After a thorough review of the game schedule, you can then begin to plan the practice schedule. Your practice schedule may also include off-ice weight training or some other

form of conditioning. If you find you have inadequate on-ice practice time, search for more ice time. If money or availability prohibit additional ice time, secure practice time in gymnasiums or similar facilities where you will be able to condition the athletes or practice tactics and systems.

SETTING GOALS

After completing the personnel analysis and the schedule review, you are now ready to establish some short-term goals for the team. This leads toward your vision of where the team should be by the end of the season. It is a good idea to break down the season into segments. I've found that the easiest way is to divide the regular season into four segments based on the number of games. Generally, the first segment is the longest because it involves the preseason period.

Let's assume that you are a high school coach playing a 20-game regular season schedule with two weeks of preseason practice prior to the first game. If the rules allow, you should try to schedule at least one scrimmage during this period. Examples of the goals to be set for this segment are as follows:

- Introduce and drill all systems of play in each of the three major zones.
- Introduce and drill power play and penalty-killing patterns.
- Practice high-speed execution of skills and play tactics.
- Cover face-offs assuming loss of the draw. If time allows, teach the offensive component.
- Cover the offensive component of a face-off won in the defensive zone and in the neutral zone.
- Condition athletes so that they are as well prepared as possible for the physical rigors of playing games.
- Prepare goalkeepers with ample shots. Practice gamelike situations that involve traffic in front of the net and situations where they must handle the puck.

It is a good idea to come up with weekly themes that further refine your segment goals. Based on the goals mentioned earlier, week 1's theme may be even-strength systems. Week 2 may involve special teams and face-offs. This does not mean that you can't practice skill sets that don't involve the principal theme for the week. Perhaps your theme for week 1 is the introduction, drilling, and refinement of even-strength systems plus an introduction to special teams play. This might be followed in week 2 by an emphasis on special teams and further refinement of even-strength systems.

In the previous example, the first segment of your plan briefly covers the systems of play. In the second segment, your goal may be to foster increased intensity of physical play and a high execution tempo. The third segment could include the refinement of face-off and special teams play. The final segment could be preparation for the playoffs with an emphasis on 1 v 1 battles for the puck, driving to the net, deflections, screens, and rebounds.

As you plan your season and establish teaching and practice goals, be aware that performance in preceding segments may force you to alter the goals for each succeeding segment. Your vision of what is possible individually and collectively may have to change. Obviously, if this occurs, your goals for practice must reflect this changing circumstance.

You may choose to quantify the goals you set for each segment relative to game performance. For example, it is possible to look at the schedule of five games and tell the players you expect to win at least four of the five games. You expect to score 25 percent of the time or more on the power play and succeed 85 percent of the time or more while killing penalties. You expect to average three-plus goals per game and allow an average of less than two per contest. Whatever goals you select for the team, remember that they must be realistic, reflecting the ability of your team as well as the ability of your opponents. Whenever possible, involve the players in this type of goal setting. As is true of all

things, people tend to be more committed and perform better when they have some ownership in the planning process.

STARTING THE SEASON

The start of your season is pivotal, and it is important to set a proper tone with the very first meeting. Expounding on the organization's philosophy and your own personal philosophy is important. Outlining the basic requirements for your players is a must. This is serious business, as it is your only chance to make a favorable first impression. You must be well organized so that there is time for all of your comments and any other agenda items that have to be taken care of, and the meeting runs smoothly and efficiently.

Effective teams are similar to high-functioning families in that there is genuine caring for other members of the group. That doesn't mean that there won't be differences among the members, as these always exist in virtually all groups or organizations. However, effective families and teams will, at critical moments, pull together toward a common goal.

How does a coach create this type of family feeling within a team? One way to accomplish this is by getting players together to do something other than play hockey. It might be a team outing such as a meal, a bowling contest, a Ping-Pong tournament, or perhaps a golf tournament. It can be a bottle drive to raise money for the team, or it can be a night where you paint the locker room and hallways inside the arena or an afternoon of charity work within the community. These types of activities are called team-building experiences, and I believe they are helpful in promoting unselfish attitudes and team cohesion.

The key concepts of communication and motivation are the "twin towers" of effective leadership and coaching. Without a commitment to first understand, then refine your skill sets in these two areas, your chances of success within the coaching fraternity are greatly diminished. You should constantly be updating your knowledge in both areas and stay ever vigilant as you watch master communicators and motivators work their magic.

The Master Plan

Depending on your own unique circumstance, a yearly planner is a must for any successful coach and program. Consideration should be given to how much time you expect to have available from players, the types and amount of equipment at your disposal, ice time availability, and so on. What follows are some generic ideas you might consider for any high school or junior level team.

Time of year	Description	Action Plan
End of season (early spring)	A few weeks of rest is required to help in the healing of bumps and bruises!	1. Light workouts of the athlete's choice. 2. Cross training activities, fun and informal. 3. Lots of stretching.
Initial conditioning phase (late spring, early summer)	Hockey players need to develop a rhythm in the weight room. This time of year can yield dramatic increases in strength and power if proper workouts are planned. Remember that abdominal strength and powerful legs are keys to successful play.	1. Weight room workouts—initiated by qualified trainers to ensure that hockey-specific training occurs. (Have players work in pairs or groups if possible to keep motivation high.) 2. Sprint work (not distance running) away from the weight room for developing quick feet and explosive leg strength.
Precamp phase (mid- to late summer)	This is the time when players get ready for training camp and the rigors of the season to come.	1. Begin ice sessions to work on conditioning. 2. Increase the intensity, leading up to one week before camp . . . then get some rest! 3. Light stretching in preparation for "2 a days" in some cases.
Training camp and early season	The time of year when teams are chosen and systems of play are introduced.	Develop your own particular training camp protocol. D Zone coverages should be introduced early on during this phase of the season. Some coaches do this during the training camp itself.
Mid- to late season	Refining individual player skills is an ongoing function of your practice planning. During this phase you must be polishing all aspects of your team philosophies, goals, and objectives.	1. Solidify forward lines and defensive pairings . . . then drill and redrill. 2. Spot your goalie! Goaltending should become obvious as to who is number 1, and who is number 2! 3. Refine special teams play along with all key aspects of play (face-off alignments, D Zone, N Zone, and O Zone).
Playoffs	This represents the end of the season, and all of your hard work will hopefully pay off!	Open the gates and let them have fun! Remember that they might be nervous, so keep them loose and in their "comfort zones." Good luck, coach!

Chapter
5

PRACTICE PREPARATION

One of the most frustrating things to watch as the parent of a child participating in any sport is a poorly conceived and executed practice. Please don't misconstrue that statement as a condemnation of my coaching brethren. Anyone who is willing to sacrifice his or her time, energy, and money to coach deserves praise, not criticism. Yet, if you intend to spend all that time doing volunteer work as a coach, why not be as successful as you possibly can? With a little homework and the information provided in this chapter, your practices will become the talk of the town! Given the seemingly ever-increasing cost of ice time, coaches must make the most of every available moment on the ice, and both parents and administrators demand it. In this chapter, we will look at the vital elements of practice planning as they relate to both short- and long-term success.

PLANNING PRACTICES

The first step in practice planning involves a review of your objectives for the week and your season master plan. Ideally, practices should be consistent with your master plan. At times, coaches must deviate from the master plan because of unforeseen circumstances. For example, injuries can cause the necessity for change. A game played where certain deficiencies are exposed can force a coach to shift from the original season plan. The coach must ask, "What do I want to accomplish in practice, and how much time should it take to reach the practice objectives?" You will also need to know that these objectives have been reached or that there has been improvement toward reaching them.

One key to any good practice is to organize the individual players into groups by assigning different-colored jerseys. Each line may have a different-colored jersey, with defensemen all in the same color or each unit of five players, three forwards and two defensemen, in the same color. If your theme is to practice the power play, give each power play unit a specific-colored jersey to wear.

Be certain that you have the necessary equipment to run your practice effectively. For example (and this might sound silly), make sure you have enough pucks. There is nothing more embarrassing than arriving at the rink to find out you only have seven pucks for a team of 20 players! Take it from someone who's "been there, done that!" If you plan to use weight vests for skating drills at the end of practice, make arrangements for them to be on the bench ready to go at the appropriate time. Make certain that you have enough cones and that they are in a convenient place when you need them. Be sure to have your coaching equipment in order—skates, stick, whistle, stopwatch, a dry-erase board with markers. In short, be prepared.

The next step in practice planning is to establish a main theme and any subthemes or objectives. The theme may be to work on a specific aspect of team play, conditioning, or perhaps high-speed execution of fundamental skills. Regardless of the theme selected, the most important concept for any hockey practice is to simulate game conditions as closely as possible. This is very difficult to do, as players have a tendency to go slower and to practice with less intensity than they play with in real games. The closer practice is to actual game conditions, the better it is for your team. If practices possess game-like tempo and work-to-rest ratios, much of the conditioning element required in preparing the team for games will be achieved. For example, if you play with three lines, this means that during games players get two shifts of rest for every shift of work on the ice. If drill repetitions in practice are consistent with

Check equipment prior to all practices and games to make sure you're prepared.

this ratio, you will be on your way to achieving a good level of conditioning for your players.

Whenever possible, try to make practices fun. Practice can't always be fun, but it sure helps the players if it is. No matter what anyone tells you, hockey is a game played by young people for fun, so don't be afraid to ask your players if they like a particular drill. Their body language will also indicate their level of satisfaction with a drill when you announce that it will be executed next at practice.

When hockey practices are well designed, the team will be practicing many skills and tactics that were not part of the original main theme. For example, your theme may be scoring goals resulting from deflections, screens, and rebounds. If you provide for defensive players to compete against the potential goal scorers in each drill, the defenders get work experience in thwarting these situations. Because your emphasis is on refining goal scoring, you may choose not to coach the defenders so that the scorers have some success. Still, if the defensive players are sharp, they will develop tactics on their own that help them stop the offense. For players, learning on their own through experience is often the best way to improve. Sometimes players are not sharp enough to figure out what works and what doesn't. At that point, the coach has to provide assistance.

At times, the theme for practice may simply be to loosen up and sharpen execution for an upcoming game. One of the main concerns for a coach in this scenario is to ensure against fatigue. The theme for a particular practice may be to perform drills that the players perceive as fun. This is often the case later in the season when players are becoming stale.

Once the themes and objectives have been established, the coach must select drills that will help the team reach those objectives. This requires a significant amount of thought. I often speak at coaching clinics that are attended primarily by youth hockey coaches. When they arrive at the clinic, they want drills. The best drills are those that are personally designed or modified to meet the objectives of your own unique practice environment. Throwing together a practice by simply assembling a bunch of fine drills without regard for purpose is an inefficient way to conduct the business of coaching. Yet it continues to happen, even on occasion at the highest levels of the game.

There is nothing wrong with using drills you've learned from books or from other coaches, but make sure they fit the purpose of your practice. A technique I often employ is to take a drill that appears promising for my purpose and modify it to ensure that it coincides completely with the practice objectives. Modifying good drills to make them even better is an important coaching skill.

PRACTICING EFFECTIVELY

Good practices begin with a meeting of the coaching staff to review themes, the day's objectives, and specific drills to be used. Assistant coaches are given their specific assignments for the day's session. As the meeting progresses, assistant coaches should be encouraged to offer opinions and suggest alterations to the practice plan and drill selections.

It is sound coaching to start practice with a brief, orally delivered outline of the workout's main theme and the expectations for the players. This sets the tone for the rest of the session. Some coaches avoid outlining the entire practice because they feel that players will conserve energy for the more strenuous drills. This is fine, but players should be advised as to the purpose of the session and the expectations for their performance.

A good practice, like a good story, has a beginning, a middle, and an end. The beginning portion is called the warm-up. Generally, the warm-up phase of practice should last at least 10 minutes but can last as long as 30 minutes, depending on the time available. The middle portion of practice includes the drills that reinforce the practice's main theme. This is a vital segment of practice. Finally, the end of practice can involve fun drills, scrimmaging, or additional conditioning followed by a cool-down period.

Before players can be asked to execute at a high tempo, their bodies must be properly warmed up. This is important for quality execution and avoidance of injury. When time allows, the warm-up should be conducted on the ice. It can begin with light skating or scrimmaging, followed by stretching. The first couple of drills after stretching should involve moderate skating, perhaps some passing, culminating with shots for the goalie.

It's best if the first several shots come from longer range, perhaps as far out as the blue line. It is also important that goalies receive shots from all three basic angles: the right and left wings and the middle of the ice. Ideally, a drill that makes the goalkeeper move across the crease from left to right and right to left should be used to conclude the warm-up phase of practice.

After the warm-up, the drills designed to

32 Coaching Hockey Successfully

attack the main theme are executed. In this segment, the highest possible tempo is necessary, and the greatest possible level of intensity must be shown. In addition, a tremendous amount of focus and commitment to execution is required by both players and coaches. This is not to suggest that the other phases of practice should be done with less than maximal effort, but clearly this portion of practice is when a coach should be least tolerant of submaximal effort and execution. This phase of practice is also the time a coach should use for scrimmaging. A properly executed scrimmage is arguably the best drill of all, and it is definitely gamelike. If the coach works the scrimmage, teaching and correcting, praising and scolding, demanding effort and intensity, it makes for a great hockey drill.

In the final phase of practice, the coach may choose to utilize high-intensity skating drills to condition the athletes. If the tempo was sufficient during the previous portions of practice, this may not be necessary. It is also a time when drills designed to be enjoyable for the athlete can be employed. This portion of practice should always be followed by a cooldown period of stretching and light skating. During this phase, the coach may choose to speak with the players about housekeeping matters or logistics or to give feedback on the day's performance.

At Bellows Free Academy, we would always have our players cool down by stretching. Afterward, while lying flat on their backs, we would have them close their eyes and envision success in certain game situations or plan how they would react after a victory in the state tournament. This relaxation and mental imagery exercise was very effective for our teams during those years. The players had been through several situations mentally before each occurred, improving their chances of reacting efficiently when it mattered most. This type of mental training helps players attain a feeling of calmness in the most pressure-packed or chaotic situations.

The coaching staff should meet briefly after practice to discuss the day's session. This meeting should focus on the objectives outlined before practice. Were the day's objectives met? Which individual players were you pleased with? Which were you displeased with? Do we need to speak with any individuals, forward lines, or defense pairs? Do we need to review and repeat segments of today's practice at the next practice or sometime soon?

What Is High Tempo in Practice?

My definition of high tempo in practice is when players are skating as fast as possible, executing skills and tactics as rapidly as possible. This type of practice usually, though not always, involves game-like drills. Players must learn to execute at tempos that meet or exceed those encountered during a game. Coaches who train their team in this way have an advantage over coaches who don't recognize and adhere to this principle when planning and conducting practices.

Practice drills that exceed the stress created by normal game conditions are potentially the best of all. Some examples are drills that involve multiple pucks, scrimmaging against seven defenders instead of five, or protecting the puck against two opponents rather than one. The only problem with these types of drills is that they may erode the confidence of some players. It is important to ensure that the players understand the purpose of these drills, which is to make the games seem easier than practice.

Keep in mind that high-tempo practices require that players have adequate rest between drill repetitions. If you are doing a drill that requires about 30 seconds of work, players should have between 90 and 120 seconds of rest before performing another repetition. This coincides with the demands of a game where players are on the ice every third or fourth shift. During games there are additional breaks for players, such as face-offs before the end of a shift. It is difficult to build these breaks into your practice drills. You may find that to maintain the tempo you desire, you may only be able to do certain drills for five minutes, perhaps less, before the tempo diminishes below the optimum level.

How long should the team be practicing a particular drill? This depends primarily on the objective(s) and complexity of the drill. A general rule of thumb is to run a drill between 5 and 10 minutes. You want to ensure that each individual performs enough repetitions of a drill, yet you also want to avoid the boredom and declining intensity that result from executing a drill for too long.

To keep the pace of practice high, the coach must be able to move the team quickly from one exercise to the next. Detailed discussions about the next drill or the previous one slow down practice. If you feel that players need recovery time before beginning the next exercise, that presents a golden opportunity to spend time talking to individuals or the team as a whole.

To keep the tempo of practice high, it is a good idea to use drills the players are familiar with. If players are unfamiliar with a drill, a detailed explanation or demonstration is usually required, and this slows down practice. Also, when players are feeling their way through a drill for the first time, they tend to execute at less than full speed. Another tip that will help you keep the pace

of practice high relates to drill logistics. Keep in mind that using a series of drills that are related in terms of where players originate their repetitions enhances the rapid movement from one exercise to the next.

CONDITIONING

To execute the skills required to play this game well, a high level of hockey-specific fitness is required. The most important thing to remember is that hockey is an explosive, anaerobic game. To be able to skate well, you need to have strong leg and buttock muscles. You must also have a well-developed set of muscles in the trunk area—the abdominals and lower back. Training for the upper-body muscles is also important and should be taken seriously, but clearly the lower body and trunk areas are the main focus.

During the summer months, I travel throughout North America working for Paul O'Dacre of the Huron Hockey School. The players we instruct are mostly between the ages of 7 and 12, however, we have 13- to 17-year-old players in our camps as well. We always emphasize optimal knee and ankle flexion in skating to these players, and well we should, because

Drills practiced in game-like situations help players condition for actual matches.

that is proper technique. In many cases, though, I am wasting my breath talking about proper knee and ankle flexion. These players simply don't have the muscle strength or stamina to execute appropriate flexion. Until they achieve the necessary level of physical development and conditioning, they will always have poor technique and perform below optimum levels in the areas of speed and agility. Lack of skating ability also compromises development in the other skill areas. The leg and trunk muscles provide the solid base on which are built the necessary coordination for other skills involving the stick and puck or checking.

This book is not intended to be a specialized conditioning resource, so I will not cover the broad and highly important topic of conditioning for hockey in great detail. However, I humbly suggest that you get your hands on the following two books with respect to conditioning. First, Dr. Jack Blatherwick's classic book titled *Over-Speed Training for Hockey,* 1994, published by USA Hockey Inc., is one of the finest texts available on the subject and is must reading for any serious hockey coach. It is available through USA Hockey, 4965 North 30th Street, Colorado Springs, Colorado 80919. Peter Twist's book titled *Complete Conditioning for Ice Hockey,* published by Human Kinetics, is another invaluable resource for hockey-specific conditioning. After reading these two impressive works, you will immediately have a better grasp on the key concepts associated with hockey conditioning.

Chapter 6

BUILDING A FEEDER SYSTEM

In today's era of free agency, draft choices, and trade possibilities, many professional hockey teams have gradually moved away from producing talent "down on the farm." While this strategy might be available, even affordable, for the big-budget operations, it's doubtful your coaching circumstances will allow you to engage in high-stakes trading as a means of improving your team. In reality, most coaches will be dependent on a substantial developmental network, or "feeder system," to supply the needed talent for their team. It is wise for you to consider some important aspects inherent to the building and maintenance of this type of system.

EXAMINE THE SITUATION

If you are coaching a junior hockey team in Canada or the United States, building a feeder system is probably not a key issue for you. Your job is to recruit or draft players into the program from feeder systems that already exist apart from your program. If you coach in a public high school or prep school environment, however, it will be important to have a solid system in place to provide you with developed talent now and into the future.

A solid junior varsity program with a full and competitive schedule and adequate practice time is the first step toward building the feeder system. You must staff this team with quality coaches who are committed to developing players for your varsity program. It is important that the junior varsity team emphasize the same principles both on and off the ice that are emphasized at the varsity level. Depending on your situation, you may need to have more than one subvarsity team. Of course, in some areas of the country, a junior varsity program may not be possible due to the number of available players in your school or the availability of opposing teams to play against.

While I was at Bellows Free Academy, we never fielded a junior varsity program. Rather, we relied on the town's bantam and midget-level programs to provide us with well-skilled and well-schooled players. I was fortunate that St. Albans, Vermont, had a fine youth hockey program with excellent coaches at every level. In an effort to develop some continuity between the St. Albans Youth Hockey and Bellows Free Academy programs, I invited the bantam coach to become a volunteer assistant with our team. I asked that he employ the same system of play utilized by our team with his bantam team, and this worked to the advantage of both programs.

If you don't have the luxury of a solid feeder system, you have a great deal of work to do. First, assess the current youth hockey program by observing the skill level of the players entering your program and their general hockey knowledge level. Follow this with an examination of the youth hockey program itself. How many players do they have playing at each level, from beginner all the way to high-school-age players? How competitive is their schedule? How much practice time do these players get weekly at each level? How effective is the coaching the youngsters receive?

After answering these questions, you will have a solid idea of what needs to be done to improve your feeder system. The biggest problem you will face may be political in nature. Attempting to dictate changes to youth hockey

Young athletes will vary in all stages of maturity and skill level.

leaders is not likely to achieve the desired results. If you approach the program leaders with tact and a sincere desire to help them improve their program without minimizing its current worth, you will likely be well received. If you approach them with the attitude that they don't know what they are doing, you will undoubtedly experience many slamming doors as you beat a hasty retreat from their boardrooms!

The two most common problems facing local youth hockey organizations, which tend to affect the local high school team, are the limited amount of ice time available and the limited number of youngsters actually playing in the program. The ice time issue is a difficult one. If your local youth hockey program is short on ice time, especially for practice, encourage them to double up the number of teams on the ice for practice. Having two and sometimes even three teams on the ice can increase the number of practice hours available each week. The issue of lack of players must be addressed at the youngest levels. Players drop out of hockey for any number of reasons as they grow up. Some lose interest, others realize they don't have aptitude and would rather focus on something else, and still others move away. The more players who begin playing the game in your local organization between the ages of five and eight, the more you will have left when they reach high school age.

Recruit Talent and Dedication

Every youngster is born with a certain amount of athletic talent. Those with the most innate talent are most likely to become the best high-school-level players. It's almost impossible to know at an early age who has the talent and who does not, so the more players you have in the program, the more likely you are to have athletically gifted individuals. That's just statistical probability, for all you math types out there! As the local high school coach, you must do everything in your power to promote the recruiting of players for the youth program and the efficient utilization of ice time. How you achieve this depends on your specific circumstances.

The amount of time youngsters spend playing hockey directly correlates with how skilled they ultimately become. Encouraging youngsters to play on their own time, not just during organized practice sessions at the arena, is vital to their skill development. Playing outdoors in unstructured situations helps players develop better than just skating in organized practices. In areas of the United States where outdoor ice is not possible, players can play street hockey, with or without rollerblades, as a complement to actual ice time. John LeClair, the best player in the history of St. Albans, Vermont, played outside almost every day. He did this even after reaching the high school level, when he was on the ice for practice or games six out of seven days a week.

The best players practice *after* practice, on the ice and outdoors.

Find Good Coaches

What if the level of coaching in the youth hockey program is substandard? Well, there are a variety of things you can do to improve this situation, which is not uncommon, especially with newer start-up programs. USA Hockey's local district offers coaching clinics throughout the season, and coaches should be encouraged to attend. Of course, it's possible they have already attended and have not applied much of the material presented. Ideally, each youth hockey organization should have an organization head coach—someone who need not necessarily even coach a team—whose primary function is to ensure that coaches in the organization are doing an effective job, as well as to provide in-service opportunities to improve their coaching skills.

Becoming a resource for the local youth coaches is important. For example, make your library of materials available to these coaches.

Encourage them to come to your practices to see how you organize and run them. If they can't attend your practices, videotape a few and make copies available to the coaches. Make certain that you dub audio explanations over the tape so that they understand completely what you are trying to accomplish with each drill. If possible, run informal clinics where you impart your coaching expertise to them in a noncondescending manner.

A common problem with youth hockey coaches in many areas of the United States is that they have limited playing experience, some having never played hockey at all. This is a particularly difficult problem when these coaches are attempting to teach technical skills to youngsters but are unable to demonstrate those skills effectively. One way you can help them solve this problem is to encourage your players to attend practices for local youth hockey teams and serve as demonstrators. Another way is to encourage youth coaches to utilize instructional videotapes, which provide excellent explanations and demonstrations of various skills.

Your high school program will only be as good as the local youth hockey program. Creating a partnership between the high school team and the local youth program will yield positive results in political terms, both on the ice and off. The power of the local youth hockey organization is often significant in terms of their influence over the school's principal and athletic director. If you create this type of partnership, you are more likely to receive support when times are difficult for your team.

Building a solid feeder system requires time, effort, commitment, and cooperation. That might sound like a tall order, but anything less will affect your program in a negative way, both short and long term. Trust me when I say that, over time, the results will more than justify your hard work.

Chapter 7

TWO PRINCIPLES FOR BETTER TEAM PLAY

In every sport, coaches talk about the importance of fundamentals because without them it is virtually impossible to become a high-level player. Further, without fundamentally sound players, it's tough to have a winning team. In hockey, you have to be able to skate, control the puck, pass, and shoot it, in combination with solid checking skills, if you intend to become a complete player. In addition to individual skill-based fundamentals, there exist some tried, tested, and true principles upon which the modern game of hockey has been built. There are two such principles that I consider hard and fast axioms of the game of hockey, and you need to understand them both. Before we can break down the game into its various components, it is important that we look at these principles as a means of giving you a solid foundation for your coaching growth.

Here's a question for you. What are we trying to accomplish in a hockey game? It's really quite simple, isn't it? We want to put pucks into the enemy net and keep pucks out of our own net, right? This may sound overly simplistic, but it's true, and the simple answer to that question leads us directly to our two principles. These principles deal with certain areas of the ice surface and positioning of players within those areas. The principles are as follows:

1. Learn to control *time* and *space*
2. Teach your players the concept of *support*

The most important events in the game of hockey are those that happen in the prime scoring area in front of both nets (see figure 7.1). What is the prime scoring area? It is the area of the ice bounded by a line extending from the goal posts to the end zone face-off dots, from the dots to the tops of the face-off circles, and then straight across the tops of the face-off circles. Successful teams play well in front of both nets. Teams can do many things improperly in other areas of the ice, but if they know how to play well in front of both nets, they immediately have a better chance of winning.

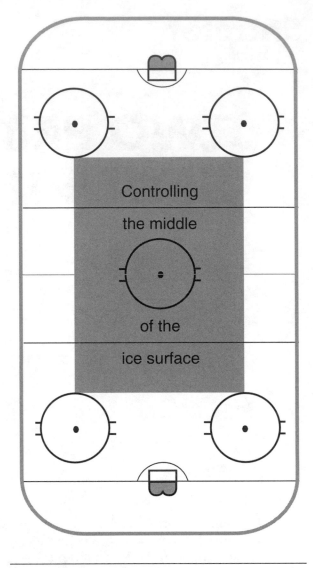

Figure 7.2   The neutral zone.

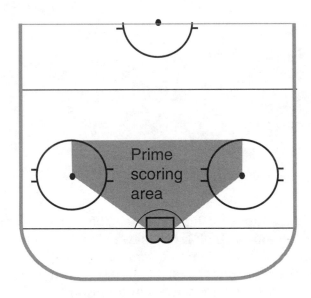

Figure 7.1   Prime scoring area.

The middle of the ice is important as well in the neutral zone (see figure 7.2). When defending, the ability to establish position so as to deflect attacks to the outside is an effective weapon. The ability to move the puck through the middle of the ice while attacking improves prospects for successful offensive play. These concepts are examined through the two key principles to which we now turn our attention.

THE PRINCIPLE OF TIME AND SPACE

The offensive team needs both time and space to execute its attacks successfully and get the puck to the prime scoring area. Everything the offense does is predicated on creating more time for the player with the puck and more space free of checking pressure from opponents. Any player, even if poorly skilled, can make a good offensive play if given enough time and space. The defensive team wants to limit the time and space the attacking team has in its effort to regain possession of the puck.

Teams that play high-pressure defensive systems with pinching defensemen tend to emphasize taking away time. They create intense pressure on the puck carrier in the hope that the opponent will make a poor decision. Other teams use more controlled defensive systems that emphasize taking away critical space first before initiating pressure on the puck, thereby taking away time.

For me, the best example of differing styles related to time and space was the 1994 Stanley Cup Eastern Conference finals between the New Jersey Devils and the New York Rangers. The Rangers were a race-horse team employing an aggressive forechecking system, pinching their defensemen along the boards in the attacking zone and in the neutral zone. Everything about their game involved putting pressure on the puck. At times, in their effort to apply pressure, two Rangers players would attack the puck carrier, creating a numerical advantage for the Devils somewhere else on the ice. At other times, it didn't matter; they forced our players into making poor plays with the puck, recapturing it and initiating a rapid transition to offense.

Our team was less aggressive in its forechecking than the Rangers were. We employed two forwards aggressively in the forecheck when we had the chance, but we never pinched defensemen. If we couldn't establish an aggressive forecheck, we would back up into a 1-2-2 trap, limiting the space we were defending to what we believed to be the most critical area, namely, the middle of the ice. When we had sufficient numbers of players in good position, we could apply pressure on the puck to take away time and force a turnover.

Each team was very effective at employing its own style. The Devils favored a "take away the important space" first approach to the time and space principle. In contrast, the Rangers favored a "take away their time" first approach. In the end, the Rangers won the series in double overtime of the seventh game at Madison Square Garden. The philosophies and systems of these two teams were not the only reasons for success or failure. Great players making great plays at critical times, scoring goals, making saves, and so on, are much more important than how players are aligned and whether they play a high-pressure, high-risk game or employ moderate pressure and a safer style. In the end, it comes down to quality execution. Both styles and all the variances between the extremes can work if properly played.

THE PRINCIPLE OF SUPPORT

The second principle, and a key one with respect to effective team play, involves learning how to support. Support means outnumbering the opponent in the area of the puck. It might also mean skating to an area of the ice so that the puck carrier has an easy pass. It means backing up a teammate who is engaged in a one-on-one battle defensively. It may mean driving to the net on an initial attack, giving the puck carrier the option of throwing the puck toward the net and creating a rebound opportunity. The principle of support is the most important team play concept of the game and is the basis from which other concepts derive. Much of the drilling you will see later in the book has its foundation in the concept of support.

If you can teach and drill the important concepts of time and space effectively, in combination with the concept of support, you are well on your way to having a successful team. Without this knowledge, and without the ability and strategies to teach these ideas, your team will suffer from inconsistency and repeated mistakes.

Part 3

TEACHING PLAY IN THE DEFENSIVE ZONE

Chapter
8

DEFENSIVE ZONE PLAY

Let's turn our attention to the "guts" of the game, namely, the defensive zone. We've all heard coaches from virtually every sport declare that "championships are won in your own end," and hockey is no different. The defensive zone is arguably the most important zone in hockey. Being able to play well defensively, not allowing the opponent to penetrate the prime scoring area for attempts at the net, is something that good teams do well. In addition, the ability to recapture the puck and move it from the defensive zone quickly is an important component for developing attacks that wind up as scoring opportunities in the attacking zone. Having a goalkeeper who can make saves when mistakes are made by the skaters is another characteristic of good teams. A goalie who handles the puck well, can set up the puck for the defensemen, or move it out of the zone with a pass or a long clear into the neutral zone is invaluable. Playing well in the defensive zone means that you will always have a chance to win. Playing well in this part of the ice requires less talent than does scoring goals or running an effective power play. Playing well in the defensive zone is about discipline, positioning, and solid work habits. Let's examine the various parameters of play in this key area of the ice.

THE GOALKEEPER

If you don't agree that this is the most important position on the ice, try going into a playoff series with a weak tender! Without a solid goalie, it's very difficult to have a winning team or to play well in the defensive zone. This is the most difficult position mentally because when a goalie makes a mistake, there is no backup. When forwards make an error, a defenseman is usually there to right the ship. When a defenseman makes a mistake, the goalie is there to help avoid disaster. Unfortunately, *no one* is there for the goalie! If a mistake is made at this position, the red light goes on. Being aware of the added pressure a goalie faces and having strategies to deal with your goalie can help immensely in the development of a successful team.

I highly recommend having someone on your coaching staff who has experience as a goalie. This individual will be able to work with goalies on techniques and tactics and will be there to counsel them on the mental aspects of playing this position. Having a former goalie on your staff is a great benefit, as they know what it feels like when certain circumstances arise. Getting advice from someone who has actually played the position will instill credibility in the minds of your goalies. Remember that goaltending is a high-pressure position, and if the goalie is not relaxed, it's difficult to play well.

This does not excuse the head coach from responsibility for knowing about the position, its physical and mental demands, or what to look for in a goalie's play. However, it makes sense to get an expert to deal with this position, because it is not at all like the skating positions of center, wing, or defenseman.

We will briefly look at the goalie from a tactical perspective and discuss the tactical skills that are needed to be effective. Our discussion and the drill suggestions related to goaltending provide a solid foundation for what to look for from a goalie without being too technical regarding the specific skills of the position. Numerous books are available on the subject of goaltending that will provide you with the depth of information needed to work effectively with players at this position. Look for several recommended texts on goalkeeping in the resources section of this book.

The goalie has to be able to make the first save while making sure to put rebounds in safe places to avoid second-shot opportunities. Goalies must be able to read plays and anticipate what the opponent may do. In addition, they must be able to communicate verbally with teammates, assisting them when they are under pressure. Finally, goaltenders must be able to set up the puck cleanly for the defensemen, pass it quickly with velocity, and move it out of the zone when the situation dictates.

There are two main tenets in stopping the puck. The first and most important is the ability to see the puck. This sounds simplistic, but many young goalies lose focus on the puck. Losing focus is usually the result of an awareness of the presence of attackers other than the puck carrier, as well as an awareness of the puck carrier's play options. It is important to be aware of all possible options but not at the expense of obtaining the best possible angle for the first play option, which is a shot. If the puck carrier chooses a different play option, the goalie's awareness will allow him to quickly move to the new angle and position in front of the net. Your goalie must learn to see the puck, playing one potential shot at a time. This is the only way to play this position well.

The other main tenet of goaltending is positioning itself. A goalie must know how to find the best possible position for each shot (angle play). It is important to obtain the best angle possible without coming out too far. As a goalie comes out to challenge a shooter, the shooter is left with less net to shoot at. This greatly improves the prospect of making the first save but inhibits the goalie's ability to move to a new angle if the puck is passed or to reposition quickly for a second shot if control of the rebound is lost. Figures 8.1a-c illustrate this principle.

In figure 8.1a, the goalie is playing very deep in the net. The puck carrier has a large portion of the net to shoot at. In 8.1b, the goalie has moved out closer to the shooter. The shooter now has less net to shoot at. In figure 8.1c, the goalie has moved too far out. If the puck is passed across the ice, as this photo illustrates, the goalie will have a very long skate to get to a position to stop the shot coming from the second attacker.

a

b

c

Figure 8.1   (*a*) too deep, (*b*) proper depth, (*c*) out too far.

99 Percent Drill

Figure 8.2   99 percent drill.

The 99 percent drill involves players coming down the wing and firing a shot from outside the face-off dots and no farther out than the top of the circle (see figure 8.2). This drill teaches goalies how far to come out of the net to challenge shooters. The basic idea is not to come out too far as necessary. Coming out farther means an automatic save but will leave the goalie in a difficult position for the next shot.

Players carry a puck down the wing and take a shot. They follow their shot toward the net and play a subsequent shot if the rebound remains near the net. The next shooter comes from the other side of the ice, making sure not to start skating toward the net until the goalie is ready. If this drill is done properly, the goalie should not allow many, if any, goals. That's why it's called the 99 percent drill.

99 Percent Drill With Second Attacker

A common mistake that many young goalies make is that they are still moving to establish position when the shot comes. A goalie must learn to be set at the time the shot is delivered to the net. If the goalie is not set, it becomes very difficult to control rebounds or to recover balance and positioning for subsequent shots after making the first save. Tell your goalies to get the best position they can and get set. If they don't get to the ideal position in time, they should stop and get set anyway. They have a better chance of making the play from a less-than-optimum position while set than they do if they are in the optimum position but are still moving.

If a goalie has proper position, the saves they have to make will often appear easy, almost effortless. When goalies are poorly positioned, the result is often very spectacular-looking saves. This often leaves the goalie in poor position to make the next play—the

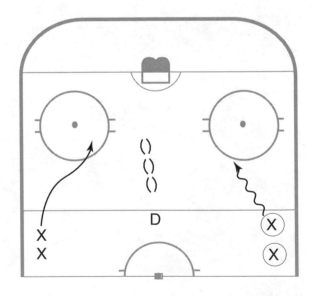

Figure 8.3   99 percent drill with second attacker.

next save. What follows are a few simple drills to help goalies learn positioning based on the situation.

The next step in this drill is to incorporate a second attacker (figure 8.3). The puck carrier carries the puck down the wing and has the option of shooting or passing. The goalie is now forced to obtain a good angle without coming too far out from the net. A good rule of thumb for goalies is to play no more than approximately one foot out from the top of the crease. The puck carrier has the option of shooting or passing the puck to the second

attacker for the shot. Check for proper position and pay attention to the control of rebounds. Finally, to create more realism, you can do the same drill with a defenseman (8.3). The defenseman does everything possible to stop a pass from being made while forcing the shot from the worst possible angle. The attackers attempt to score on the initial play and follow the shot for any rebound opportunities. If a rebound occurs, the defenseman should attempt to clear the rebound or keep the attackers from getting a second shot at the net.

Dot Drill

A great drill for goalie movement and positioning is the dot drill (figure 8.4). Two players are positioned on the face-off dots in an end zone, each with a pile of 10 pucks. On command, the goalie gets into position for the first shot. After the goalie stops the first shot, the original shooter passes a puck across the ice to the other player, who receives the pass and

takes the shot. Meanwhile the goalie has had to move quickly to a new position and get set for a shot. After taking the shot, the second shooter then makes a pass across the ice to the original shooter. This pattern continues until the 20 pucks have been shot. This is also a great conditioning drill for goalies.

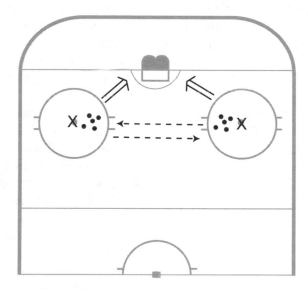

Figure 8.4   Dot drill.

Playing in Close Situations

For most goalies, the shooting situations that occur near the net and offensive attack options initiated from behind the net can be very difficult. When the puck is near the net, it is natural for all the players on the defending team to feel some anxiety, especially the goalie. With the puck near the net, the game can become more chaotic in the minds of the defenders. The only way to ensure that the chaos of defending these situations doesn't lead to paralysis is to practice defending them often.

The first practice situation involves an offensive player skating out from the corner along the goal line (figure 8.5). The attacker must move with as much speed as possible and has the option of cutting in front of the net to take a shot or faking a cut to the front, then moving behind the net and coming out the other side for a shot. It is important for the attacker to skate along the goal line while approaching the net. By skating behind the goal line, the attacker initially poses less threat of cutting in front, and it is easier for the goalie if the attacker continues to move behind the net. By skating along the goal line, the attacker becomes a legitimate and immediate threat to go in front or behind. The goalie must be able to follow the attacker's movements without cheating. If the attacker carries the puck too close to the net, the goalie has the option of using a poke check to keep the attacker from releasing a shot. The dia-

gram in figure 8.5 illustrates a simple drill for practicing this situation.

Two markers (cones, gloves, etc.) are placed in front of the net on either side to limit the space available to the attacker when coming to the front of the net. Attackers are positioned on both sides of the rink near the corners. Subsequent attacks at the net come from opposite sides. Be sure the goalie has enough time to get back in position before allowing the next attacker to begin.

The next step in this sequence involves a second attacker who is positioned on the near-side face-off dot (figure 8.6). The first attacker executes the same pattern, skating toward the net with the puck. The puck carrier now has the option of cutting to the front for a shot, moving behind the net and to the other side for a shot, or passing the puck to the second attacker for a shot. The important teaching point is to remind the goalie to play one potential shot at a time. By remaining square to the puck carrier, the goalie can avoid playing a potential shot from the puck carrier and one from the second attacker at the same time.

The last phase of this drill sequence involves a third attacker positioned on the far-side face-off dot (figure 8.7). Now the puck carrier has the option of cutting out in front or moving behind the net, taking the shot himself, passing to the near-side dot for a shot, or passing to the far-side dot for a shot. When the third attacker is included, talk to the goalie about positioning the stick so as to block a pass to the far dot. If the attacker gets too close before passing the puck and the goalie can deflect the pass, it's one less shot to stop. Playing these types of situations requires the goalie to have very specific technical skating

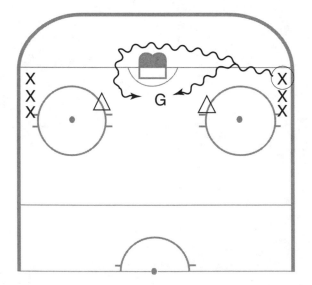

Figure 8.5 Defending the goal with attacker coming from the corner along the goal line.

skills. To add more realism to this drill, add a defender in front of the net so that it becomes a 3 v 1 situation. Finally, add a second defender to make it a 3 v 2.

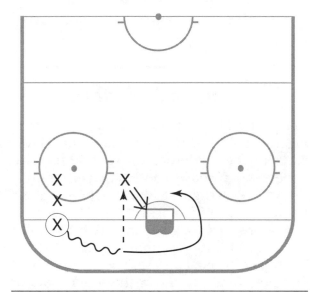

Figure 8.6 Defending the goal with attacker on the near-side of the face-off dot.

Shots from the point with player traffic in front of the net are difficult situations for many goalies. Player traffic can obstruct the goalie's vision and pucks can change direction quickly, creating a feeling of uneasiness. It is important to practice this type of situation so that the goalies become comfortable and confident in their abilities to stop the puck under these circumstances.

An easy way to begin teaching goalies how to deal with screened shots is to use another goalie to establish a screen in front of the goal. A coach or player may then fire pucks on either side of the screen or through the screening player's legs. The goalie in net attempts to see the shot through the legs of the screening player or to either side. During games, it is often impossible to find the puck through a screen. When this is the case, the goalie must establish the best position possible relative to the puck and then cover as much net as possible.

More advanced drills to practice this situation would involve 2 v 2 or 3 v 3 battles in front of the net while defensemen shoot pucks

Figure 8.7 Defending the goal with attacker on the far side of the face-off dot.

from the point. The offensive players in these battles would be concerned with establishing screens and attempting to deflect pucks and get to rebounds for second shots.

Deflected shots are yet another difficult situation for the goaltender to play. When playing potential deflection shots, the goalie should establish the best position possible. This is done by getting as close as possible to the attacker attempting to deflect the puck. The closer the goalie is to the deflector when the deflection occurs, the more likely the puck is to hit the goalie. It is very difficult to react to deflections. The best defense is to limit the space between the deflector and the goalie.

Deflecting/Redirections

The next drill involves deflecting or redirecting shots. In the first exercise, one player stands in the middle of the ice and attempts to deflect shots fired by another player shooting from the point (figure 8.8a). The shooter at the point has the option of shooting between the deflector's legs, to his right, or to his left. The deflector's position is from 7 to 15 feet above the top of the goal crease. The goalie should come out of the net no farther than a foot or two beyond the goal crease. In a real game, being positioned beyond that makes it difficult to recover if the puck changes position on the ice quickly. The second exercise involves a player standing in the corner, passing to the point, then moving toward the net for a redirect (figure 8.8b).

Figure 8.8   (*a*) Deflecting and (*b*) redirecting the shot.

The initial training for this situation involves placing two boards on either side of the net, angled toward it. The coach can then shoot pucks off either board, and the goalie can react to the caromed shots.

After allowing goalies to face situations involving only one deflector, look to create more gamelike situations. An excellent exercise for practicing this situation is to create a 3 v 2 in front of the net with two point players. The two point players must stay at the blue line. They are encouraged to make passes between themselves and also to take shots. Because there are three offensive players in front of the net and only two defenders, it is relatively easy for one of the attackers to get open in front to deflect a point shot. The attackers should play any rebounds in front. If the rebound goes to the corner, the attackers should try to retrieve the puck and send it back to the point for another shot and potential deflection. Each drill repetition can be allowed to go on for up to 30 seconds. If the defenders completely clear away a loose puck, the coach may throw out a second puck in order to complete the 30-second work interval.

This concludes our discussion of goalkeeping as it relates to its primary function—stopping pucks. Our discussion focused on the tactical aspects of stopping pucks and situations that goalies must be able to handle effectively. There is much more to learn about goalkeeping for all serious coaches. As mentioned previously, take the time to read the books and view the tapes related to this position that you will find listed in the selected resources at the end of the book.

DEFENSIVE ZONE PLAY WITHOUT THE PUCK

We have already discussed the principle of playing well in front of both nets. It's easy to talk about the importance of playing well in front of your net, but exactly how should a coach teach and drill this principle so players will execute well?

Begin with a discussion of the prime scoring area, stressing the importance of this area of the ice. Explain that most goals are scored from this part of the ice and that very few are scored from outside this area. When a goal is scored from outside this area, it is usually because the goalie has made a poor play.

Next, explain to the players that if all five skaters are positioned within this area, the prospects of denying a scoring opportunity from the prime scoring area are enhanced. All five skaters cannot stand still and wait for the opponent to bring the puck to the prime scoring area. This means that players will have to leave their initial positions in the middle of the ice to force the opposing puck carrier outside of the prime scoring area. Players must understand that before leaving the prime scoring area, they must be sure that this area is being covered properly by teammates.

Making certain that the area in front of the net is covered first is just common sense. Why would a player ever want to leave the front of the net to chase a puck carrier who is behind the goal line or near the boards when no teammate is available to cover the front of the net? It shouldn't happen, yet it occurs frequently during games at all levels of play. One reason is that players become impatient or are focused only on the puck, unaware of who or what else is around them. Another is that players often forget that they must not only do their own job, but must be prepared to support teammates who fail to do theirs.

Alignments

There are two methods for aligning players in the defensive zone. The first and most common method is to use the center as a low forward supporting the defensemen around the front of the net and in the corners (figure 8.9). In this formation, called the 2-1-2, the wings are primarily responsible for covering the opposing defensemen (points). Assuming the opposition has an alignment of three forwards and two defensemen, it creates a 3 v 3 situation down low and a 2 v 2 situation at the point.

The other method is to use both wings down low in support of the defensemen while the center covers both opposing defensemen

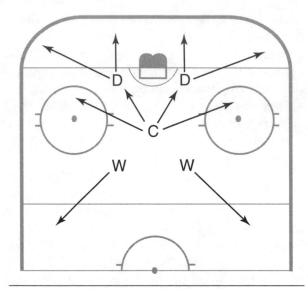

Figure 8.9   Aligning players in the defensive zone.

(figure 8.10). Obviously, the center cannot cover both offensive defensemen at once, so the tendency is to shade toward the puck-side defenseman. This creates a numerical advantage of four defenders vs. three attacking forwards down low in the defensive zone. This formation, usually called the 1-2-2, is less common than the 2-1-2 but can be effective, especially if your defensemen are not reliable. The potential problem with this formation is that it can make it difficult to form an attack quickly once the puck has been recaptured in the defensive zone.

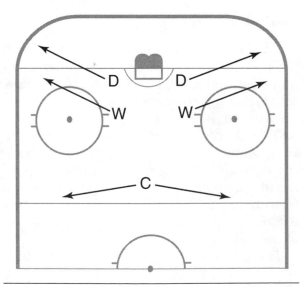

Figure 8.10   Using wings to support the defensemen.

We will focus our attention on defending the defensive zone with a 2-1-2 formation. As we work through the explanations and drills used for teaching this system of play, you will be able to figure out how to create a similar set of drills if you want to utilize the 1-2-2 alignment.

2-1-2 Defensive Zone Coverage Fundamentals

Address these fundamentals when playing the 2-12 defensive zone.

Head on a Swivel

Playing solid defense requires that all players continuously look around, particularly when they are away from the puck. The puck has a mesmerizing quality for any hockey player, but especially for younger players. Its alluring power can consume professional players, too, even seasoned NHL'ers. Because situations change quickly, players must be looking around at all times, constantly assessing the play. Positioning is equally important to stopping the attacking team, and when defenders are looking around, they are much more likely to move their feet and assume a better position relative to the attackers and their offensive play options.

The fundamental principle of constantly looking around must be emphasized at practice and in games. When running a drill that involves coverage in the defensive zone, check your players to make sure they are playing with their head on a swivel. Demand that they do it. During games, watch players who are away from the puck and make certain they are looking around. Reinforce this principle as often as possible.

Playing 1 v 1s

We are discussing 2-1-2 zone defense, but it still comes down to 1 v 1 confrontations. If players win their 1 v 1 battles, your opponent will have the puck for less time in your defensive zone and is therefore less likely to score. When a defensive player commits to attacking an opponent, initiating a 1 v 1 confrontation, the first step is to read what level of puck possession the opponent has. There are three basic puck possession levels. The first occurs when an opposing player has full control of the puck with his head up and is looking toward the middle of the ice or the net. The second level is when the puck carrier has full possession of the puck but is facing the boards and is not completely aware of all play options available to him. The third level of possession involves the puck being near the attacker's stick, perhaps rolling along the boards or bouncing around between his skates. Determining the level of possession dictates how quickly and aggressively the defender can approach the opposing player and which defensive techniques should be utilized. This determination must be made instantly and instinctively.

Let's assume the attacking player has full possession looking toward the middle of the ice or the net. The defending player must attack at an angle, preferably driving the opponent down toward the backboards. If the angle of attack is straight or "head on," the player in control of the puck can use fakes and skate to either the left or right. If the defender approaches at an angle, one lateral skating option is denied to the opponent. The defender's stick should be in front of his body, in one hand. As the defender approaches the attacker, the defender will be prepared to extend the stick to poke the puck away or deflect a pass attempt. At a distance of about 10 feet from the attacker, the defender must align his skates under his body, gliding under control. If the defender skates too aggressively, the attacker will be able to spin away easily. If possible, the defender should finish the attacker with a body check but make certain that the opponent is controlled and therefore unable to beat the defender to the front of the net. In this particular situation, it is often better not to finish the body check. When the opponent has this level of possession, the defender must think to contain first, keeping the puck carrier from getting to the prime scoring area.

When the opponent has full possession of the puck but is facing away from the net, the defender can be slightly more aggressive. The defender should still approach at an angle, driving the puck carrier toward the goal line. Good offensive players know when attackers are coming too fast, out of control, and can spin away easily. When the opponent turns away from the angling defender, the puck is always exposed. A poke check with one hand on the stick is used, followed by a body check designed to stop the opponent's momentum.

In the last scenario, with the puck loose along the boards, the defender can and should be far more aggressive, looking to take the body of the opponent and allow a supporting teammate to regain possession of the puck. In this situation, the defender may not need to angle, but should look to control the opponent physically as soon as possible.

Playing Quick-Developing 2v1s Deep in the Defensive Zone

Playing 1 v 1 situations well and winning those battles is a staple of good defensive play, but in every game, there are numerous times when someone is beaten 1 v 1. Sometimes, it's just for a second or two, and the remaining players near the net must play a quick 2 v 1 attack.

Players caught in this situation must first recognize that they are caught in a 2 v 1 situation. This recognition comes from playing swivel-headed and having the necessary awareness. The second element is common sense in that players must defend the prime scoring area first, shading toward the most dangerous player with their stick on the ice, ready to deflect any pass attempts.

Playing Against Enemy Forwards

Playing against enemy forwards in front of the net when a point shot is imminent is one of the more difficult situations for young players to learn to play effectively. The fundamental guideline in this situation is to try to keep the body between the attacker and the net without allowing oneself to be completely tied up with that attacker. The most important technical element is to make sure that the defender has two hands on the stick. If a defender gets caught with only one hand on the stick, they will not have the necessary strength to ward off the attacker or clear the rebound. Ideally, the defender should try to wall off the attacker so that the goalie has a clear line of vision. Not getting tied up completely is important because if the rebound lands nearby, the defender needs to be able to clear the puck from in front of the net. Also, a quick 2 v 1 can develop in front when a teammate loses position on one of the attackers. If tied up with one opponent, a defender cannot react to this situation. At the moment the shot is fired, the defender should look to lift the attacker's stick, preventing a deflection.

The fundamental technique for walling off opponents and remaining free is for a defender to push the opponent quickly with two hands on the stick, walling off and creating a cushion between himself and the attacker. Usually, a crosscheck-type action is required and must be aimed at the midsection of the attacker's body to avoid a penalty. The coach must be aware of what level of aggressiveness with the stick the defenders will be allowed to employ without being assessed a penalty.

When playing against attackers who are large and difficult to move near the net, defenders must begin by somehow getting the attacker off balance. A physically large or powerful attacker is easy to neutralize once he's lost his balance. Slight tugs with the stick directed at the feet followed by a quick push-off are often effective. Pushing down with the stick on the small of the back will also cause an attacker to lose balance. The defender must be careful not to knock the attacker to the ice, as this usually results in a penalty unless the puck is directly adjacent to the attacker.

Using the Body

Whenever prudent, defenders should finish their checks, hitting the opposing player who is in possession of the puck or who has just released a pass or shot. In modern hockey, attacking teams like to cycle the puck. This means that the three attacking forwards try to remain in motion in the attacking zone, and when they face checking pressure and don't have a direct pass available, they will bump the puck back down along the boards for a teammate to skate to. After bumping the puck down the boards, the original puck carrier may skate to the net. If attacking forwards are hit and their skating momentum is interrupted, this offensive play tactic is less effective. If attackers are allowed to skate freely, cycling the puck, it's only a matter of time before one of them beats a defender to the net and a scoring chance occurs.

Positional Guidelines and Responsibilities

Every position has responsibilities and rules to the team. They are described here.

Defensemen

The two defensemen cover the area in front of the net and into the corners from roughly the face-off dots to the side boards to the back boards. The right defenseman works in the right quadrant and the left defenseman in the left quadrant. When one defenseman is working his area, the other should be in front of the net (figure 8.11). The exact position of the defenseman covering the front of the net is determined by the positions of the attacking forwards. For example, it makes no sense for the defenseman covering the front to be standing next to the goalie, three feet from the net, if two of the opposing forwards are working in the corner and the third forward is at the top of the circle on the puck side.

In figure 8.11, the left defenseman is attacking the puck carrier in the corner. The second opposing forward is near the puck carrier, and the defending team's center is positioned to support the left defenseman, ready to get the puck if it comes loose and ready to challenge the second attacker if the puck comes to that player. The net front defenseman in the diagram is initially positioned too close to the goalie. As you can see, the third opposing forward is high, away from the net, so it makes sense for the defenseman covering the front of the net to move out a bit higher,

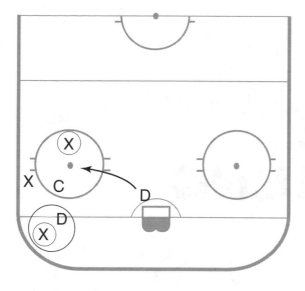

Figure 8.11 Positioning defensemen.

closing the gap. Thus, the net front defenseman can challenge the attacking high forward if the puck is passed in their direction.

Low Forward/Center

This player's role is to act as a third defenseman. The area of coverage responsibility is the same as for the two defensemen. This player must have sound stick-checking ability, body-checking technique, and the ability to play swivel-headed, always aware of the ever-changing play situations in the defensive zone. The low forward is the first forward back in the defensive zone. In our 2-1-2 system of defensive zone coverage, we want the center to be the low forward as much as possible. However, as the forwards skate back to defensive zone coverage position after an attack, the center may be the last player back into the defensive zone. Because the area down low around the front of the net is the most important area to protect initially, the

first forward back, in this case, a wing, must know the low forward's responsibilities and be able to execute this role until there is a safe opportunity to switch positions with the center.

The low forward can be either the first or second player to attack the puck carrier or contend for a loose puck in the corners, away from the front of the net. In most cases, the defenseman will be the first player involved and the low forward/center becomes the supporting player, ready to gain control of a loose puck or get involved in a 1 v 1 confrontation with a second attacker.

High Forwards/Wings

The last two forwards (wings) back into the defensive zone are primarily responsible for covering the points, the other team's defensemen. The strong-side wing should cover the opposing defenseman somewhat tightly, two stick lengths away, and from the inside out. Playing from the inside out allows the wing to be in the shooting lane, ready to block a shot if the puck comes to that defenseman. If that defenseman leaves the point and heads for the net, the two-stick-length cushion and inside positioning will make it easier for the strong-side wing to recognize and cover.

The weak-side wing covers the point player away from the puck side and plays four or five stick lengths away. This wing's primary role is to cover that point player, but the gap is greater because this player also has "help" responsibility in front of the net if one of the defensemen or the low forward gets beaten down low.

The centers must also know how to perform these two jobs in case they become the fourth or fifth player skating back into defensive zone coverage position.

Chapter 9

DEFENSIVE ZONE DRILLING

Before you begin reading this chapter, a word of warning is in order. This section of the book contains a ton of information, and for good reason. The importance of the defensive zone goes far beyond coverages to include concepts such as defensive zone face-offs, breakout patterns, specific assignments by position, and so on. You will find all of that plus more in the pages to follow. In addition to drills, I will also provide additional explanations when warranted with respect to areas we have not yet looked at. Don't get overwhelmed by this information, but simply take it in stages. Over time, the concepts you read about here will become second nature to you and your players. Remember, Rome wasn't built in a day!

INITIAL DRILLS FOR TEACHING DEFENSIVE ZONE COVERAGE

1 v 1 Low Drill

Forwards are positioned in line along the half wall with defenders positioned in line at the tops of the circles (figure 9.1). One defender is positioned with both feet on the edge of the face-off circle, facing away from the corner. A forward is ready with a puck in the corner, facing the glass. On cue, the forward turns with the puck and attacks the net while the defenseman turns and attempts to keep the forward from reaching the net and getting a shot on goal. The repetition ends when either the attacker is pinned to the glass, a goal is scored, the defender clears the puck from the defensive zone, or approximately 20 seconds have elapsed.

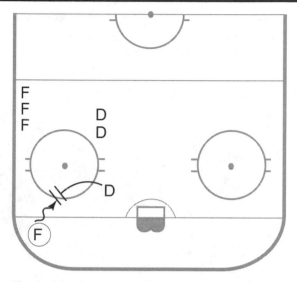

Figure 9.1   1 v 1 low drill.

A variation to this drill is to practice a 1 v 1 low corner battle. In this scenario, the forward is again facing the glass, but the defenseman or defending low forward is right behind the attacking forward when the cue to begin the drill is given (figure 9.2). Again, the attacking forward is attempting to reach the net for a shot, and the defender is trying to either pin the attacker against the boards and glass or take the puck and pass it out of the defensive zone. Repetition ends when either the attacker is pinned to the glass, a goal is scored, the defender clears the puck from the defensive zone, or approximately 20 seconds have elapsed.

A final variation of this drill involves a 1 v 1 with a chip down the wall. In this variation, the coach chips the puck along the boards, where it is chased by the attacker and defender and the ensuing 1 v 1 battle takes place. Repetition ends when either the attacker is pinned to the glass, a goal is scored, the defender clears the puck from the defensive zone, or approximately 20 seconds have elapsed.

Figure 9.2   1 v 1 drill with defensemen behind attacking forward.

2 v 1 Low

One attacker is positioned at the hash mark against the boards with a puck. The other attacker is positioned against the boards along the goal line (figure 9.3). On cue, the attackers attempt to make a play that results in a shot on goal. The defender attempts to keep the shot from occurring. It may not be possible to stop a shot on goal, so the defender must concentrate on forcing a shot from a poor position, away from the prime scoring area. Repetition ends at the coach's discretion. A variation of this drill is to begin the attack from behind the net.

Figure 9.3   2 v 1 low.

2 v 2 Low

The coach initiates the drill sequence by chipping a puck into the corner, where it is fought for by an attacker and defender. A second attacker and defender get involved at any time (figure 9.4). Again, the attackers seek to get a shot on goal; the defenders attempt to deny a shot and get the puck out of the defensive zone. Repetition ends when a goal is scored, the defenders clear the puck from the defensive zone, or approximately 20 seconds have elapsed.

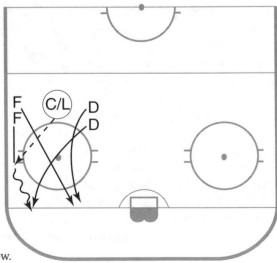

Figure 9.4   2 v 2 low.

A variation of this drill consists of 2 v 2 Low with point shots. This drill is the same as the previous 2 v 2 except that one or two defensemen are placed along the blue line. At any time, the attackers may pass the puck to the point for a shot by one of the defensemen positioned there (figure 9.5). The point shot must come from the blue line. The defensemen who are shooting are not allowed to slide any closer to the net than 10 feet from the blue line. The defenders must now wall off the attackers as the shot comes and try to clear away any rebounds. Repetition ends when a goal is scored, the defenders clear the puck from the defensive zone, or approximately 30 seconds have elapsed.

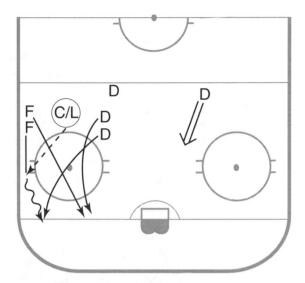

Figure 9.5 2 v 2 low with point shots.

3 v 2 Low

Three forwards attack against two defenders. One defender must always pressure the puck carrier, leaving the other defender to play a 2 v 1 (figure 9.6). The defender left to play the 2 v 1 must always shade toward the most dangerous of the potential shooters. The defender who attacks the puck at any point must sprint back to position at the front of the net, at which time the defensive partner may initiate pressure on the next player in possession of the puck. This is a 30-second drill. If a goal is scored before 30 seconds have elapsed, the coach provides another puck.

Figure 9.6 3 v 2 low.

Similar to the 2 v 2 Low with point shots, try the same drill again except that when the attackers pass the puck to the defenseman at the blue line for a shot, the two low defenders are now playing an outnumbered situation in front of their net and must not get tied up with any single attacker (figure 9.7). Again, this is a 30-second drill, and more than one puck may have to be used to complete the repetition if the defenders clear the puck or the attackers score.

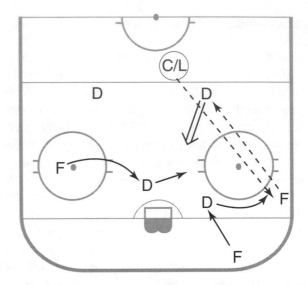

Figure 9.7   3 v 2 low with point shots.

Bread and Butter: 3 v 3 low

We call this our "bread and butter" drill because it is the one we use most often to practice our defensive zone coverage down low. It is a 30-second drill. If a goal is scored or the puck is cleared by the defenders before 30 seconds have elapsed, the coach provides an additional puck. In figure 9.8 you can see the Bread and Butter drill with an added point player. This is a variation that may be used to proceed on outlet for the offensive players.

Figure 9.8   Bread and butter drill.

5 v 2 High Forward Drill

The purpose of this drill is for the high forward to practice coverage responsibilities based on the position of the puck. The five attackers are positioned in the attacking zone, one in each corner, one in the high slot, and two at the points along the blue line (figure 9.9). The two defenders must go from covering the point when the puck is on their side of the ice to covering the high slot when the puck is on the opposite side. The attackers pass the puck around the perimeter for approximately 15 seconds while the coach checks for proper positioning by the two defending forwards. After 15 seconds, the attackers are allowed to make a pass to the attacker in the high slot. Whenever the puck is at the point, both defending forwards should be tight on the attacking defensemen.

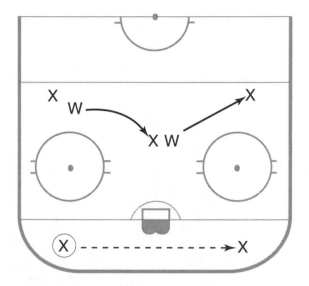

Figure 9.9   5 v 2 high forward drill.

5 v 5 Defensive Zone Coverage With Multiple Pucks

This 30-second drill is simply a 5 v 5 scrimmage in the defensive zone. The attackers are attempting to score, and the defenders are attempting to clear the puck from the defending zone. If a goal is scored or the puck is cleared before 30 seconds have elapsed, the coach throws in another puck. This drill can be done with the defenders playing with their sticks turned over so that they are unable to play the puck. This makes it easier for the coach to check for proper positioning.

5 v 5 Defensive Zone Coverage Conditioner

In this drill, the coach allows the scrimmage to continue for 10 to 15 seconds. At that time, the whistle is blown, and the defending team must skate to the nearest side board, across the ice to the other side board, then back to coverage positions. At that point, a second puck is provided by the coach. The drill ends after the third puck is cleared from the zone or a goal is scored. This can be made into a fun competition if you have units of five. The unit allowing the fewest goals is the winner.

Funnel Drill

The purpose of this drill is to teach the transition from backchecking to defensive zone coverage. A unit of five players breaks out from an end zone, with one player carrying the puck through the neutral zone. A second unit of five is positioned in the neutral zone with their own puck, making passes and skating lightly (figures 9.10a-b). At the whistle, the neutral zone unit attacks and the unit that initially broke out of the defensive zone leaves the puck they were carrying and backchecks to defensive zone coverage position. The coach checks for proper reads and movement to correct positions by the backcheckers based on whether they were the first, second, or third forward back. The repetition ends when either a goal is scored or the puck is cleared from the defensive zone.

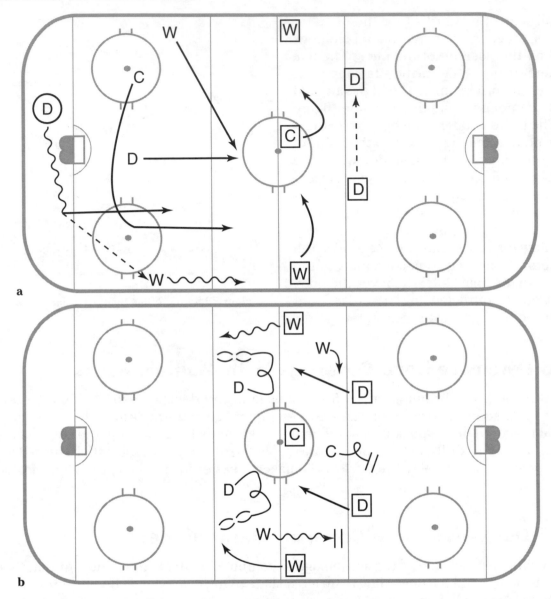

Figure 9.10   Funnel drill.

COVERAGE AFTER LOSING A DEFENSIVE ZONE FACE-OFF

Players must always assume that the face-off will be lost and therefore should be sprinting to their coverage assignments. The fundamental rule on any defensive zone draw is that defensemen must line up opposite the opponent's wings, the center lines up opposite the opponent's center, and the wings line up opposite the opposing defensemen. This is

the one moment in the game where a complete man-to-man style is preferable for the first few seconds after the puck is dropped.

How do you align your players for a defensive zone face-off? The answer is based on how the attackers are positioned following the principle of center on center, defensemen on wings, and wings on defensemen. This is important because your team must assume that the face-off will be lost to the opponent. Figure 9.11 illustrates a standard three-across

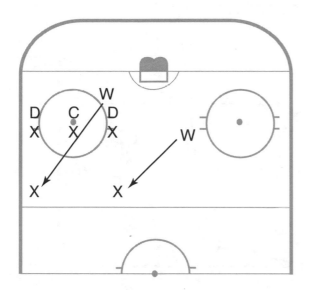

Figure 9.11 Standard three-across alignment.

1. The goalie or one of the skaters shoots the puck out of the zone.
2. One of the skaters, most often a defenseman, carries the puck out of the zone.
3. A few quick, well-timed passes are executed, and the team advances the puck to the next zone and perhaps beyond with a coordinated attack.

The ideal situation is to be able to get the puck out with either a carry or a pass, perhaps two, so that possession is maintained and the attack can continue. However, the bottom line is to ensure that the puck gets out of the defensive zone. Successful teams can read the pattern and intensity of the enemy forecheck and select the appropriate option. At times, regardless of how skilled the players are, they just have to get "down and dirty" and fight to get the puck back in the neutral zone.

Remember, too, that breakouts begin with the goaltender, who has two main jobs to perform. The first is to play the puck, if possible, either by setting it up for a defenseman to possibly make a breakout pass or by passing it. The goalie's second job is to communicate verbally with both defensemen. All goaltenders must tell the defensemen how much time they have, how many forecheckers are coming, how close they are, and finally, what to do with the puck.

We use a full-ice warm-up drill to begin developing this type of puck skill for our goalies and the communication that must exist between the goalie and defensemen. The drill begins at one end, with two players skating and passing a puck while coming up the side boards (figure 9.12). At the center red line, the puck is dumped in and ringed around the boards. The goalie leaves the net and stops the ringed puck. The player who dumped the puck in assumes the role of defenseman, skating to retrieve the puck and instructing the goalie to leave the puck, ring it (near side), or reverse it to the weak side. Meanwhile, the second skater assumes the role of a winger and is available for a pass on either

alignment by the attacking team and coverage assignments for the defenders.

Notice that the wings head toward the opposing defensemen at the point on the drop of the puck. Notice also that the defensive left wing skates through the face-off circle on the way to covering the opposing right defenseman. In this case, the defensive left wing is taking an inside-out path to his coverage assignment.

What happens if an opponent uses a different alignment? This is where the principle of wingers on opposing defensemen, center on center, and defensemen on opposing wings becomes very important. Coaches need to pay special attention to opponents who use variations on the three-across alignment.

BREAKOUTS FROM THE DEFENSIVE ZONE

Successful hockey teams seem to get control of the puck quickly and advance the puck out of their defensive zone with ease. By minimizing the amount of time spent in the defensive zone, good teams reduce the probability of allowing goals. There are three ways to get the puck out of the defensive zone:

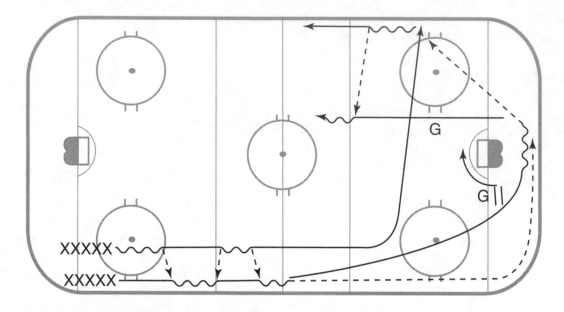

Figure 9.12   Communication drill for goalies and defensemen.

the near-side or far-side boards based on what was communicated. The two skaters then carry the puck back up the ice, returning to the starting point. Both goalies should be working to enhance the flow of this drill, keeping more players moving. Thus, after the first goalie makes his play, the second goalie is in position to work with the next two advancing skaters. At first, the coach may have to use the whistle to control the timing of repetitions. After doing the drill a few times, the team should begin to develop the proper timing between repetitions without needing the regulatory whistle blasts from the coach. Finally, to make this drill more realistic, a third player can be added who acts as a forechecker, pressuring the goalie.

The most difficult play for defensemen to make is going back to retrieve the puck with their back turned away from the attacking forecheckers and their teammates. Thus, it's a plus when the goalie can set up the puck so it's easy for the defenseman to maintain his skating speed as he retrieves it. When a defenseman is coming back for the puck under pressure and can't see who's chasing him and which teammates are open, it's comforting for him and effective to have verbal direction from the goalie.

GOALIES

• Always try to leave the puck behind the goal line extended. This is important because if the defenseman attempting to retrieve the puck mishandles it, it is less likely to wind up in the net. Obviously, if the goalie sees that there are no opposing forecheckers around, he can leave the puck in front of the goal line extended.

• Leave the puck away from the boards. It's very difficult for defensemen to retrieve a puck under forechecking pressure, but it's even more difficult when they have to dig it away from the boards. Goalies must learn to take the time to set up the puck away from the boards.

• Leave the puck on the player's forehand. Every hockey player I have ever watched is better at handling the puck and making a pass on the forehand side than on the backhand. If the goalie can set up the puck so that the defenseman can retrieve it on the forehand, the defenseman has a much better chance of making a good play. To do this, goalie must realize which defenders shoot left or right-handed. Success at getting the puck out of the defensive zone is often determined by how the goalie sets up the puck for the defensemen.

DEFENSEMEN

As mentioned earlier, the most difficult play for defensemen is coming back to get the puck with their back turned to the charging enemy forecheckers. The tactical skills required are difficult to execute, especially under pressure. These skills must be practiced often and with proper execution demanded by the coaching staff.

- Always pivot to the outside. Defensemen are usually skating backward when the opponent dumps the puck into the zone and must pivot from backward skating to forward skating. By pivoting to the outside, the defenseman can see how close the opposing winger is and how fast that player is coming. He can also see whether or not he has a teammate in support position on the near-side wall behind the oncoming forechecker.

- Look over the inside shoulder after pivoting to the outside and collect information on what's coming in the form of forecheckers from the weak side and what support is available from teammates.

- Look once more to the strong side. Approach the puck from the side, if possible, at an angle that allows for maintaining speed. Defensemen often approach the puck skating directly toward the backboards and are forced to slow their speed in order to pick up the puck. When under immediate pressure, look to approach the puck so that a play can be made immediately using the forehand.

- Pick up the puck with your stick and hands in front of your body and slightly to the forehand side, using both hands to hold the stick. This ensures a smooth collection of the puck. If a defenseman fumbles the puck as he attempts to gain control of it, he has less time to make a good play and is more likely to get hit by an onrushing forechecker.

- Develop the ability to feel which side the forechecker is attacking from and be prepared to escape with the puck by turning to the opposite side. The forechecker has to be very close for this to work. If the forechecker is too far away, he can easily adjust his skating to check the defenseman's escape move.

- It is a good idea to practice giving false information or fakes as you approach a puck when the opponent is close behind. Good fakes can leave forecheckers crashing into the boards and leave the puck-retrieving defenseman with plenty of time to make a play.

- Be prepared to use the net as an obstruction to oncoming forecheckers by cutting sharply, as close to the net as possible, using the net as a pick and leaving the forechecker to chase from behind.

Defensive Partner

The defenseman attempting to retrieve the puck against heavy forechecking can have a much easier time of it if he gets help from his partner. There are three fundamental ways the other defenseman can help his partner:

- Step into the skating lane of the oncoming forechecker; this is commonly called a pick. Defensemen are allowed to do this for their partners provided they do not use their stick to impede the forechecker's progress or deliver a body check. By simply skating into the forechecker's intended line of pursuit, a defenseman gives his partner more time to collect the puck, make a good play, and avoid being crunched on the boards.

- If a defenseman has enough time to retrieve the puck without being pressured too aggressively, his partner may choose to give him the option of passing the puck from corner to corner behind the net or of going to the front of the net and reversing the puck so the partner can retrieve it.

- In general, always communicate verbally with the other defenseman so he knows what he should do with the puck and how much time he has to do it. Simple key phrases like, "He's right on ya," "Time, lots of time," "Over," or "Ring it" can make your partner's life much easier.

DRILLS FOR DEVELOPING
TACTICAL BREAKOUT SKILLS FOR DEFENSEMEN

Pivot, Look, Forehand Drill

The defenseman starts by skating backward from the face-off dot outside the blue line. A puck is then dumped in so that it lies close to the boards in the corner (figure 9.13). The defenseman pivots to the outside and looks over both shoulders while maintaining speed. He must approach the puck from an angle so that it is on his forehand as he turns up ice with it, and he is not allowed to skate behind the net with it. He must skate at full speed with the puck as far as the face-off dot before passing to the next defenseman in line. The drill is run out of both corners simultaneously, and after a player has executed from the right corner, he moves to the other line so his next repetition is done from the left corner. The coach can choose to begin this drill with a point shot followed by the dump-in.

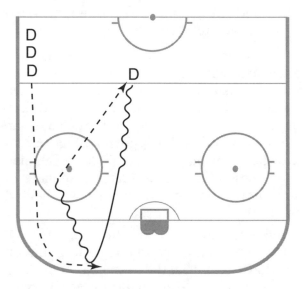

Figure 9.13   Pivot, look, forehand drill.

False Information Drill

One defenseman starts at the dot with a puck and throws it off the backboards (figure 9.14). The "D" immediately starts to retrieve the puck while being pursued closely by another defenseman acting as a forechecker. Since the defenseman has no time to approach the puck at an angle, he is forced to approach it directly and to use fakes to avoid getting crunched on the boards. Convincing fakes, smooth puck retrieval, and quick turning ability are required. Repetition ends when the defenseman is able to skate the puck to the dot or the forechecker forces a turnover.

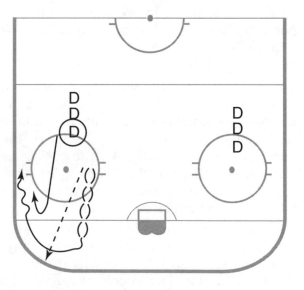

Figure 9.14   False information drill.

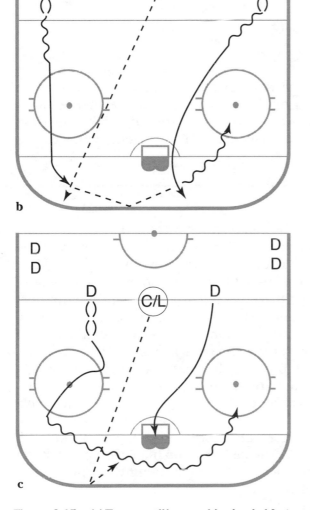

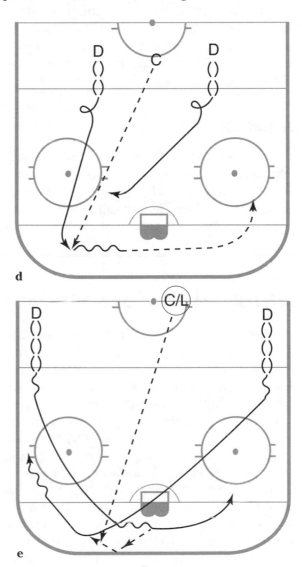

Partner Communication Drill

Two defensemen start by skating backward from the face-off dots outside the blue line (figures 9.15a-e) as a puck is dumped into one corner. One defenseman pivots to retrieve the puck, and his partner calls out the play he wants his teammate to execute after retrieving the puck. His call options are "Turn up," "Wheel," "Over," "Ring," and "Reverse." "Turn up" means turn up ice toward the boards on the side of the puck. "Wheel" means carry the puck behind the net to the other side. "Over" means a defenseman-to-defenseman (D-to-D) pass behind the net. "Ring" means fire the

Figure 9.15 (*a*)Turn up, (*b*) over, (*c*) wheel, (*d*) ring, (*e*) reverse.

puck along the boards to the weak side. "Reverse" means carry the puck behind the net and throw it back to the area he came from so that his partner can retrieve it.

Partner Options Drill

This drill involves two defensemen working together against one forechecker (figure 9.16). The two defensemen skate backward from the face-off dots, and a puck is dumped in. A single forechecker applies pressure on the defenseman attempting to retrieve the puck. The other defenseman must read how much time his partner will have to retrieve the puck. If the forechecker is close, he should look to skate into the forechecker's path, giving his partner more time to retrieve the puck. If the forechecker is not close, he may choose to slide to the opposite corner for a D-to-D pass or go to the front of the net for a possible D-to-D reverse.

Figure 9.16   Partner options drill.

Read Drill

One defenseman starts from the dot, skating backward. A forechecker dumps the puck, and the defenseman turns to pick it up while being chased by the forechecker. His partner, without communicating verbally, goes to either the strong-side or weak-side boards around the top of the circle. The puck-retrieving defenseman must recognize which side his partner is going to and move the puck up that side of the ice.

CENTER OR FIRST FORWARD BACK

The center or first forward to get back into the defensive zone is responsible for supporting the defenseman on the breakout from a position somewhere between the two face-off dots. The exact position the center occupies between those dots at any moment in the breakout process is determined by the position of the puck and the degree of possession the defenseman has. In general, the center's skating pattern should mirror the path of the puck. If the puck is being carried by the left defenseman in the left corner, the center should be shading to the left side. If the puck is passed D-to-D behind the net, the center must follow the pass across the ice.

The center can never be too low (too close to the goal line extended) as he mirrors the puck. Centers often get into trouble when they are out too high (too near the blue line) and therefore not in good position to support the defensemen if the puck turns over to the opponent. Being out too high can also be a problem if the puck is passed to the wing on the boards. The center must stay below the winger on the boards to provide proper support when that winger receives the puck. Again, if something goes wrong with the winger's attempt to make a play on the wall while the center is too high, a quick 3 v 2 can result near the net, giving the opponent a chance to score.

WINGS

The responsibility of the right and left wings on the breakout is fairly simple but often difficult to execute under game conditions. They must be available to receive an outlet pass from the defensemen and then make a second pass so that possession of the puck is maintained and the attack can continue up ice. If it is not possible to make a good pass so the attack can progress, the wing must be able to either get the puck out over the blue line or protect the puck along the boards until support arrives from the center. One problem for wingers is that they must execute all this under rather intense checking pressure. Another problem is that they are often stationary, making it difficult to avoid being hit while making the play. Wings must communicate verbally, just like the defensemen and goalies. If they hustle back to make themselves available for a defenseman and are open, they have to yell for the puck.

The weak-side wing has a very easy job to perform. As it becomes obvious that the puck will move to wing on the other side, he must skate across the zone to the middle of the ice, just below the blue line, providing support. It is important for the weak-side wing to control his skating speed. He should be able to read the play and determine what level of possession his teammate on the other side will have and how much pressure that wing is under. If his teammate can make the play cleanly, then he should be flying through the middle of the ice, yelling for the puck, which can be passed directly or off the boards, depending on the defensive positioning of the opposing players.

The first step in developing wingers' ability to make the necessary plays on the breakout along the boards is to develop their ability to execute a quick Mohawk turn and then catch a pass. To execute a Mohawk turn, the wing skates back toward the goal line about 10 to 15 feet from the side boards. The wing then pivots quickly to backward skating so that he is facing up ice as he receives the pass and quickly turns back to forward skating. When done properly, this forward-to-backward and backward-to-forward move while catching a breakout pass looks like one skill, even though it involves two change-of-direction pivots and a pass reception The wing must also be sneaking looks toward the middle of the ice to ascertain support and also toward the opposing defensemen to determine if checking pressure is coming. Too often, wings are so intent on looking only for the puck being passed that when it arrives, they are surprised to learn that what they intended to do with it is no longer an available option.

The second step is teaching wings how to receive passes coming along the boards (rings). The key teaching points for catching a ringed pass and making the appropriate play are as follows:

- Be at least one stick length away from the boards as you prepare to receive a ring.

- Look toward the middle of the ice and toward the nearest enemy defenseman to see where support is available and where checking pressure will come from. Because the puck is hugging the boards, it is not necessary to look at it the entire time it travels to the wing. Collecting information before receiving the puck is vital to making the right play once the puck arrives.

- Always try to play the puck with the stick first. Never play it with the skates unless the checking pressure is so intense that the only option is to protect the puck along the boards and wait for support. If skates are used to receive a ringed pass, two touches are required before a subsequent pass can be made: the puck touching the skates and then being touched by the stick. This may take too much time. Also, the puck often deflects off the skate and into the middle of the ice. Finally, by using skates to collect the pass, players must have their backside pinned to the boards, inhibiting their ability to move.

If checking pressure from the opponent will arrive before the puck can be collected, the wing has three options:

1. Stop the puck along the boards and protect it with the body while waiting for support.

2. Stop the puck or deflect it off the boards out of the zone.

3. If the pressure is coming from an opposing defenseman pinching down along the boards, bump that defenseman and lift his stick so that the puck slides out over the defensive blue line.

If the wingers are deep (below the tops of the circles) in the defensive zone, the puck is unlikely to get out if deflected or shot off the boards when an opposing defenseman pinches. This play option usually works best if the winger plays the ring higher in the defensive zone, between the tops of the circles and the blue line.

BREAKOUT DRILLS FOR WINGS AND CENTERS

Mohawk, Receive, and Skate

The forwards form a line outside the blue line. A coach or defenseman is positioned near the side of the net with pucks. A forward skates toward the passer, executes the Mohawk turn, skates across the blue line with the puck, and then returns for a shot on net.

Mohawk, Receive, and Pass

Use the same format as in the previous drill with the addition of a player acting as the center. The center must come straight at the passer from the middle of the ice and curl toward the wing, executing the Mohawk turn and receiving the pass (figure 9.17). For the center, this involves swinging low and controlling skating speed so that he is still at least slightly on the defensive side of the puck when the wing is ready to make the next pass. The wing moves the puck to the center, and they skate with the puck beyond the blue line, returning to attack the net 2 v 0.

Figure 9.17　Mohawk, receive, and pass.

Mohawk, Receive, and Make Play Under Pressure

Use the same format as in the previous drill but add a checker. The center and wing go back toward the puck. The pass comes from the coach or defenseman, positioned at the side of the net, up to the wing. The checker must control his skating so that he arrives to challenge the wing a second or so after the wing has received the pass. Again, the wing makes the pass to the center, and they continue across the blue line with the puck and head back to the net for a 2 v 0. The checker doesn't need to continue pressuring the center and wing after the puck has crossed the blue line. After you are satisfied that the players can execute successfully under the current level of pressure, you can allow the checker to arrive earlier in his effort to pressure the wing.

Receiving Rings

A coach is at the side of the net with pucks and the wings are positioned outside the blue line. A wing begins skating back inside the blue line, pivots to backward to see if there is any checking pressure, then collects a pass along the boards. The wing carries the puck across the blue line and then back to the net for a shot (figure 9.18a-d).

a

b

c

d

Figure 9.18 Receiving rings.

Receive Ring and Make Play Under Pressure

As in the last drill, a coach is at the side of the net with pucks and the wings are positioned outside the blue line. A wing comes down for a ringed pass fired along the boards by the coach. The next wing in line pinches down, applying checking pressure similar to what an opposing defenseman would provide (figure 9.19a–c). A third player can be used to perform the role of the center. Once the puck gets outside the blue line, the wing playing the ring and the supporting center attack the net 2 v 0.

a

b

c

Figure 9.19   Receiving rings under pressure.

We've just covered a large amount of information on the tactical skill requirements for each position related to breakouts. It is impossible to overemphasize the importance of all these "little things" as they relate to the development of your players and the execution of breakouts by your team. When a team fails in its attempt to get the puck out of the zone, it is usually due to poor execution of basic hockey tactics and skills (a defenseman didn't look around as he went back for the puck, or his partner was lazy and didn't block out; a wing was open but didn't yell for the puck; a goalie didn't trap the puck and set up nicely for the defenseman; the center got too high too quickly and didn't provide proper support; a wing misplayed a ring; etc.). These skill techniques are not enjoyable to practice. For forwards, the fun of the game is scoring, and that's what they want to practice. As the coach, you know that winning hockey and the responsibility for developing your forwards completely involves more than just shooting pucks and learning how to play in the attacking zone.

'Team Drill
for Practicing Breakouts

1-2-3-4-5 Progression

A unit of five players is positioned in the neutral zone. The coach dumps the puck in and sends one fore-checker to disrupt the break-out (figure 9.20). After the unit of five successfully leaves the zone, they continue to the other end of the ice for a shot on goal. A coach is positioned in the corner with pucks, and after the shot is taken, he passes a puck to one of the forwards, who carries that puck back toward the other end. On reaching the center red line, he dumps the puck and forechecks against a new unit of five waiting in the neutral zone to break out. The other four players on the original breakout unit return to the side boards. After each unit executes a

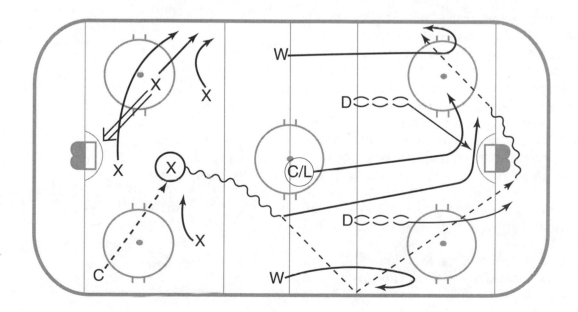

Figure 9.20   1-2-3-4-5 progression.

breakout against one forechecker, the coach sends two, followed by three, and so on (figure 9.21). Finally, when the progression reaches the full 5 v 5 complement of players, the coach with the pucks at the far end can yell to the forecheckers what type of forechecking pattern to employ on the next repetition, such as 2-1-2 or 1-2-2.

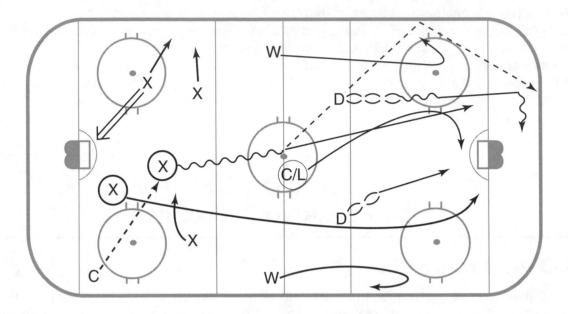

Figure 9.21   5 v 5 progression.

BREAKOUTS FROM DEFENSIVE ZONE FACE-OFFS

This is the easiest area of breakouts to teach because all players are at or very close to their correct positions on the ice at the time the puck is dropped. In this segment, we assume that when the puck is dropped, our team gets possession. In game situations, the players should never assume a win on a defensive zone draw. Instead, they should assume a loss and then adjust to a win. The only exception to this principle would be if the team is behind by a goal or two late in the game and you've put in a special face-off play designed to spring a player free for a scoring chance.

About 90 percent of the time, the puck should be moved to the weak side, away from the side where the face-off took place. This is common sense, considering that all the opposition players are positioned on the strong side when the puck is dropped. The simplest breakout play is to get the puck to the weak-side wing. The fastest way to accomplish this is with a ring (figure 9.22). If the puck is won

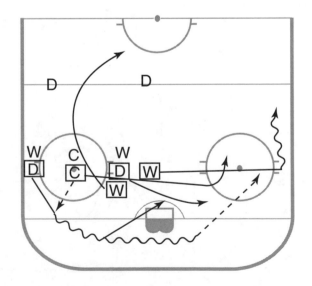

Figure 9.22   Puck to weak-side wing.

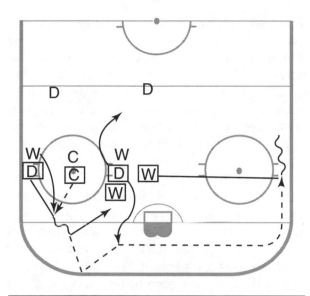

Figure 9.23 Chip to partner then ring.

boards, making it harder for the opposing winger to tie him up and easier for the defenseman to ring it. Therefore, in figure 9.19, the board defenseman would be a right-hand shot. What if you have two left-handed shooters and the face-off is to the goalie's left? The board defenseman must work to get inside position on the enemy winger opposite him so that he can still play the puck on his forehand without exposing it (figure 9.23). If the board defenseman is unable to establish good puck protection position and gets tied up, he can chip it behind the net for his partner to ring up the boards.

If your opponent is anticipating that the board defenseman will retrieve the puck on the face-off and has their board wing jumping quickly, your adjustment could be to block out with the board defenseman and have your inside defenseman go get the puck and send the ring to the weak side (figure 9.24).

It is possible to break out on the strong side, but you must give the impression that you intend to go to the weak side. In figure 9.25, the defenseman retrieving the puck off the draw begins to skate toward the weak side and then reverses the puck to the center. This play works best if your team has been consistently breaking out to the weak side and the opponent is starting to rotate their players too quickly in that direction.

back by one of your defensemen, and he takes the time to carry it behind the net and make a stick-to-stick pass to the weak-side wing, the opposing players have the same amount of time to adjust their positions to cover the play.

When the plan is to get the puck over to the weak side quickly, adjustments can be made to make it easier. First, place your defensemen on their off sides if you intend to have the board defenseman ring the puck. This puts him on his forehand with his stick toward the

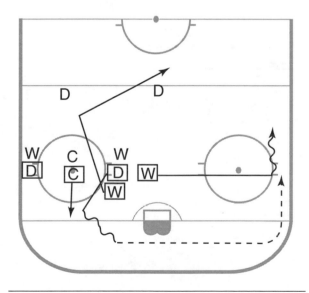

Figure 9.24 Ring to the weak side.

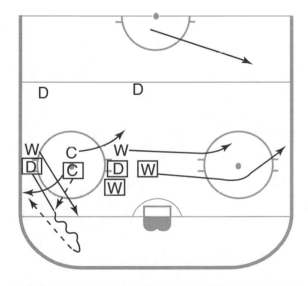

Figure 9.25 Weak side with reverse puck to center.

CONTROLLED OR SET-UP BREAKOUTS

Your team should have a plan for a controlled breakout that is used when your puck-carrying defenseman sets up behind the net and the opponent sets up a trapping forecheck, waiting for your defenseman to move out from behind the net. What pattern you select is up to you, but it should include multiple pass options so that you can adjust to whatever the opponent's formation dictates. In any controlled breakout, you are looking to create speed in the attack. To accomplish this, it is usually wise to have at least one forward act as a stretch man. By posting a forward high, somewhere in the neutral zone (depending on the two-line offside rules, he could be posted at the center red line or the attacking blue line), you force the defensive team to pull one or both of its defensemen back, allowing more space to generate speed and make passes (figure 9.26). The posted forward acting as a stretch man is also a pass option by using the boards or glass. If the players bringing the puck up the ice run into difficulty, they can always fire the puck up to the stretch man. At the very least, the puck is now outside the defensive zone. Figure 9.24 shows one example of a set-up breakout, with explanations for a few of its options. You can easily design your own to take advantage of the individual talents of your players.

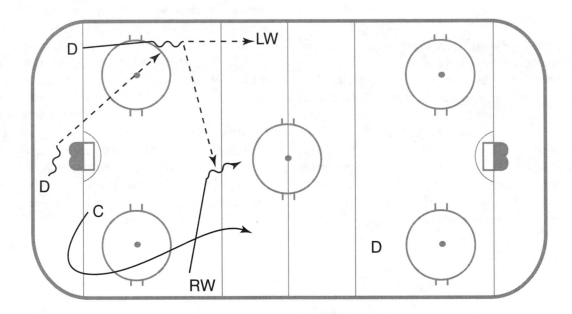

Figure 9.26   High forward in the neutral zone.

Part 4

TEACHING PLAY IN THE NEUTRAL ZONE

Chapter 10

THE NEUTRAL ZONE AND TRANSITION

In this chapter, we will focus on many aspects of an often overlooked part of the game, namely, play in the neutral zone. For our purposes, the neutral zone is defined as the area of ice between the two blue lines. Many hockey coaches today typically describe the neutral zone as extending from the tops of the face-off circles in both the attacking and defensive zones.

SUCCESSFUL NEUTRAL ZONE PLAY

Creative offensive play and effective defensive strategies in the neutral zone have gained more attention during the past 25 years, due in part to the 1972 Summit Series between Team Canada and the Soviet National Team. This exhibition series had enormous influence on the offensive elements of neutral-ice play. At that time, North American teams were playing a very linear game, with wings staying in their lanes and centers always in the middle of the ice, much like the old table hockey games. The Russians were very good at controlling the puck with their defensemen while their forwards skated to openings laterally and diagonally, organizing and executing a combined attack with all five players. Russian forwards were encouraged to skate to any area of open ice, unconfined by a coach's declaration to "stay in your lane." For example, right wingers often ended up on the left wing's side and defensemen wound up playing forward. In some cases, the Russians would approach the attacking blue line in possession of the puck and turn back to regroup, hoping to form a better attack. That Canadian team of 1972 was made up of NHL players who were less creative and collectively less organized than their Russian counterparts. When the heavily favored Canadians only managed to win the series by a single game, North American coaches began to look at the effectively played elements of Soviet hockey. Offensive play in the neutral zone was one of the areas where we learned a great deal from the Soviets, and as a result, today in North America teams at all levels of hockey play a more fluid, less linear game in the neutral zone.

When your team possesses the puck, you are on offense. When your opponent has the puck, you're on defense. Fair enough, and quite simple, right? But . . . hockey is a game where the puck changes hands hundreds of times at a high rate of speed over the course of any game. Therefore, the ability to anticipate a change of possession and subsequently change position on the ice and apply skating speed or rapid puck movement is vital to successful play. Successful coaches emphasize and drill the transition element consistently. In the modern game, transition is the essence of hockey. The following quote from Ken Dryden's book, *The Game*, says it best.

Ken Dryden's view of hockey as a fragmented and transition-dominated game is completely accurate. This is why hockey is so exciting to watch, fulfilling to play, and extremely challenging to coach.

Trapping

In recent seasons, the majority of NHL teams have implemented variations of neutral zone trapping defenses. Ironically, these trapping defenses are not new to the game. Variations of the 1-2-2 neutral zone trap have been played in the NHL since the 1950s and perhaps even earlier. In today's game, television commentators and members of the print media are more sensational, if not sophisticated, in their coverage of hockey relative to the trap. They describe how the trap is being used, often incorporating "imaginative" depictions of its real importance into their narratives. They imply that teams which don't appear to have equal talent relative to their opponent, yet still manage to win, must be doing something innovative or tricky.

When we won the Stanley Cup in New Jersey in 1995, the television and print media marveled at the effectiveness of our trapping

"Then came the Challenge Cup. I don't know when it happened. I don't know how. I don't know if I understand it the same way that the Soviets understand it. I am convinced only that it happened—that the Soviets fundamentally changed their approach to the game, which they understand finally that hockey is not a *possession* game, nor can it ever be. Possession was what they were supposed to be about: passing, team play, always searching for the open man, regrouping to start again if their possession seemed threatened. But a puck cannot be physically carried up the ice like a football; and a hockey player is not protected from physical battering as a basketball player is. He can be overpowered, the puck can be wrested from his stick by one or two or more opponents, with little recourse except to pass it on to someone else soon harassed the same way. A possession game is hyperbole. The puck changes teams more than 6 times a minute, more than 120 times a period, more than 400 times a game, and little can be done to prevent it. And when it is not changing possession, the puck is often out of possession, fought after, in no one's control. It is the nature of the game, North American or European. There is sustained possession only on power plays. There is possession involving several seconds at other times only when a team regroups to its own zone to set up a play. If possession a team style, it will be frustrated. Worse, if it is attempted, it will make a game cautious and predictable.

Instead, hockey is a *transition* game: offense to defense, defense to offense, one team to another. Hundreds of tiny fragments of action, some leading somewhere, most going nowhere. Only one thing is clear. A fragmented game must be played in fragments. Grand designs do not work. . . ."

in both the offensive and neutral zones. The rap was that we rarely forechecked aggressively—that we were passively waiting for our opponents to attack and make a mistake that would lead to counterattack opportunities. The media gave far too much credit to the "trap" and too little credit to the aggressive play of our forwards in attacking opposing defensemen and punishing them with body checks. Later, the media depicted our style of play in villainous tones, suggesting that it had disfigured the game and that somehow we were cheating while making the games boring. We were accused of hooking and holding more than our opponents were. The reality was that we did far less hooking and holding because our team worked harder and played a more intelligent positional game than most of our opponents. For the media, it would have made for more interesting writing and television commentary had the star-laden Pittsburgh Penguins, Philadelphia Flyers, or Detroit Red Wings beaten us. After all, how could a team without Jagr, Francis, Lindros, LeClair, Yzerman, or Federov possibly win? We won because we had great players too, perhaps not as glamorous or statistically prolific as our opponents, but no less effective. We won because we played together as a team, because every player put the team ahead of himself, and because each player played at or near the top of his game for two months.

Hockey experts have often spoken about how important it is to play well in the neutral zone and theorize that somehow playing well offensively and defensively in the neutral zone has a direct impact on winning. I wanted to test that theory for myself, so in 1993, I conducted a study to determine the importance of neutral zone play. As part of the study, I analyzed scoring chance variables from all three zones, both for and against, from the 1991-92 season at the University of Maine. These variables were examined in relation to the scoring outcomes of each match played. The results suggested that generating offense from the neutral zone and limiting offense generated by the opponent from this zone had a statistically significant impact on the

score of the game. Conversely, offensive and defensive play in the form of scoring opportunities from the other two zones did not show a strong relationship with the final score of the game. Admittedly, this was a sample of convenience and not extensive in either scope or duration; however, the study did provide some valuable data with respect to scoring chances.

After studying these results, some might conclude that if you play well in the neutral zone, you have the best possible chance of winning. This is only partly correct, however. The bottom line is that you can give up a ton of scoring chances that originate in the neutral zone, but if your goalie plays well and your defensemen limit the quality of those opportunities, it often doesn't matter. You can generate substantial numbers of scoring chances from neutral-ice play, but if your players can't finish those chances by scoring, they are of little consequence. The neutral zone is certainly important, but games have always been won and lost based on what is executed in the area in front of both nets.

Neutral Zone Forechecking

Let's examine some ways in which your team gains territorial control of this vital area of the ice surface. A good place to begin is by looking at various neutral zone forecheck schemes.

There are two fundamental ways in which a team can forecheck in the neutral zone (figures 10.1 and 10.2). The first is to commit two forwards to attack the opposing defensemen, forcing a pass up the ice quickly, often before their forwards are in position to receive the puck. This leaves the forechecking team with two defensemen and a forward back to play against the three enemy forwards (see figure 10.1). The second way is to forecheck with one forward against the two enemy defensemen, leaving four players back to defend against the three enemy forwards. Once the coach has decided which of these two forecheck styles to use against opposing defensemen, there are then a variety of options with respect to deployment and responsibilities

Figure 10.1   Forecheck in neutral zone with two forwards.

of other players. If you have a very quick group of forwards and mobile defensemen, all of whom have good anticipation skills, a two-player high-pressure system may work well for you. If you have slower players, I definitely recommend a one-player system (see figure 10.2).

Two fundamental rules apply to playing the 1-2-2 zone trap. The primary rule is to defend the middle of the ice first (figure 10.3). The initial position of forwards F2 and F3 must be no nearer the side boards than an imaginary line drawn through the face-off circles from end to end. From these positions, F2 and F3 can attack a puck carrier from the inside out. If they are unsuccessful in stopping the puck carrier's advance, at least the puck carrier is traveling along the boards with limited op-

tions rather than in the middle of the ice with multiple options. The second rule involves defending lines. If you are coaching a junior team where two-line passes are not allowed, you may choose to trap before the blue line. In this way, the opponent can only advance the puck as far as the red line with a pass, assuming your trap is set before the puck carrier reaches the blue line. If you are coaching a high school team, you don't have the two-line pass rule to work with, so you must defend the red line, not allowing your opponent the option of a dump-in without risking an icing call. This entices them to pass the puck into the middle of the ice, precisely what you hope for so that there is a good chance for an interception and subsequent counterattack.

Figure 10.2   Forecheck in neutral zone with one forward.

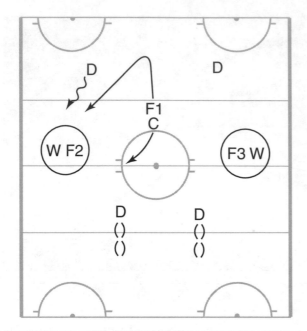

Figure 10.3   1-2-2 zone trap.

The University of Maine "man-to-man 1-4" is a very effective method of playing neutral zone defense, assuming that you have talent equal or superior to that of your opponent. This system relies more on individuals performing specific roles, and if one individual fails, often there is no support available from other players.

I recommend using the 1-2-2 zone trap regardless of your team speed and skill level. It teaches good positioning by forwards and ensures good numbers at your defensive blue line, should the opponent reach that far, and of course, they will on occasion! It encourages opponents to put the puck into the middle of the ice, the area from which it is best to initiate counterattacks. Finally, it keeps your defensemen in the middle of the ice, with the play directly in front of them, from where they can easily react defensively and can initiate counterattacks.

The next chapter will provide you with a variety of neutral zone drilling sequences. Once your players master the concepts and skill sets inherent in these drills, your team will become a difficult one to play against in the neutral zone.

Chapter 11

NEUTRAL ZONE AND TRANSITION DRILLING

Chapter 9 provided detailed drills for the defensive zone, and this chapter is structurally similar in that I include a multitude of activities for a wide range of neutral zone situations. Some drills can be run with your team to reinforce sound neutral zone forechecking. Other drills emphasize the importance of face-offs in this zone and maximizing your chances off these common game situations. Again, slow and steady wins the race here! Do not try to incorporate all these activities over a short time or your players, and probably your coaching staff as well, will get that deer-in-the-headlights look!

INITIAL DRILLS FOR TEACHING NEUTRAL ZONE SKILLS

1 v 1 Angling

A puck is chipped 15-20 feet from a defenseman, who retrieves it while being pursued by a forward acting as a forechecker (figure 11.1). The objective for the defenseman is to carry the puck to the center red line. The objective for the forward is to keep the defenseman from reaching the red line. The key teaching point for the forechecking forward is to attack the defenseman from one side. If this tactic is used, the defenseman has only one way to go, the side dictated by the positioning and angling of the forward.

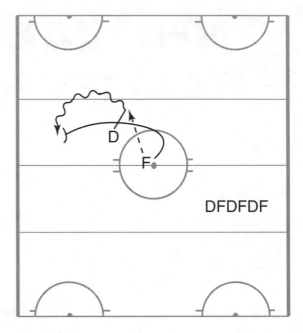

Figure 11.1   1 v 1 angling.

Angling v 2 Defensemen

The puck is chipped 15-20 feet from two defensemen, who retrieve. Again, the defensemen must attempt to reach the center red line with the puck, which they should be able to do. The forward angling the two defensemen is successful if no more than one pass is made between them (figure 11.2).

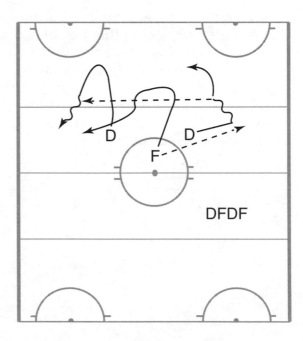

Figure 11.2   1 v 2 angling.

Trapping 2 v 3

The puck is again chipped 15-20 feet from two defensemen, who retrieve and attempt to gain the red line (figure 11.3). F1 angles, making sure no more than one D-to-D pass is made. Once play is forced to one side by F1, F2 sets a trap to force the puck carrier before the red line. F3 comes across in the middle.

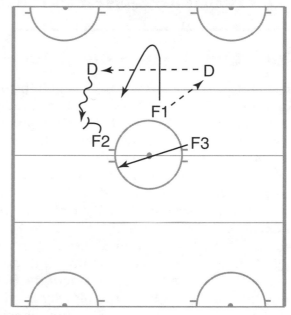

Figure 11.3   Trapping 2 v 3.

5 v 5 Neutral Zone Scrimmage

A coach is positioned in the neutral zone with pucks. Two groups of five players are also positioned in the neutral zone. The coach throws out a puck and the game is played live. The team in possession of the puck tries to attack and at the very least reach the red line for a dump-in. The team without the puck uses a neutral zone forechecking pattern to deny the opponent's attack. The coach can throw out a second puck after blowing the whistle. When the whistle blows, the players leave the first puck and begin to play the new puck. The coach can throw out several pucks at once but should allow the play to continue to some form of conclusion with the last puck (e.g., a goal is scored or the prespecified time limit, say, 45 seconds from the start of the drill, has elapsed).

THE NEUTRAL ZONE AND FACE-OFFS

It is no exaggeration to say that championships have been won and lost, even at the highest levels of play, due to the use of a specific face-off alignment. Failure to properly defend neutral zone face-offs may result in fast break chances for an opponent, and this in turn can lead to scoring opportunities.

Coaches should never underestimate the importance of practicing face-offs in the neutral zone. Failure to do so could have dire consequences, especially when the heat is on during a close game. If properly executed, a face-off can lead to impressive neutral zone forechecking that will inevitably result in turnovers. Let's look at a couple of ideas you might consider when preparing your players to forecheck from face-offs in the neutral zone.

NEUTRAL ZONE FORECHECKING OFF A LOST FACE-OFF

Face-Off Outside the Attacking Blue Line

Assuming a 1-2-2 trap forecheck, when the draw is lost, the center should try to break through the opposing center and begin to steer the play (figure 11.4). Unless the opposing center is asleep and does not block out, the center will not be able to get between the two enemy defensemen quickly enough to prevent the first D-to-D pass but should be able to prevent any subsequent D-to-D passes. The wing on the wide side should widen out with the opposing winger on that side to an area no closer to the boards than an imaginary line drawn through the face-off circles. As the center steers the puck his way, the wing must force the play by moving forward before the center red line, not allowing the opposing defensemen to reach the red line and dump the puck in. The winger who started nearest the boards should come to the middle of the ice and look for any passes attempted through the middle. The wide-side defenseman should widen out and back off.

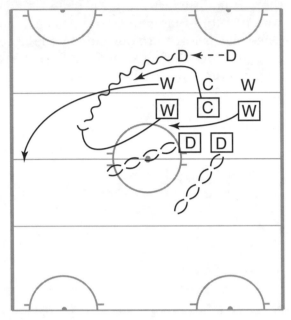

Figure 11.4   Face-off outside the attacking blue line.

Face-Off Outside the Defending Blue Line

When the opponent wins the face-off from this position on the ice, their defensemen have already reached the center red line and can dump the puck in. Keeping in mind that one of the basic purposes of a trapping formation is to defend lines, it makes no sense to commit a second forward to trap the opposing defensemen, since they already have the puck at the red line. Thus, the center should break through the opposing center after losing the draw and pressure their defensemen (figure 11.5). The wings should hold up the opposing wingers so that when the puck is dumped in, the defensemen will have more time to retrieve it under less forechecking pressure. The board-side defenseman should slide toward the middle of the ice and prepare to retrieve the dump while the wide-side defenseman steps forward and gaps, tightly protecting the middle of the ice. This method of neutral zone defense after a lost draw near the defending blue line is very similar to the University of Maine style discussed earlier.

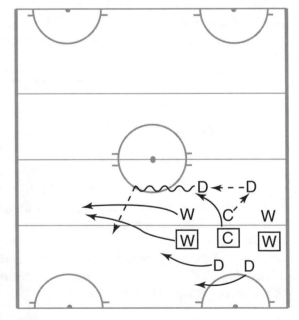

Figure 11.5   Face-off outside the defending blue line.

BACKCHECKING THROUGH THE NEUTRAL ZONE

While players must understand the importance of neutral zone forechecking, they should also come to realize the need for solid backchecking technique through this zone.

There are two basic concepts associated with backchecking through the neutral zone. The first encourages backcheckers to ignore the puck carrier and look to establish coverage of enemy attackers not in possession of the puck. This leaves the puck carrier for the defensemen to attack. With this method, defensemen are encouraged to gap tightly, not allowing the puck carrier time or space to maneuver. The second idea is for the first forward back to pressure the puck carrier, if possible, and force a pass. The basic guideline for the first backchecking forward is to pressure the puck carrier if the backchecker can reach the puck carrier before the center red line. If that is not possible, the backchecker should allow the defenseman to play the puck and then look to cover another attacking forward from a position in the middle of the ice.

I believe strongly that getting forwards to backcheck through the middle of the ice and pressure the puck carrier as they do so is the most effective way to play. When a puck carrier has both a defenseman in front and a backchecker closing in from the back or side

area, it makes for a very uncomfortable feeling! This also allows the defensemen to continue to read the play as they back up or retreat. Quite often, the backchecking forward forces an errant pass by the puck carrier, and the defensemen can retrieve the puck and start the counterattack.

To be effective with this method of backchecking, the players must communicate verbally, and in particular, the defensemen must talk to the backchecking forwards. For example, if the opposing puck carrier has reached the center red line, the defenseman should say to the backchecking forward, "Take the middle, I've got the puck." If the defenseman sees that the backchecking forward has a good angle at the puck carrier and can establish contact before the red line, the defenseman should say, "Take the puck." Forwards can communicate with defensemen just as easily, letting the defensemen know what their intentions are. Verbal communication makes backchecking easier and more effective.

Drills to Teach Backchecking

Here are some ideas to use when reinforcing the neutral zone backcheck. Remember to share with your players that there is nothing glamorous about this part of the game, but if success is to be realized, everyone must commit to hard work back through the neutral zone.

2 v 2 Communication and Decision Drill

Three forwards are positioned with their skates on the blue line. The forward in the middle of the ice has the puck. A defenseman is waiting to defend against the attack at the center red line (figure 11.6). On the whistle, the forward in the middle passes the puck to one of the forwards along either side, and the two forwards attack. The forward who passed the puck to initiate the drill becomes the backchecker. The puck carrier is pressured, if possible. At some point after the attackers have reached the red line, the backchecker and the defenseman must communicate as to who is to cover which attacker.

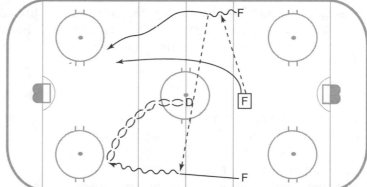

Figure 11.6 2 v 2 communication and decision drill.

Breakout 5 v 0 Into 3 v 3 Attack

A unit of five players breaks out from one end zone and carries the puck into the neutral zone while a forward waits at the far blue line (figure 11.7). When the group of three forwards reaches the red line, they make a pass to the forward waiting at the blue line, who returns the puck to them and backchecks, creating a 3 v 3 situation. As the coach, you are looking for good communication and backchecking execution. Allow the drill to continue as a 3 v 3 down low.

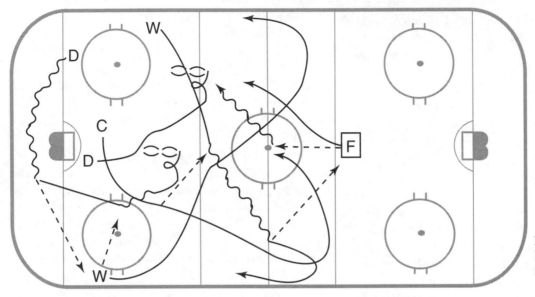

Figure 11.7
Breakout 5 v 0 into 3 v 3 attack.

1 v 1 Defense

The ability of defensemen to play 1 v 1 situations effectively is a staple of winning hockey. If your defensemen are beaten in this situation, even-numbered attacks quickly become odd-numbered attacks, and the results are usually disastrous. There are really only two ways that an opponent can beat a defenseman in a 1 v 1 situation. An attacker might skate around the defenseman using outside speed or simply put the puck into the defenseman's personal space and slide right through. Proper execution of the following principles and tactics form the guide for teaching this part of the game.

Gapping

The gap is the space between the puck carrier and the defensemen. An ideal gap is approximately two stick lengths. Defensemen must begin gapping as soon as it is clear the opponent will gain possession of the puck. Defensemen should be backing up at approxi-

mately the same speed at which the attackers are moving forward. Improper speed will mean either the gap will grow too wide or the opponent will blow past the defensemen to the free space behind. Ideally, the defensemen should be able to force the puck carrier to make a decision.

Body Position

The defensemen should try to establish a position more toward the middle of the ice, lining up their outside shoulder with the inside shoulder of the attacker. This helps keep the attacker to the outside and away from the middle of the ice.

Stick Position

Defensemen must have their sticks directly in front of their body at all times, usually at arm's length. When combined with proper body position, this stick position encourages the attacking forward to keep to the outside. It also keeps the attacker outside the defenseman's personal space. If an attacker is allowed to get too close to a defenseman on the initial attack, it is easier for the attacker to win the one-on-one battle. A common mistake made by young defensemen is having the stick to the side of their body instead of directly in front.

Foot Position

The defensemen must try to skate backward with their feet never more than shoulder-width apart. Having the feet too far apart makes it difficult to pivot from backward to forward and skate with an attacker that tries to skate wide with speed. Whenever possible, the defensemen should avoid using cross-over steps to move laterally. If an attacker catches a defenseman in the middle of a cross-over step going one way while the attacker is moving in the other direction, the result is the attacker walking in alone on the net.

Eyes

The defenseman's eyes should be focused on the chest of the opposing puck carrier. If a defender looks at the puck or at the head of the opponent, chances are greater that they will be outplayed with fakes. By looking at the chest of the puck carrier, the defenseman can still see the puck and use the stick to poke check.

Poke Checking

The defensemen should attempt to poke check the puck while keeping their body in proper alignment and position. That way, if the poke check is missed, the body is still in position to make contact with the attacker. A common mistake made by young defenders is to lunge with their entire body when poke checking. If the poke check fails to dislodge the puck from the attacker's possession, the defenseman will be unable to turn and continue pursuing the puck carrier.

2 v 2 Situation

A common play situation in hockey is the 2 v 2 rush pitting two defensemen against two attacking forwards. When broken down, it is nothing more than two 1 v 1 situations added together. Therefore, the 1 v 1 principles of play for defensemen are the key elements for defending against 2 v 2.

What the forwards should be trying to do against the defensemen in the 2 v 2 attack is to isolate one defenseman, creating a 2 v 1 against that defender. There are two basic methods for accomplishing this (figure 11.8). The first is a linear approach, bringing both attackers to one side; the second is a crossing attack where the forwards attempt to cut across in front of the defensemen and get them both on one side of the ice, leaving the other side of the ice free.

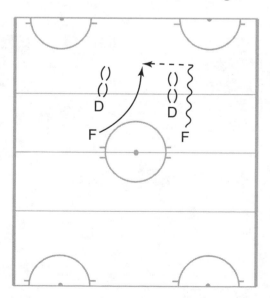

Figure 11.8
Linear approach in 2 v 2.

Linear attacks are easy to defend. The defenseman away from the point of attack only has to slide over to maintain the two 1 v 1 relationships, denying the opponent's attempt at isolating his partner. Crossing attacks are more difficult to defend, but if each defender holds his position on the ice, sooner or later one of the attacking forwards will return to his side. Defensemen can deny the use of crossing attacks as a play tactic by simply establishing a good gap initially. If the gap is tight to begin with, the enemy forwards will not have the space to move laterally. Thus, the best way to defend against crossing attacks is to prevent them from developing in the first place.

DRILLS FOR DEFENDING 1 V 1 RUSHES

Bob Johnson, Backward Acceleration 1 v 1

I first saw this drill used by Bob Johnson's Calgary Flames back in the 1980s. It was a great drill then and remains so today. Forwards are positioned in the corners at diagonally opposite ends of the ice. Defensemen are placed on the inside hash marks (figure 11.9a-b). On the whistle, the forward takes off on a straight line along the wall. The defenseman must accelerate backward from a standstill and make the play on the forward.

Figure 11.9   Bob Johnson backward acceleration 1 v 1.

Canadian Olympic 1 v 1

This drill is similar to the Bob Johnson 1 v 1 because it involves backward acceleration by the defenseman. It is different in that the forward will be able to generate much greater speed, putting additional pressure on the defenseman. Forwards are lined up at diagonally opposite blue lines. Defensemen are positioned in the center ice face-off circle (figure 11.10). On the whistle, forwards begin moving with pucks, skating across the ice underneath the blue line. Two defensemen are positioned at the blue line, waiting for the corresponding forward to attack. The defensemen are not allowed to begin their backward acceleration until the forward begins to turn up the ice and the puck has crossed the blue line.

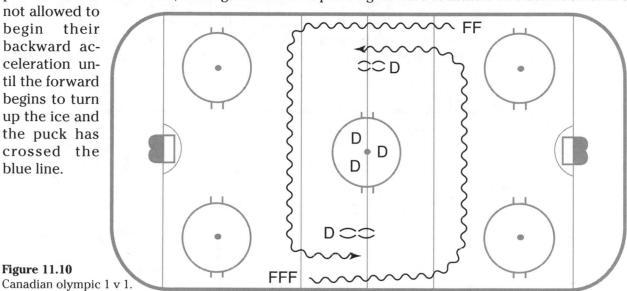

Figure 11.10
Canadian olympic 1 v 1.

Lemaire Multiple 1 v 1s

This drill involves three to five repetitions of 1 v 1 rushes. The emphasis is on gapping and use of the stick to poke check. One defenseman jumps out from the side boards to go against the forwards, who are lined up at the red line. The defenseman skates forward to the bottom of the face-off circle, stops, and then starts to skate backward (figure 11.11). As soon as the defenseman begins to skate backward, the forward begins the attack. After the shot is taken or the puck is poked away by the defenseman, the defense-man returns to the bottom of the circle at full speed, stops, and turns backward, ready to take on an attack from a new player.

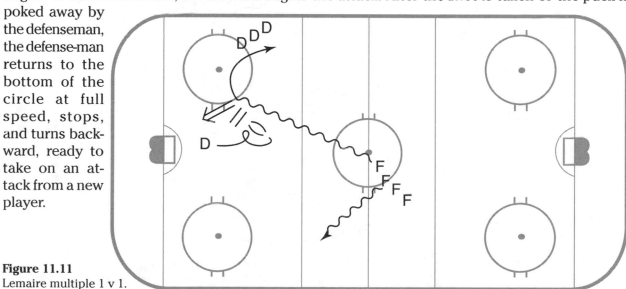

Figure 11.11
Lemaire multiple 1 v 1.

DRILLS FOR DEFENDING 2 v 2 ATTACKS

Michigan Tech Continuous 2 v 2

This drill begins with a coach passing a puck to two forwards breaking out from an end zone. The forwards skate into the neutral zone with the puck and are met by two defensemen (figures 11.12, a-b). At some point while the attacking forwards are progressing through the neutral zone, the coach blows the whistle. The forwards then turn and throw the puck back to the coach and regroup on him. Meanwhile, the defensemen must stop and skate forward, reestablishing the appropriate gap. The coach passes the puck back to the forwards, who attack 2 v 2. Play continues in the attacking zone until a goal is scored or the defensemen clear the puck up the wall to two new forwards, and the sequence is repeated.

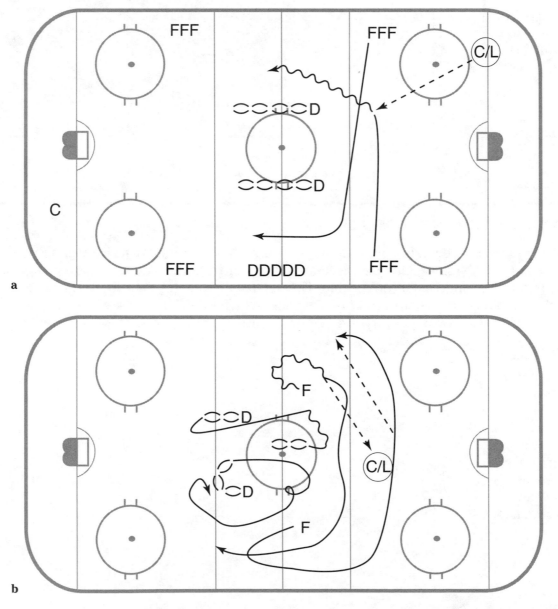

Figure 11.12   Michigan Tech continuous 2 v 2.

Cunny 2 v 2 Conditioner

Players work together in pairs in this half-ice 2 v 2 drill. The player rotation sequence is simply offense, defense, then rest. The drill starts with two offensive players skating across the center red line, one with the puck, to attack against two defenders (figure 11.13). The play continues until a goal is scored or the puck is cleared out to the neutral zone. Once the puck is cleared to the neutral zone, the next two players attack, beginning with a cross at the center red line. The two players initially on offense must sprint up to the neutral zone to establish a good gap and play the subsequent attack.

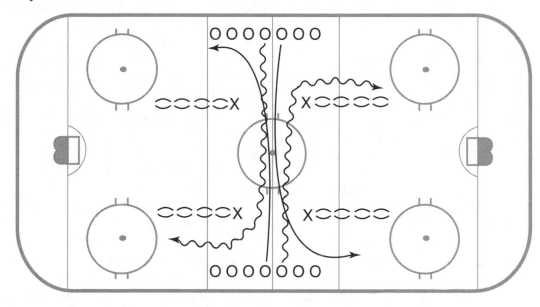

Figure 11.13   Cunny 2 v 2 conditioner.

DEFENDING AGAINST ODD-MAN ATTACKS

It is wise to avoid giving the opponent odd-man attacks, but even the most careful and well-disciplined teams allow a few during the course of any game. There are four categories of odd-man attacks: breakaway 1 v 0, 2 v 1, 3 v 2, and 4 v 3. We will focus on the two most common odd-man attacks, the 2 v 1 and the 3 v 2.

When a 2 v 1 or 3 v 2 is occurring on the ice, the reality is that the situation is even strength between the two teams. Remember, there is a goalie in the end zone as well, making the situation a 2 v 2 or 3 v 3. The key point here is that you must maximize the use of your goaltender by having this player involved in the tactics used to defend these situations.

There are two basic methods for defending 2 v 1s and 3 v 2s. First, the defenders can back up in the middle of the ice, hoping to slow down the play until backchecking help arrives. With this method, it is likely that a shot will be allowed. The goal of the defenders is to make certain the shot comes from as wide an angle as possible, making it an easy one for the goalie to defend. As the shot is about to be taken, the defender must make sure that no more passes can be made, allowing the goalie to be aggressive in cutting down the angle.

The second fundamental method is to force a puck carrier before he is ready to make his play, hopefully causing him to hurry and make a mistake. In the 2 v 1 rush situation, this might mean a slide somewhere below the tops of the circles by the defenseman, attempting to stop both the shot and the pass. The goalie knows that the defenseman will slide and that the puck carrier will attempt a hurried shot or pass through the sliding defenseman. With this information, the goalie can play slightly deeper in the net unless absolutely certain that a pass across cannot be completed.

I recommend the former method, where the defenseman plays the 2 v 1 situation from an upright position. The problem with sliding to block the pass and shot is that if the shot or pass gets beyond the sliding defenseman, that defenseman is out of the play, at least temporarily. This means that two attackers will be facing the goalie without support from the defenseman.

Here's how we teach defensemen to play the 2 v 1 rush:

• Try to play between the two attackers with the stick out and on the ice and with the gap as tight as possible, discouraging passes between the attackers. It is much easier for the goalie if only one of the two attackers carries the puck. This means that the goalie will not have to shift position in front of the net, reacting to passes made by the attackers.

• As you position yourself between the two attackers, shade slightly toward the most dangerous player, the one nearest the middle of the ice. Also, be aware of which player might be on the off-wing side, which will provide a more favorable shooting angle. Know, the identity of the players attacking against you. If you are facing Wayne Gretzky, you know he will want to make a pass rather

than shoot. If you have a good player coming at you along with a poor player, allow the poor player to get the puck early and give away the shot.

• Take multiple looks as the play progresses toward the net. Defensemen get into trouble because they look only once or twice and, at the critical moment, don't know where the non-puck-carrying player is, and therefore allow a pass to get through. Taking multiple looks helps the defensemen adjust their body and stick position to the appropriate area because they are constantly aware of the relationship between the puck carrier and an attacker without the puck.

• If possible, fake a thrust toward the puck carrier, enticing the attacker to make a pass that you can intercept. At the very least, the puck carrier might more wider away from the thrust.

• Once you reach an area below the tops of the circles, return both hands to the stick, always keeping the stick on the ice in the middle of your body while maintaining position between the two attackers. It will be necessary to turn your body to an angle of approximately 45 degrees, with your back to the attacker without the puck.

• Once the shot is taken, be prepared to clear the rebound; don't allow yourself to be tied up with either of the attackers exclusively.

DRILLS FOR DEFENDING 2 V 1 ATTACKS

Dot 2 v 1

Forwards are lined up behind the neutral zone face-off dots. Defensemen are positioned along the boards on either side of the ice at the red line. The drill begins with a defenseman stepping away from the wall and making a pass to one of the two

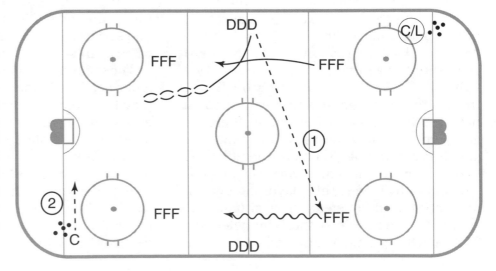

Figure 11.14 Dot 2 v 1.

forwards. The forwards begin an attack against that defenseman, who has pivoted to backward to take on the attack (figure 11.14). The forwards execute the attack, and after play culminates with a shot or the defender breaks it up, the coach blows the whistle and throws out a second puck for a quick 2 v 1 near the net. The whistle is also the cue for a new defenseman and two new forwards to begin a 2 v 1 sequence at the other net.

Montreal 2 v 1

Forwards are lined up outside the blue line. A defenseman starts in the middle, even with the hash marks, and skates forward toward the attackers, stops, and begins to skate backward. At that moment, the forwards begin their attack (figure 11.15). After getting a shot or after the play is broken up, the defenseman skates forward toward the next two attackers. The defenseman plays four 2 v 1 attacks in succession and then the next defenseman jumps in to face his own series of four attacks.

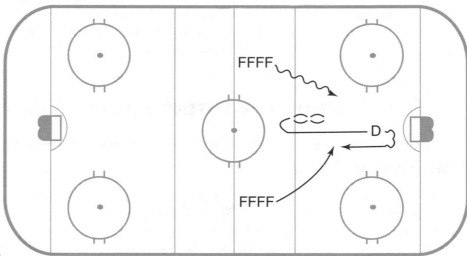

Figure 11.15   Montreal 2 v 1.

DEFENDING THE 3 V 2 RUSH SITUATION

As with 2 v 1s, it is important to limit the frequency with which these situations occur. The majority of 3 v 2s occur because the forwards fail to keep a high player in attack or offensive zone grind situations. When the puck is turned over, none of the three forwards is in position to backcheck. Another cause is more simple—forwards just don't hustle, failing to come back quickly. The third reason is that the high forward commits to an opponent near the boards, the puck is passed around that player, and the opponent activates a defenseman offensively, who beats another of the forwards up the ice.

When introducing your athletes to the tactics and strategy for defending against the 3 v 2 rush, you need to convey two main ideas. First, they must try to force the opponent to put the puck in one of the outside lanes. This limits the opposing puck carrier's options and simplifies the defensive problem. It also takes more time for a play to develop from the outside lanes, so your backcheckers have more time to return to a support position in the middle, hopefully turning the situation into a 3 v 3. Second, your defensemen must think of this play as a 2 v 1 on the puck side and a 1 v 1 on the weak side and position themselves accordingly.

Tight gapping by the defensemen and having them close to each other in the middle of the ice as the play begins is the key to getting the opponent to move the puck to an outside lane. Once the puck is in the outside lane, the puck-side defenseman should play the situation like a 2 v 1 and make certain to shade the player in the middle lane, using good stick and body position to deny a pass to the middle attacker. The weak-side defenseman should take the opposing player, who drives to the net without the puck.

If your defensemen have gapped tightly and forced the puck to a wide lane as it traverses the defensive blue line, the attacking team has two options. The easiest play to defend is option 1. It is played as a 2 v 1 on the puck side, and because there is no switching of lanes, the defenders have easy reads and very simple positioning problems to contend with. Option 2 is more difficult, and there are two ways to play it. One is to have the weak-side defenseman go with the forward driving to the net from the middle lane without the

puck. This means that the puck-side defenseman must recognize the middle-lane drive and know that the weak-side forward will be coming across to provide support. This player cannot retreat too near the net because this will make it difficult to deny the back diagonal pass. The second way to play this situation is for the puck-side defenseman to retreat and play between the puck carrier and forward driving toward the net from the middle lane. The other defensive partner can then look to come across with the attacker who is advancing from the weak side.

DRILLS FOR DEFENDING 3 v 2 ATTACKS

Continuous 3 v 2

All forwards and defensemen are positioned in the neutral zone. The drill begins with three forwards coming down into an end zone, receiving a pass from a coach, and then turning to attack against two defensemen (figure 11.16). The 3 v 2 continues until the defensemen get the puck and pass it to a new set of forwards attacking in the opposite direction or until the puck winds up in the net. If a goal is scored, a defenseman must take the puck out of the net and start the next attack.

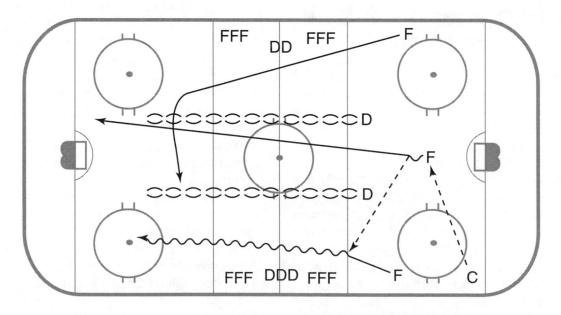

Figure 11.16   Continuous 3 v 2.

5 v 0 Breakout Into 3 v 2

The puck is dumped into an end zone. The defensemen retrieve it and initiate a breakout with three forwards (figure 11.17). The forwards pass and carry the puck to the far blue line, where they turn and attack the two defensemen who started the breakout. The defensemen must hustle up the ice and establish the appropriate gap.

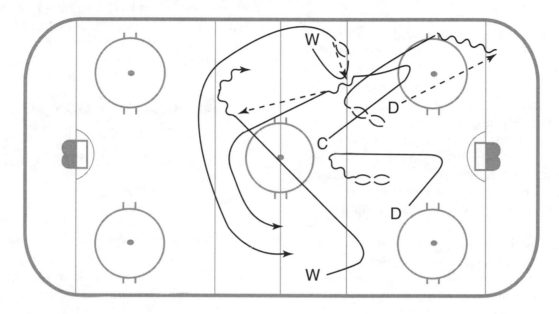

Figure 11.17   5 v 0 breakout to 3 v 2.

OFFENSIVE HOCKEY IN THE NEUTRAL ZONE

Speed, speed, speed! Extreme pressure is placed on the defenders when speed is employed on the initial entry from the neutral zone into the attacking zone. Speed sometimes allows attackers to isolate and beat defenders one-on-one. Speed allows the attacking team to take advantage of temporary odd-man situations that have developed. As the coach, you cannot overemphasize employing speed in your attacks. One of the most profound differences between the best teams and players and those at the next-best level is simply how fast each can execute skills and tactics. Emphasis on improving speed of execution is a must in attempting to optimize the talent of your individual players and the team as a whole. If your team doesn't

have a lot of speed, it will look a whole lot faster if your players can move the puck quickly.

When speaking at coaching symposiums, I've often used the analogy that I can do anything that Mario Lemieux, Wayne Gretzky, or Ray Bourque can do. When I make this statement, coaches in the audience look up quizzically, no doubt wondering if I've lost my mind or perhaps have an enormously inflated ego and no sense of reality. I go on to say that it is not skill alone that is impressive when looking at the abilities of these great players; rather, it is the speed at which they can execute their hockey skills and playmaking tactics.

When playing against quality opponents, speed alone likely will not be enough to cross the blue line successfully and get a chance at the net. It also requires quick puck movement, support, and the tactic of directing the attack so as to isolate one of the defenders.

RAPID PUCK MOVEMENT AND CHANGING THE POINT OF ATTACK

Nothing is easier to defend against than a player who carries the puck too long. The reason is that carrying the puck too long gives the defending team time to cover the puck carrier's play options. Eventually, time and space are adequately limited, and the puck carrier is forced into a dead-end situation where the only options are to turn the puck over or dump it to a safe place on the ice. Conversely, each time the puck is passed, the defending team is forced to react to a brand-new set of defensive problems. From this new point of attack, the pass receiver has a whole new set of angles and attack options.

> Perhaps the most important point to be made about rapid puck movement is the one made by my old youth hockey coach 30 years ago. Huskey Poirier was fond of saying, "Boys, head man that puck. The puck moves ahead much faster when passed than when it is carried." If speed is important to successful attacks from the neutral zone, then rapid puck movement is a tactic that must be utilized consistently. Rapid puck movement makes teams that don't have much individual skating speed play at a much faster pace.

SUPPORT AND CREATING ISOLATION 2 v 1s

Attacks are successful when either of two things occurs: (1) an attacker defeats a defender in a 1 v 1, or (2) two attackers isolate a defender by using close support to create a 2 v 1 before the defender can get support help from a teammate. Against quality opponents, the latter must be part of your team's tactical repertoire.

ADVANCED SKILLS FOR FORWARDS APPLIED TO THE NEUTRAL ZONE

Forwards must be able to

- make and receive passes while skating at full speed horizontally, diagonally, or laterally,
- receive a pass while skating toward the puck carrier and execute either a Mohawk turn or tight turn,
- shield the puck from pinching enemy defensemen after receiving a pass near the wall and be able to make either a direct or indirect pass to a teammate,
- handle the puck with speed and drive around or through a backward-skating defenseman to get to the net or buy time to make a play, and
- execute tactical passing plays such as pass and follow, cross and drop pass, saucer pass, and indirect (off the boards).

DRILLS FOR DEVELOPING
NEUTRAL ZONE OFFENSIVE SKILLS FOR FORWARDS

Diagonal Shooting

The purpose of this drill is to get forwards to skate across the ice diagonally at full speed, receive a pass, and continue to the attacking zone for a shot (figure 11.18). This helps them get into the habit of coming across the ice to support the player with the puck. Demand that the receiver yell for the puck.

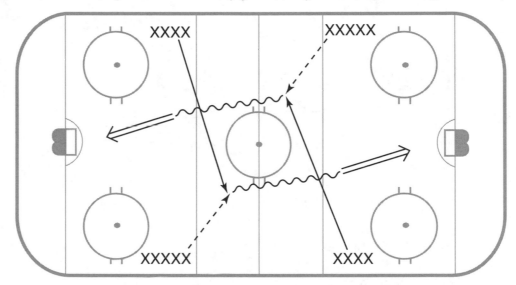

Figure 11.18   Diagonal shooting.

Curl Shooting

This drill simulates a support situation similar to diagonal shooting. In this case, the player comes across and tries to get a pass at or near the attacking blue line in the middle of the ice. In a game, this is the type of play that would result in splitting the enemy defensemen and would culminate in a breakaway shot (figure 11.19).

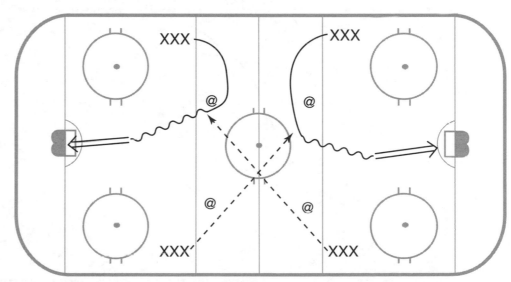

Figure 11.19   Curl shooting.

Turn-Up Shooting

This exercise involves a player coming back toward the puck carrier (figure 11.20), receiving the pass, and then turning up ice, finishing with a shot on goal.

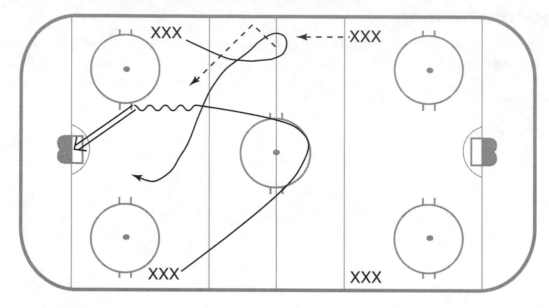

Figure 11.20   Turn-up shooting.

A variation of this drill is to use a turn-up shooting 2 v 0. In this drill, the forward comes back to the puck (figure 11.21), receives the pass, and then bumps the puck to a teammate who has come across from the other side of the ice to provide support.

A third variation is to use a turn-up shooting with pinch. This drill is the same as turn-up shooting 2 v 0 except that a defensive player is added to come from behind the pass receiver, applying pressure.

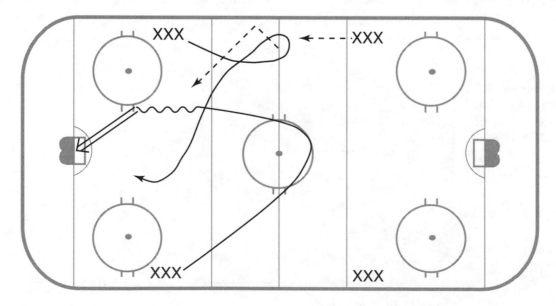

Figure 11.21   Turn up shooting 2 v 0.

DEFENSEMEN AND NEUTRAL ZONE OFFENSIVE PLAY

The primary role of defensemen in neutral zone offense is to initiate the attack with a good pass. This situation is not unlike a breakout from the defensive zone. It will be difficult to impossible to generate offense from this area of the ice if your defensemen are unskilled and poorly drilled in the fundamental tactical elements important for success in this area of the ice.

Advanced Skills for Defensemen in the Neutral Zone

Defensemen must be able to

- get to the puck quickly and, whenever possible, collect it and turn so that they are prepared to make a pass on the forehand. Being on the forehand increases the chances of a good, hard pass. There are few, if any, players at any level who are as good on the backhand as on the forehand.

- pass while skating forward, moving laterally, and skating backward.

- make a variety of passes—long ones, short ones, stick-to-stick, off-the-boards, and area passes.

- be able to scan the ice while waiting for a pass from a partner and have some idea what to do with the puck when the pass arrives.

- support their partner from a back diagonal position.

- jump up at the right time to support the attack as it enters the attacking zone.

Neutral Zone Passing for Defensemen

In this drill, four defensemen will be working between the blue lines, making passes. Any additional defensemen act as token forecheckers between the blue lines, providing moderate resistance. There are two pass plays to be practiced with this drill: D to D to W and D to D back to D (figure 11.22). D to D to W is an effective and automatic way to break 2-1-2 neutral zone forechecking patterns, and D to D back to D to weak-side W is an effective way to break 1-2-2 trapping patterns.

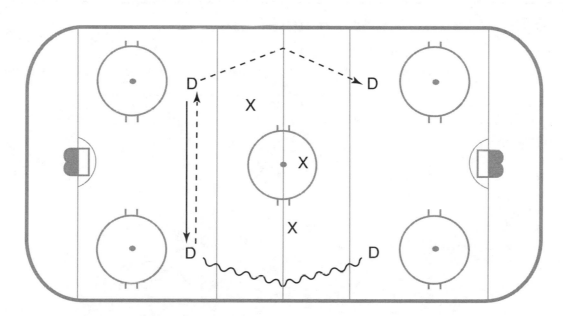

Figure 11.22   Neutral zone passing for defensemen.

Neutral Zone Passing 2 v 1

The purpose of this drill is to teach defensemen to work together in passing the puck against one forechecker and advancing it under control to the center red line. The puck is chipped out to the area between the top of the circle and the blue line. Two defensemen go back, one retrieves the puck, and they skate toward the red line, passing the puck between them against one forechecker.

Quick Up Drill

A puck is placed between the top of the circle and blue line at diagonally opposite ends of the ice. On the whistle, a defenseman goes back to retrieve it, looking over both shoulders, similar to what happens on a breakout from the defensive zone (figure 11.23). The defenseman must then surround the puck so that it is on the forehand and, on the first touch, pass it to a forward coming back along the wall to provide support. The drill continues with the forward moving down the ice for a shot on goal.

A variation of this drill is to add a forechecker to chase the defenseman retrieving the puck and making the pass to the forward supporting on the wall.

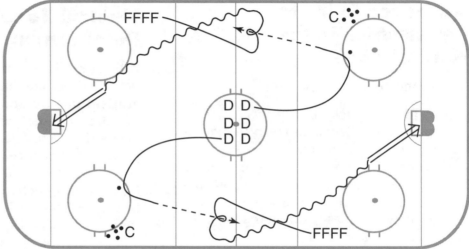

Figure 11.23   Quick up drill.

D to D to W With Shutdown and Pass

This exercise is the same as the D to D to W with three shots drill outlined in the section on developing neutral zone offensive skills for forwards except that the forward carrying the puck into the attacking zone carries to the top of the circle, turns toward the boards, and makes a pass to the defenseman coming late (figure 11.24). This defenseman accepts the pass and shoots, with one forward positioned at the net.

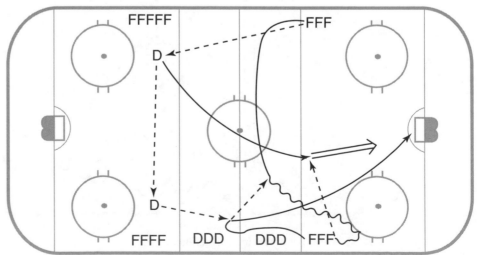

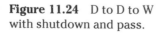
Figure 11.24   D to D to W with shutdown and pass.

WIDTH AND DEPTH IN THE ATTACK

This section covers an area of the game that is partly neutral zone and partly offensive zone in orientation. It involves what some coaches call the initial entry to the attacking zone. Over the years, I've found that the best way to teach the principles of width and depth in attack is by using the drill progression that follows.

The player with the puck must attack with speed whenever possible. There are times in a game when the puck carrier must slow down and wait for teammates to provide support. When teaching the initial entry to the attacking zone, however, it is best to emphasize speed early in the teaching process and assume that the necessary support is there.

As noted earlier, hockey is a game of time and space. Offensive hockey involves the *creation* of time and space while attempting to generate a scoring opportunity, whereas defensive hockey is about *limiting* time and space in order to get the puck back. Carrying the puck and attacking with speed has the effect of driving the defenders back and creating space for a pass behind. Sending a second attacker to the net has a similar effect on the defenders. If the defenders don't respect the speed-driven thrust toward the net, then your attackers need not worry about a pass behind to a third attacker. They can simply get to the net or get the puck to the net because the free space is behind the enemy defense. The following series of drills demonstrates the "drive drill" activities.

Drive Drill 1 v 0

Players are assembled at diagonally opposite blue lines. On the coach's whistle, a single player from each line attacks toward the opposite blue line, skating around a cone while moving with speed down the wing. The player continues to drive down the wall for a shot on goal.

Drive Drill 2 v 0

This drill has the same format as the preceding drill except a second attacker is added who drives the middle lane and continues toward the net (figure 11.25). The puck carrier moving down the wing now has the option of shooting, with the possibility of a rebound, or passing to the second player heading for the net.

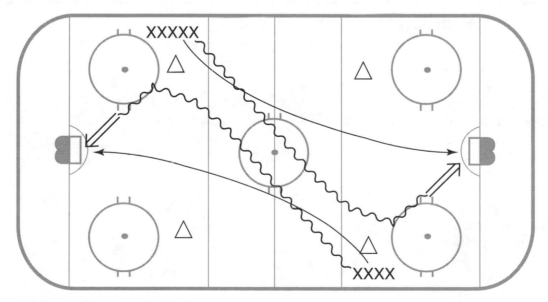

Figure 11.25   Drive drill 2 v 0.

Drive Drill 3 v 0

The format of this drill is the same as before, but with a third attacker added. The first player carries the puck wide; the second player goes down the middle lane, driving to the net; and the third attacker fills the other lane and then comes to the middle to provide support for a possible back diagonal pass and shot from the high slot.

Drive Drill 4 v 0

Using the same format as before but with a fourth attacker, the puck carrier now drives wide and, instead of shooting or making a play immediately, turns toward the boards and looks for the fourth attacker (figure 11.26). Adding the fourth attacker simulates the second-wave-of-attack principle whereby a defenseman joins the

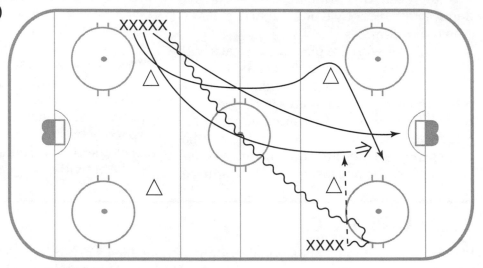

Figure 11.26   Drive drill 4 v 0.

play late, and if the opposing team's backcheckers are asleep, this "second-wave" player comes open just inside the attacking blue line.

The drive drill variations described to this point assume the puck enters the zone from a wide lane, but there are times when the puck enters from the middle. When the puck enters the attacking zone through the middle, it usually means that the opposing defensemen have backed off so that the free space to make plays in is in front of rather than behind them. We use the same drill format to simulate and drill the play options available in this situation.

Drive Drill Middle Lane Carry 2 v 0

The first player goes wide without the puck. The second attacker carries the puck into the middle lane and then cuts toward the teammate without the puck (figure 11.27). The player without the puck moves across and behind the puck carrier for a drop pass or fake drop. Both continue on for a shot on goal.

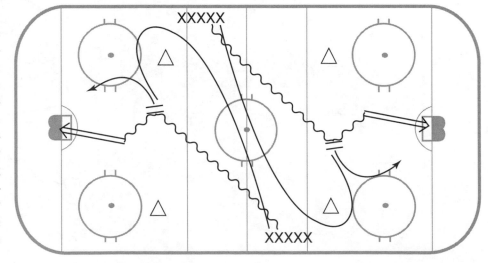

Figure 11.27   Drive drill middle lane carry 2 v 0.

Drive Drill Middle Lane Carry 3 v 0

The first player skates wide, the second skates the middle lane with the puck, and the third fills the empty lane (figure 11.28). The puck carrier has the option of cutting across toward either forward. The forward without the puck must recognize when the puck carrier is moving closer, then slow down and provide support from behind for the drop or at least the potential drop pass. The forward away from the play drives to the net.

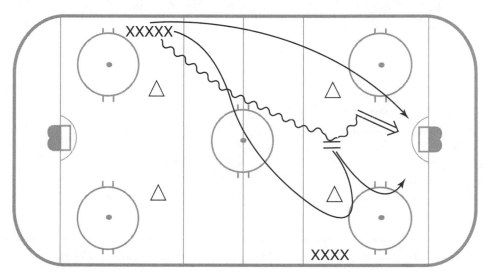

Figure 11.28 Drive drill middle lane carry 3 v 0.

Double Cross and Drop

Again, the first player skates wide, the second skates the middle lane with the puck, and the third fills the empty lane. The puck carrier has the option of cutting to either side for a drop pass. The other forward comes across for a second drop pass.

RAPID COUNTERATTACKS AND NEUTRAL ZONE REGROUPING

So far, we have covered the importance of speed utilization, the execution of offensive skills related to the neutral zone, and the offensive support and attack principles required for successfully getting a shot at the net. Now it's time to put all of this together into a combined system of play. Understand that there are two fundamental types of combined offensive play. The first consists of a rapid counterattack where the puck is pushed back toward the opponent's net immediately after it is retrieved. The second type is a controlled regrouping where a coordinated attack is employed. In this situation, the emphasis is on generation of speed through changing the point of attack by defensemen and on the support skating of forwards.

Rapid counterattacks are the essence of modern hockey, and that essence is best described as "transition." The anticipation of and rapid transition to a change of possession is often what separates winners and losers in the game of hockey.

Drills for practicing rapid counterattacks are difficult to design because the basic notion of a rapid counterattack suggests spontaneity while defying structure and control. Keeping that in mind, here are some drill suggestions you might like to try.

4 v 5 Neutral Zone Counterattack

Beginning at the top of the circles, two defensemen and two forwards are given a puck and asked to advance it to the red line and dump it in. A unit of five players is positioned in the neutral zone (figure 11.29). They are charged with taking the puck from the unit of four before they reach the red line and counterattacking rapidly upon creation of the turnover.

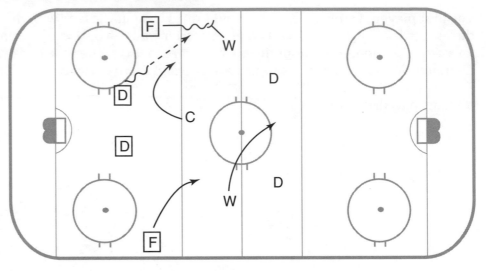

Figure 11.29   4 v 5 neutral zone counterattack.

Two-Puck Counterattack and Funnel Drill

A unit of five players breaks out of one end without pressure. Meanwhile, a second unit of five waits in the neutral zone, moving around with a puck and making passes (figure 11.30). The breakout unit moves with the puck into the neutral zone at full speed. On the whistle, the unit waiting in the neutral zone attacks in the opposite direction. The breakout unit leaves the

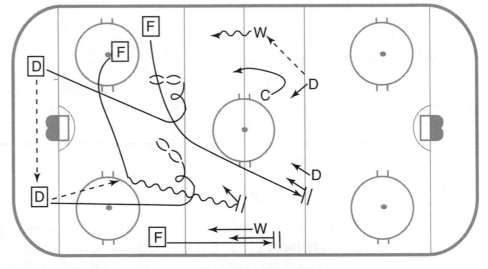

Figure 11.30   Two-puck counterattack and funnel drill.

puck they were carrying and makes the transition to defense by funneling through the middle.

There are numerous times during any game when rapid counterattacks are not possible because the opponent is well positioned or your forwards are not in support positions ready to attack. When this happens, it is necessary to organize a more controlled and deliberate attack known as neutral zone regrouping.

NEUTRAL ZONE REGROUPING

Neutral zone regroups almost always involve a D-to-D pass that allows your team to achieve two things. First, the pass itself changes the point of attack, thereby forcing opposing players to adjust their positions on the ice. This creates a whole new set of defensive angles and options that must be covered. Second, it allows time for the attacking forwards to get into support positions and begin to generate speed for the new attack. Neutral zone regroups are a less desirable option compared to rapid counterattacks because they allow opponents time to coordinate and implement their defensive formation. Obviously, whenever a rapid counterattack is available, it should be the first option.

An important key to successful regrouping and attacking from the neutral zone is recognition of the opponent's positioning on the ice and forechecking pattern. Some teams use two forwards to forecheck the two defensemen. When this is the case, it is sometimes difficult to make the D-to-D pass. To make this pass, the defenseman without the puck must quickly get in a back diagonal position. If both players remain at the same depth, the D-to-D pass may not be possible or might be intercepted.

Against two-man neutral zone forechecking patterns, the defenseman receiving the D-to-D pass has the following options.

For defensemen, selecting the correct play under the pressure of heavy forechecking will be easier if the defenseman about to receive the D-to-D pass has taken a quick look up ice before receiving the puck. Knowing which options are available prior to handling the puck often makes the difference between a successful and an unsuccessful pass. Obviously, the forwards have to be coming back quickly to support positions, preferably filling all three lanes.

Against 1-2-2 forechecking patterns, the defensemen usually have more time to make the first D-to-D pass. The defenseman who receives the D-to-D pass has to advance with the puck. The defensive partner, after making the first D-to-D pass, must skate to a support position in the middle of the ice and behind.

In chapter 10, I wrote about the influences of Soviet hockey on modern neutral-ice offensive play. One of the features of Soviet-era hockey was the interchanging of positions by the forwards in regrouping situations. When I first witnessed this, I thought the Soviet forwards were following some predetermined pattern. It seemed as though they were programmed, drilled, and made to execute this pattern like a football team running a sweep play. We now know that it was not a predetermined pattern as much as it was players moving to support the puck and give the puck carrier passing options. Predetermined patterns of motion and interchanges of position by forwards simply do not work on our rinks most of the time due to the lack of space. All motion and player interchanges must be executed based on the principle of support and on the forechecking pattern and pressure created by the opponent.

The work of the forwards in neutral zone regrouping must begin with filling at least two of the lanes. Thus, if the puck-carrying defenseman is being pressured, that player has two short pass options available (figure 11.31). The defenseman in possession of the puck must have the option of moving the puck right up the boards on the puck side or into the middle. This is called triangulation of support.

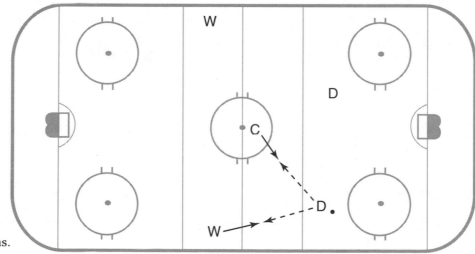

Figure 11.31
Short pass options.

Once the pass is made from defenseman to defenseman, the forward in the middle lane then determines the pattern of support. For example, the forward in the middle lane may swing toward the defenseman initially controlling the puck and continue toward the boards (figure 11.32). The wing on that side would then come across the ice to provide support in the middle lane. If the wing on the other side comes back to the boards, a new support triangle is created.

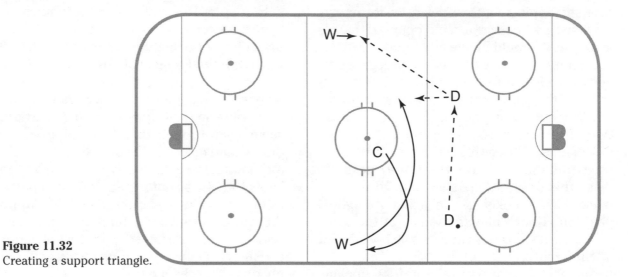

Figure 11.32
Creating a support triangle.

This type of exchange allows the forwards to generate some speed in the neutral zone in attempting to carry the puck into the attacking zone. It is a simple play—a simple exchange of positions between wing and center.

Another pattern forwards can use to generate speed employs the offensive principles of stretching and overlapping. The weak-side forward on the regroup immediately stretches by flying across the ice, looking for a pass between or behind the enemy defensemen (figure 11.33). This long pass to the stretching forward is the first option for the defenseman with the puck. Even if the stretching forward doesn't get the puck, his presence is a threat and keeps the enemy defensemen back while creating space in front of them for other passing options.

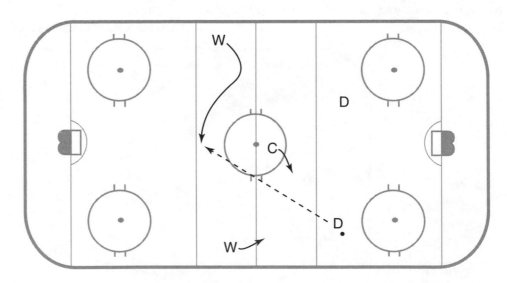

Figure 11.33
Stretching and long penetrating pass.

If a D-to-D pass is made, the center flows with this pass, and the winger on the original puck side continues behind the center (overlapping) at a reasonable distance and slightly different depth (figure 11.34). The defenseman

receiving the D-to-D pass then has the option of passing the puck to the center in the middle, either directly or indirectly with a pass off the side boards, or to the wing overlapping behind the center.

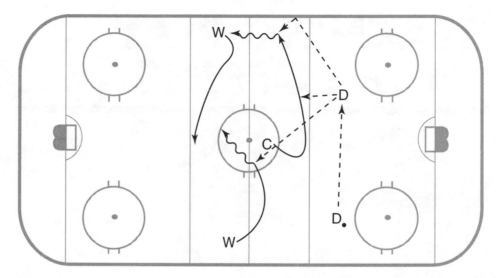

Figure 11.34
Double flow regroup.

Remember, the pattern you choose to have your forwards employ in the neutral zone is not that important. What is important is that the players have the appropriate skills required to execute within this pattern. Of equal importance is the notion that players skate

for the purpose of providing support, not to fulfill the grand design of a fancy regroup pattern. Finally, keep in mind that what your team does in the neutral zone, however pretty, doesn't mean anything unless the players can execute around the enemy net.

Part 5

TEACHING PLAY IN THE OFFENSIVE ZONE

Chapter 12

OFFENSIVE ZONE SKILLS AND STRATEGIES

We have only scratched the surface elements of offensive zone play in discussing initial attacks into this area from the neutral zone. Now we'll analyze the remaining principles of play and situations that pertain to this part of the ice surface. Quality plays finished off in this zone result in goals that win hockey games. For this reason, the section on scoring goals appears in this chapter. Coaches must understand that poor plays made here are often the first in a series of mistakes leading to goals scored against. They must also understand that defensive strategies and formations that influence events in the neutral and defensive zones are initiated in the offensive zone.

FORECHECKING:
DEFENSIVE HOCKEY IN THE OFFENSIVE ZONE

When the opponent has the puck or it is loose in the attacking zone, the strategy and tactics employed by a hockey team to get possession of the puck are called forechecking. Obtaining possession of the puck in the attacking zone through forechecking can also lead to an immediate scoring opportunity.

Forechecking is often used to establish the pace and set the tone of a hockey game. If a team forechecks with aggressive skating, provides good support, and finishes body checks, it sends a message to opponents that it is serious about winning the game. Attempting to dictate the pace of a game through forechecking has been part of the grand strategy of hockey games since the sport began. Forechecking with trapping tactics, less aggressive though these are, can frustrate an opponent early in the game and establish a slower pace. When on the road or playing an opponent with greater talent, this is often an intelligent strategic ploy. The main concept operating here is initiation. Initiation of the play forces an opponent to react to your strategy and tactics. When your players feel that they are dictating the pace and flow of the game, it is a great confidence builder for the team.

How to Dump the Puck In

Why dump the puck in? Why give up possession of the puck so that the other team has a chance to get it and come back at you? The answer is fairly simple. When you are approaching the center red line or the attacking blue line and the likelihood of a successful entry is poor while the likelihood of a turnover and counterattack by the opponent is high, why not dump it in? Playing the odds makes sense here. If the puck is dumped in, you have a chance to get it back. That's good. If the puck is dumped in, the opponent has to return it 200 feet to score a goal on your net, and your team has all the time it takes the opponent to do this to organize and execute a defense. That's good, too. If the puck is dumped in, your forwards have a chance to put a body on the opponent, and that is also good. If the puck is not dumped in but rather turned over to an opponent who counterattacks, well . . . that's not so good!

If you plan to forecheck aggressively, this strategy usually starts with a precision dump-in. In other words, throw the puck into the attacking zone in a manner that gives your team the best possible chance to get it back. While I was with the New Jersey Devils, we had a player on our "Crash Line" who was very good at dumping the puck intelligently so he and his linemates could get a body check on the enemy defensemen and get the puck back.

Mike Peluso often made jokes about what he called "The Seven Ways to Dump the Puck Correctly." Mike had the players and coaching staff doubled over with laughter while skating around the rink, warming up for practice, as he demonstrated each of his dump-in variations combined with equally articulate and enthusiastic explanations of the hows and whys. He would further joke about how some of our more skilled players should attend his summer hockey school offering dump-ins as the exclusive curriculum. Mike made light of this part of the game, but all professional players and coaches know that being able to get the puck deep in the offensive zone is extremely important if you want to establish a forechecking game.

The first rule for effective dump-ins is to keep the puck away from the opposing goalie. In today's hockey game, many goalkeepers are very skilled at trapping pucks behind their net and setting them up for their defensemen or making an outlet pass themselves, acting as a third defenseman. This may not be a concern for many of you because the goalies in your respective leagues don't have such skills, but it's still a good idea to teach the tactic of dumping the puck properly. If your players move on to higher levels, it will be one less reason for their new coach to yell at them.

The second rule for effective dump-ins is to make it very difficult for opposing defensemen to collect the puck. This means that the closer the puck remains to the boards, the harder it is for the opposing defensemen to collect and the better the dump-in. The most difficult and intimidating play for many defensemen is retreating to collect a dumped puck stuck tight to the boards with a large, fast, nasty opponent hunting them down. The following are three different dump-in strategies for you to try.

The Ring

The ring, or hard around, keeps the puck tight to the wall so it is difficult for opposing defensemen to collect. It has to go behind the net, past the opposing goalie, so it has to be fired with maximum velocity. Some rinks have deep corners that slow the speed of the puck, so this must be taken into consideration. It is often wise to ring the puck into the glass. This usually keeps opposing goalies from venturing behind the net to trap the ring for fear of a bad bounce off the glass stanchions, resulting in the puck bouncing into or in front of the net.

The Near-Side Chip

This is an effective tactic against opposing defensemen who like to play very tight gaps in the neutral zone. Softly chipping the puck off the boards behind a defender on the puck side will cause it to settle in the corner, away from the goalie.

The Cross Corner

This dump-in is executed by a player who is skating down the wing and then shoots the puck across the front of the goal, off the backboards, so that it resides in the opposite corner. Cross-corner dump-ins are my least favorite method because even though the puck is kept away from the goalie, it often bounces off the wall nicely and is easy for the opposing defensemen to collect. It also means that the puck must be dumped across two opposing defensemen, who may intercept it. It can be effective if the winger on the side the puck is being dumped toward has speed and will arrive at the caromed puck about the same time as the enemy defenseman.

One Drill to Teach All Three Types of Dump-Ins

Dumping the puck is usually advisable when the attackers are faced by an equal or greater number of defenders somewhere in the neutral zone. One of the easiest ways to introduce this tactic is with a simple 2 v 2 drill (figure 12.1) where the players execute either a near-side chip, a ring, or a cross-corner dump-in, depending on how the play develops.

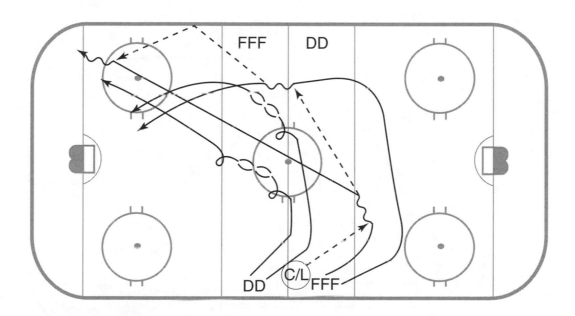

Figure 12.1   2 v 2 drill.

2 v 2 Dump-In and Forecheck Drill

All players are standing in the neutral zone along the boards. Two forwards skate out toward one of the blue lines and receive a pass from the coach, then turn to attack toward the other blue line. At the same time, two defensemen step out to challenge the attack by the forwards. The forwards must execute one of the three dump-in types based on how the play develops. If the play develops as a tight gap 2 v 2 on one side of the ice (figure 12.2), the best dump-in is a near-side chip. If the play develops with one forward on each side of the ice (figure 12.3), either a cross-corner dump-in or ring is likely to be the most successful play option.

There are two keys to coaching during the execution of this drill: (1) making sure the players recognize which is the appropriate dump-in tactic to select; and (2) precise execution of the

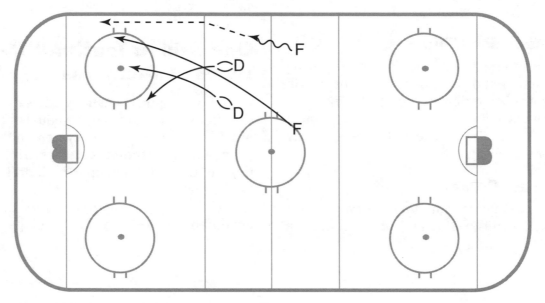

Figure 12.2   2 v 2 dump-in and forecheck drill.

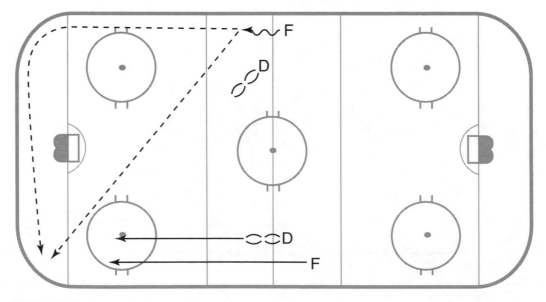

Figure 12.3   Cross corner or ring.

dump-in so that the goalie can't get to the puck and it is difficult for the defensemen to retrieve the dump-in and/or to make a play once it is retrieved.

The coach allows the drill to progress until the defensemen fire the puck out of the zone, the goalie freezes the puck, or a goal is scored.

INDIVIDUAL SKILLS FOR EFFECTIVE FORECHECKING

To be a great forechecker you must be fast and agile.

Skating Speed, Skating Mobility, and Just Plain Hustle

Effective forechecking begins with skating speed. Skating speed creates havoc with the breakout patterns of the opponent. Utilizing skating speed means that the opponent will always feel the pressure inherent in the lack of time this skill creates. If you have a fast team or a fast line of forwards, it is usually wise to have them forecheck aggressively whenever possible. The mobility element of skating cannot be overemphasized. Being able to change direction rapidly by either turning sharply or stopping and starting are keys to effective forechecking.

What needs to be said about hustle? It's obvious that the pure desire to get the puck back by simply working hard is at least as important as any fancy skating techniques. I mention this only because I've sometimes found myself so engrossed in the systems and strategies of the game that I've forgotten about what has always been the most important key to success—hard work!

If your players aren't blessed with skating speed and agility, it will be more difficult to forecheck aggressively. More conservative forechecking patterns such as trapping patterns are usually better options for those types of players. During a few seasons at Bellows Free Academy, we used three units of

five players. We had two units that were very mobile, and they forechecked aggressively. We had a third unit that was far less mobile, and their primary forechecking pattern was very similar to the trap that is so popular in modern hockey.

The ideal scenario is to have all your lines forecheck both aggressively and conservatively, depending on the situation. For example, after the puck has been dumped in for the purpose of a change, it makes no sense for two forwards to race out and attack aggressively when the opponent has full control of the puck. When an opposing defenseman is stopped behind the net with the puck, it makes no sense to chase him out, letting him use the net as a screen to skate the puck out of the zone. This is a time when a more modest forechecking pattern should be used. Players should also be able to recognize when a quality dump-in has taken place and there is a chance to forecheck aggressively. To forecheck this way, players have to anticipate a quality dump-in and a chance to forecheck. It is easy to back off into a conservative pattern if the play is misread; however, it is impossible to forecheck aggressively with any effect if players aren't anticipating such an opportunity and skating accordingly. Without anticipation, the opportunity to employ high-pressure forechecking tactics is lost.

Steering and Angling

Steering and angling combine to form the fundamental tactical skill associated with good forechecking, whether the forechecking pattern is highly aggressive or more controlled in nature. Steering refers to the initial positioning of the first forechecker. If, through positioning, this player can influence the opponent to move toward a specific area of the ice, he can then angle the puck carrier and use proper skating and stick position to continue in that direction while denying certain pass options to the puck carrier. The first forechecker's linemates can then read the direction of the play, anticipate what is likely to happen next, and get in good position to take advantage of subsequent events.

Figure 12.4   Steering—notice position of forechecker to deny one side of the ice.

Steering is more obvious to the naked eye when a trap is being used. Let's assume that the opponent is attempting to break out, beginning with a defenseman standing behind the net. Let's further assume that the center swings behind the net with the intent of picking up the puck and coming up the wall with speed. If the first forechecker establishes position to the side of the net toward the intended swing, the opposing center will likely choose not to take the puck (figure 12.4). The defenseman behind the net will have to start

the breakout coming up the other side.

In an aggressive forechecking situation, the first forward forechecking has to use speed and skating agility to establish a favorable steering position. For example, if the intent is to forecheck hard 1-2-2 and keep the play on one side of the ice, the first forechecker will have to skate to an inside position (that is, toward the middle of the rink) as he chases the opposing defenseman (figure 12.5). By establishing this position (steering), he creates an opportunity to angle the puck carrier

Figure 12.5   Forecheck hard 1-2-2.

farther in the intended direction.

Angling, the next phase of forechecking fundamentals, involves two principal elements: skating path and stick position. When a forechecker approaches the puck carrier from the side, skating along an elliptical path, the puck carrier has only one option: passing to reverse the flow of the play. And if the forechecker has his stick on the ice, to deny that pass, the puck carrier's only option is to continue along the path being forced by the forechecker. If all of the elements of steering and angling are properly executed, the forechecker can continue to close in on the puck carrier and take him out of the play with a body check.

DRILLS FOR TEACHING FORECHECKING FUNDAMENTALS

Basic Steering and Angling 1 v 1

The coach dumps a puck into the corner. The defenseman turns to get the puck. The forward forechecks the defenseman by first establishing a steering position to the inside and then angling the defenseman toward the boards.

1 v 1 Angling vs. Skating Speed

For this drill, a cone is set up on the ice. In situation A, the defenseman is allowed to carry the puck with speed behind the net and try to beat the forechecker to the blue line (figure 12.6). The only thing the defense-man is not allowed to do is stop behind the net. In situation B, the defenseman is allowed to get to the net and come up the ice with speed. The forechecker must go around the cone, angle off the puck-carrying defenseman, and finish the body check, if possible.

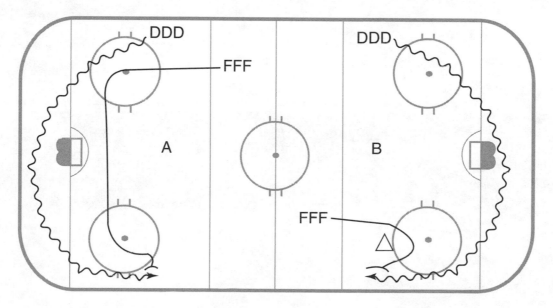

Figure 12.6   1 v 1 angling vs. skating speed.

1 v 1 Steering and Angling in a Trap Situation

In this drill, the forechecker is pitted against two offensive players. The forechecker's job is to keep the puck on one side of the ice, not allowing more than one D-to-D pass. The forechecker's body denies skating space and stick position denies the pass (figure 12.7). There is no body checking in this drill because the first forechecker's role in a trap situation is to set up the puck carrier for an attack by a teammate. The offensive players should be instructed to attempt a second D-to-D pass, if possible.

Figure 12.7   Steering and angling.

BODY CHECKING

When forechecking aggressively, the job of the first forechecker is to steer and angle the play, and when he closes on the puck carrier, he should finish his check. Normally, when utilizing trapping systems, the first forechecker does not finish his check. Many of the important techniques for effective body checking were described in the chapter covering the defensive zone. Use the angling drills presented previously to practice body-checking technique.

Pinching by Defensemen

What is pinching? This term refers to defensemen trying to hold the puck in the attacking zone by sliding down the boards against opposing wingers. It involves use of the stick and perhaps the body to keep the puck in the offensive zone. The defenseman sliding down has to remember that the primary purpose is to keep the puck in the offensive zone. I often laugh to myself when I observe a defenseman pinching down on a winger and just going for the big hit, when he could have kept the puck in first and then finished the opposing winger with a body check. If a defenseman does pinch and misses the puck, he must take the opponent with a body check and not allow the player to move freely up the ice.

Personally, I'm not a big proponent of pinching. Our rule with the Albany River Rats was that defensemen are not allowed to pinch unless they are 100 percent certain of getting the puck. Otherwise, we back off. It's a much safer way to play the game. We've scored countless odd-man rush goals against our opponents resulting from foolish decisions made by defensemen at the blue line. And whenever we've lacked the discipline to back off and allowed our opponents similar odd-man rushes, the puck has wound up in our net too often for my liking.

Having said that, if you find yourself trailing your opponent on the scoreboard late in a hockey game, it may become necessary for defensemen to pinch. In this case, we encourage pinches. The key to effective pinching is, first and foremost, good anticipation. If the defenseman arrives at the same time as the puck reaches the winger or a bit sooner, he has a good chance of keeping the puck in the attacking zone. Keeping the stick on the ice to jam the puck and the body, particularly the shin pads, alongside the boards is equally important.

CONCEPTS FOR EFFECTIVE FORECHECKING

To be a great forechecker you must take several things into consideration.

Time and Space

From our discussion of defensive play in other zones, we know that getting the puck back from the opposition involves limiting their time and space to force a change in possession. When forechecking aggressively, a team is placing more of its emphasis on the time element. When trapping, a team concentrates more on the spatial area. However, these two principles are applied together, neither exclusive of the other. If your team forechecks aggressively, it will forecheck more effectively if it employs intelligent angling, a spatial element. When using a less aggressive trapping system, concentrating on limiting space, the team must still apply aggressive pressure at the right moment.

The First Player

Regardless of the system, the first forechecker cannot allow the puck to be carried past him. If he allows the puck to be advanced beyond his position on the ice by someone skating with it, he has not done his job. Frankly, when this happens, the forecheck is usually dead in the attacking zone, and it is best to re-form in the neutral zone and try to regain possession of the puck there.

When forechecking aggressively, the first checker must not be concerned with the puck.

Their job is to apply pressure, force a pass, and finish the check. The stick blade should be on the ice for a possible disruption of a pass while on the way to finishing the check.

The Second Player

The job of the second player in any system is to read the actions of the first forechecker and anticipate where the opponent will send the puck. If it is obvious that the first checker will turn the play up the boards on the puck side, the second player should anticipate this and be in an appropriate support position. The third player should likewise adjust his position to the middle of the ice in the event that the puck is moved into that area. Having numbers around the puck is key to forechecking successfully.

High Player or Third Player

This term is very common and refers to an extremely important concept in forechecking or offensive zone play. It means that at least one of the forwards must remain closer to the defending goal than to the puck. No matter how good a team is at forechecking, the opponent will make a good play to break out the puck a significant percentage of the time. Thus, it's necessary to have a forward in position to support the defensemen against an oncoming rush. Staying above the puck allows the high player to go in either direction. If the forecheck develops positively, the high player can dive in and become part of the play to keep the forecheck alive or can go to the net.

Beating the Opponent Back

Whenever forecheckers attack the opposing team, they must remain mindful of the concept of getting back onto the defensive side of the opponent after the puck has been moved past them. In today's hockey, teams activate defensemen on a consistent basis, and if your forwards go down to forecheck, execute a body check, but allow the opposing defensemen to beat them back up the ice, it gives the opponent a chance to create odd-man rushes against you.

The first two or three strides are always important. If a forward has a good burst immediately after finishing off an opponent, he gains great position to backcheck or turn to forecheck the opponent again.

Forechecking Systems

If your players possess good fundamental forechecking techniques and understand and can apply the principles of effective forechecking, you should be able to employ any type of pattern with good prospects for success. I recommend that you use only one or two forechecking patterns. Good forechecking involves anticipation and aggressiveness, skills that are fostered when players can react automatically and instinctively, without thinking. If you ask players to know and execute too many patterns, thinking begins to occur on the ice, and a disease called "paralysis by analysis" will invade the minds of your players.

Aggressive Systems

Hard 1-2-2

The first forechecker is responsible for applying pressure on the puck, preferably from the inside out. This keeps the play on one side of the ice. The second player provides support along the boards on the puck side (figure 12.8). The third player either covers the boards on the weak side or comes directly to the middle. If the third forechecker covers the middle, you can allow the defenseman on the weak side to pinch.

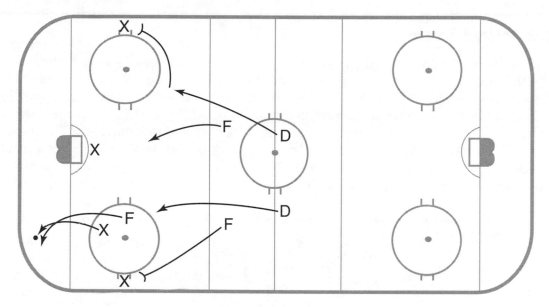

Figure 12.8 Hard 1-2-2.

2-3 Pick a Side

This is the basic forechecking pattern the University of Maine has employed in winning two NCAA titles in the decade of the '90s. The first two forwards forecheck aggressively on the opposing defensemen. Again, the first forechecker normally tries to establish inside-out pressure, denying the opposing defensemen the chance to get to the net (figure 12.9). The third forechecker picks the side he thinks the puck will go to. Most often he would go to the strong side. The weak-side defenseman pinches on a ring.

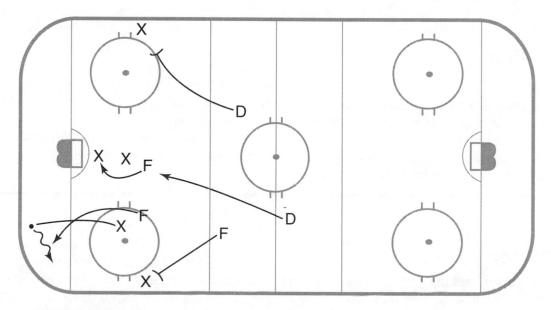

Figure 12.9 2-3 pick a side.

Weak Wing Lock

In this drill, the first two forwards forecheck aggressively. The job of the first checker is a bit different than in the previous two systems. Instead of forcing inside out, the first checker forces outside in, trying to drive the puck toward the weak side, then either chases the opposing puck carrier behind the net or cuts back across the front of the net (figure 12.10). The second forward should be on the other side of the net to greet the puck carrier if this happens. The third player automatically goes to the weak-side boards to cover the opposing weak-side winger so that a ring to that side is covered. If the opponent breaks the forecheck, the third or high player must then cover that forward or that lane so that the defensemen can cover the strong-side and middle lanes.

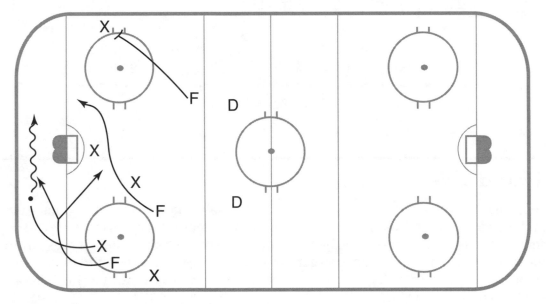

Figure 12.10   Weak wing lock.

Left Wing Lock

In recent years, the Detroit Red Wings have employed this system to perfection, and the Czech National Team has used it for as long as I have been involved in hockey. The first two forecheckers are rather aggressive. The third forechecker covers the opponent's right wing or the boards in that area. The defensemen are offset a bit, with the left defenseman in the middle of the ice and the right defenseman ready to pinch down on the opposing right wing. If the opponent breaks the forecheck, all three lanes are covered.

Trapping

Traps are forechecking patterns used when the opposing puck carrier has stopped behind the net. Chasing a defenseman behind the net in this case would mean sacrificing the first forechecker without forcing a pass. When this situation occurs, some form of controlled or trapping forecheck is advisable.

Man-to-Man Trap

Please excuse the gender-specific term, but I cannot force myself to say "person-to-person" trap! I've seen variations of this system employed by the Buffalo Sabers and New York Rangers of the mid-1990s, along with the Rochester Americans of the AHL and Boston University of Hockey East. For teams and coaches who like an "in your face" style of play, this can be an appealing form of trapping. Its strength is that the breakout team's players are covered so tightly that there is little the offense can do beyond gunning the puck off the boards into the neutral zone, provided they have posted a forward there. The down side is that firing the puck out is about the only effective option against this system, so that's what offenses generally do to avoid turnovers. The puck may indeed be turned over somewhere in the neutral zone, but two and perhaps three forecheckers are caught inside the blue line, eliminating any type of puck control counter-attack. Because of the tag-up offsides rule, this may not matter much to coaches who are content to have their defensemen fire the puck back in, get the forwards to tag up, and reestablish the forecheck.

For this trapping drill, the first forechecker stops in front of the opponent's net and is responsible for the defenseman in possession of the puck. The second forward positions himself head up with the other defenseman, who usually will go to a corner. The third forward mirrors the opposing center, who customarily swings into the empty corner. The two defensemen are responsible for covering the opponent's wings.

1-2-2 Zone Trap

The main idea behind the 1-2-2 zone trap is to force the opponent to skate or pass the puck into an ambush area. Luring the opponent to the ambush site, combined with proper execution of the trap at the critical moment, often leads to a turnover. Even though this formation is established

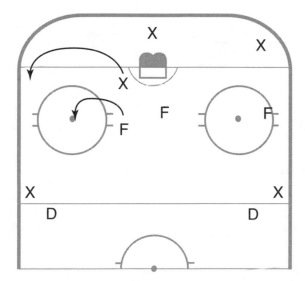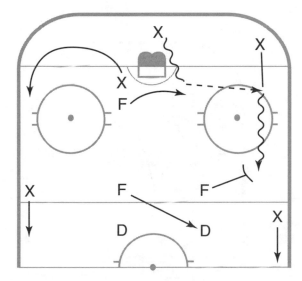

Figure 12.11   (*a*) 1-2-2 zone trap, (*b*) 2-1-2 neutral zone forecheck.

in the attacking zone, the ambush sites are usually closer to or inside the neutral zone (figure 12.11a-b).

The foundation principle of the 1-2-2 zone trap is to play the lines, limiting the space and available play options for the attacking team. There are two ambush areas: one near the wall at the blue line and another near the wall at the center red line.

In leagues where the two-line offsides rule is used, this type of trap is easier to execute effectively. If the ambush occurs before the puck carrier reaches the first blue line, the player with the puck can pass only as far as the center red line. If the ambush site is set just before the red line, the opponent can't dump the puck into the attacking zone without risking icing and a subsequent defensive zone face-off. In U.S. high school and U.S. junior hockey, the lack of this rule makes it more difficult to create the type of turnovers you want from this system if the offensive team is well prepared.

The first player is the helmsman and is responsible for steering the play to one side of the ice, toward one of the ambush areas. Once the play moves up one side, this player is responsible for keeping it there, preventing the opponent from bumping the puck backward and reversing the flow. The first technique in steering is proper initial positioning.

The first player should not be positioned head up with the defenseman in possession of the puck behind the net, but should be sliding to one side or the other. The ideal is to set up so that the defenseman behind the net must come out on the backhand side. The second technique is to use your stick to discourage a pass backward to the middle of the ice.

The initial positioning for the other two forwards is just outside the blue line inside the dots (figure 12.12). In this way, they are in position to challenge any pass made up the middle, and from this position, the strong-side forward can attack at the ambush site, once the play has been directed there, and the weak-side forward comes through the middle of the ice, looking to intercept pass attempts into that area. The defensemen are positioned in the middle of the ice and have no pinching responsibility. They wait for an errant pass and are there to provide the first counter-attack pass.

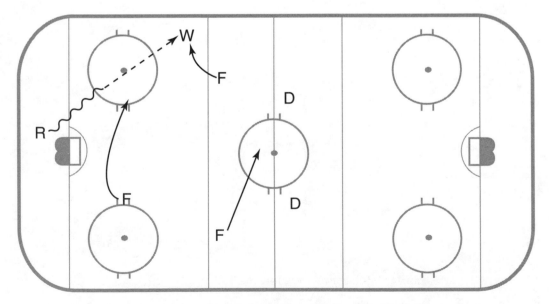

Figure 12.12   Initial positioning for two forwards outside of blue lines.

DRILLS FOR FORECHECKING SYSTEMS

Half-Ice Drill

This is the simplest and perhaps oldest drill for practicing forechecking systems. Two units are positioned between the red line and blue line, one breaking out and the other forechecking (figures 12.13 and 12.14). The puck is dumped in and the forecheck begins. The problem with this drill is that it isn't gamelike. Ten players just don't stand around between the blue and red lines waiting for the forecheck to begin. However, it does provide the coach with an opportunity to assess and instruct forechecking reads, reactions, skills, and positioning. One way to practice this in a half-ice situation is to start with a face-off at the offensive blue line dot. The coach throws the puck off the draw to the forechecking team's defensemen, who can get a dump, and forechecking can begin.

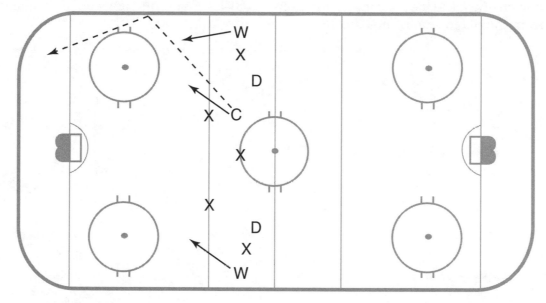

Figure 12.13   Forechecking drill.

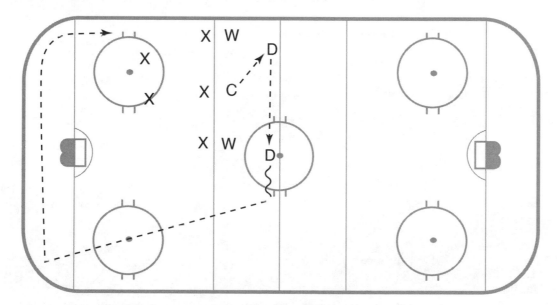

Figure 12.14   Half-ice drill for forecheck starting with face-off.

Flow Forechecking Drill

For this drill, the coach is positioned in one end zone with pucks. Pucks are also placed behind the net. Two forwards are in front of the net and one forward is in the high slot on the puck side (figure 12.15). The drill begins with a pass from the coach to the high slot for a shot. The coach then passes a second puck to the defenseman at the point for a shot with traffic. The coach then passes a third puck to the weak-side defenseman sneaking down from the point for a shot. The defenseman who takes the last shot while coming in from the point then goes behind the net, gets a new puck, and starts a breakout of the players in the zone. Meanwhile, a unit of five waits in the neutral zone.

On reaching the red line, the breakout unit dumps the puck in and forechecks the group that was waiting in the neutral zone (figure 12.16). Once that group breaks the puck out of the far end, they advance down the ice 5 v 0 for a shot, followed by a shot in the high slot, a point shot, and a shot from the defenseman sneaking down, a new breakout, and so on.

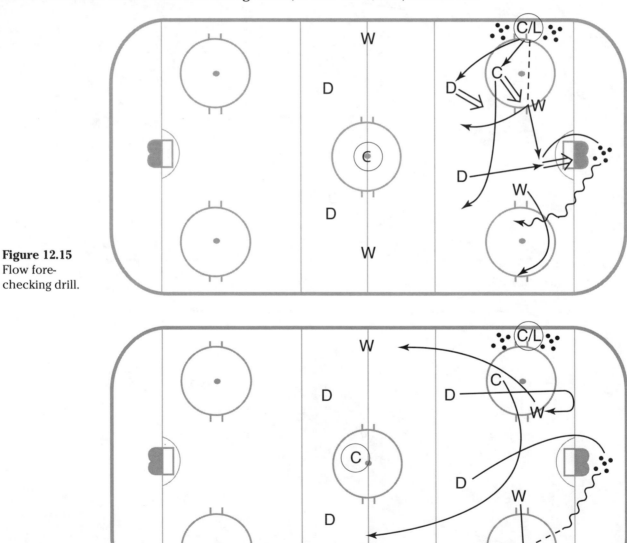

Figure 12.15
Flow fore-
checking drill.

Figure 12.16
Forechecking group
in the neutral zone.

OFFENSE IN THE OFFENSIVE ZONE

The most important and exciting part of playing in this zone is scoring goals. Scoring goals is arguably the most difficult part of the game to teach. Many coaches believe it is a purely instinctive skill that is impossible to teach. There is a measure of truth to this notion. If you believe that goal scoring is largely instinctive, those instincts still have to be nurtured and developed through practice. The best practice occurs when a player works alone in unstructured environments.

Having had the good fortune to watch John LeClair develop, it is interesting to think back on how he developed his goal-scoring ability as a youngster. He played hockey every chance he got on the outdoor rinks of his neighborhood. His scoring prowess was refined through countless hours of personal prac-

tice, with only his imagination to constrain him. What he learned in the backyard he was able to apply in the organized games he played throughout his minor hockey career. I believe that many of the goal-scoring situations he faces today as an NHL player are ones he faced a million times while growing up, some against opponents at Mr. Benoit's rink and some in his own mind as he practiced alone.

So was John LeClair born a goal scorer, or did he develop the skills he needed? No one knows for sure. However, I think it's safe to say that he would not be the goal scorer he is today if he had not practiced for endless hours as a youngster. The lesson here is simply that the more you practice something, the better you become.

© Rob Trigali Jr/Sportschrome

John LeClair's diligence and persistence make him one of the best NHL players today.

Unfortunately, for most high school and junior-level coaches, it is not possible to conduct long, involved practice sessions to improve goal-scoring abilities exclusive of all the other elements of the game you must practice. The key is to encourage players to improve their shooting skills on and off the ice as often as possible. There aren't many players in the history of hockey who have scored lots of goals despite having a below-average shot. It all starts with a good, accurate shot, quickly released and possessing good velocity.

As coaches, it's not about having every player on the team reach 50 goals in a single season; rather, it's about helping 10-goal scorers reach 15 goals, 20-goal scorers get to 25, and so on. It's about developing the myriad specialized skills and tactics that have been identified over the years as being of importance to goal scoring.

Scoring goals involves numerous elements, the first of which is shooting ability. Shooting consists of a hierarchy of subelements. First, get the shot on net. If the shot misses the net, a goal cannot be scored. Second in importance is a quick release. A quick release of the shot usually means the goalie has less time to position and set himself to make the save. Third in importance is the velocity of the shot. Helping players improve their quality of execution in these three areas is one way of improving their goal-scoring ability.

Seldom mentioned but vitally important is the concept of orientation. In other words, knowing where the net is—where the defenders and goalie are. Just watch your players skate toward the net to take a shot during a practice drill. I think you will find that most of them don't look at the net until the last moment, just before releasing the shot. The surprise of what a player sees at the last moment often leads to poor execution of the shot. If a player has looked up to find the net early, they will instinctively position their entire body so that they can successfully place the shot in the intended location.

Connected to the principle of orientation is the concept of the "shooter's illusion." What the shooter sees is not what the puck sees.

The true angle and the actual openings can only be seen with realism by looking through the imaginary eyes of the puck. Players must understand that their eyes are between five and seven feet above the puck. This means that a player almost always sees openings in the high areas of the net. If the shooter were to lie down on the ice and look at the net from behind the puck, he might see that there are no openings up high. Also, when a shooter carries the puck on his forehand, he tends to see more net on the side of his eyes. The true angle is three to six feet to the right or left of the eyes, depending on whether the shooter is right or left handed. Often players tend to shoot the puck across their own bodies to the side of their head. A shooter may not see any opening on the stick side, but that is where the opening may actually be—the true angle.

The shooter's illusion can be easily demonstrated on the ice by taking four lengths of rope and attaching one to the top of each post and the other two to the bottom of each post. Join the four lengths of rope together 30 to 40 feet from the net, and place a goalie in the net. Make sure the goalie stands inside the crease. Next, stand with the puck on the stick and talk about what you see. Have your players come behind you and ask them to confirm what you've described as the available openings for the shot. Now, have the players take turns kneeling down behind the puck, at the true angle, and discuss what they see as openings for the shot.

For the last part of this lesson, ask the goalkeeper to come out an additional three to five feet. The result of the goalie's action to cut down the angle by telescoping out toward the puck is that there is much less net to shoot at or perhaps none at all. If the goalie has shut off the angle completely, then the shooter must change the angle if he wishes to score. By skating laterally, pulling the puck toward the body, or pushing it away from the body, a player can change the angle and create new openings. This can provide the opening needed to score. As the shooter executes one of these moves, the goalie will be forced to move to establish position on the new angle. As the goalie moves, there is normally a brief moment when holes exist, especially between the pads. A quick curl and drag of the puck followed by a shot right at the goalie can often result in a goal between the goalie's legs. Moving the puck similarly and shooting back against the flow of the curl and drag motion can work well too, especially if the goalie is very quick and tends to overplay shots.

Finally, talk about getting goalies to move by using stick feints. Faking shots and disguising the intended line of the shot by opening and closing off the blade of the stick can be very effective tactics. The modern goalie tends to go down into a butterfly very quickly, so a well-executed fake can result in the goalie going down and exposing the top of the net to the shooter.

The simple tactic of driving to the net without the puck and stopping in front can also be effective. It allows the player with the puck to simply throw it either at the goalie's feet or at the traffic moving toward the net. Quite often, pucks bounce into the net in strange ways when this tactic is employed. In practice drills, never allow players to skate past the net into the corner. Make certain that players going to the net without the puck stop in front. Also, make certain that players taking the shot follow it and look to play any rebounds.

Scoring goals often involves much more than shooting and going to the net hard without the puck. Frankly, when playing against top-quality goalies, you'll find they nearly always stop the first shot if allowed to see it clearly. Against top-quality goalies, it is often necessary to obstruct their line of vision with screens or distract them with traffic. It may also be necessary to shoot to create a rebound opportunity rather than shooting to score. Goalkeepers who move out aggressively to cut down the angle and deny any open net must be hit with the first shot. If the first shot hits a goalie on the leg pads, he will often be unable to control the rebound. Goalies who wander out well above the crease area can easily make the first save in most cases, but if they don't put the rebound behind the goal line or to the side boards, they have a long way to move to cover the next

shot. Shooters who don't recognize this miss the net with their shots, exactly what the opposing goalie wants.

One of the most important tactical aspects of scoring rebound goals is the ability to get the puck high into the net with the rebound shot. Modern goalies at all levels are almost always down on the first shot. If a shooter has the ability to get the puck up quickly on the rebound shot, the chances of scoring are enhanced considerably. Point out to players that to get the puck up quickly, they must have leverage. This means that the closer the puck is to the shooter's body, the easier it is to get it up into the top area of the net. Starting the shot from nearer the heel of the stick blade provides additional leverage for the shooter, making it easier to get the puck upstairs.

Getting traffic in front of the goalie for the purpose of deflecting a shot, changing its direction, can also be an effective tactic. It is fairly simple to deflect a shot traveling along the ice, but it's more difficult to deflect shots that are elevated. It is easier to deflect a shot from a stationary position than to deflect it into the net while skating across the front of the goal. To improve goal scoring from deflections, all of these scenarios must be practiced.

Being able to score off tight plays near the net or stuffs and wraparounds from behind the net are important tactical goal-scoring skills. This type of scoring tactic requires not only skill, but also courage. Often when shooters attempt these plays in game situations, they are wiped out after the shot.

POINTS OF EMPHASIS FOR SCORING IN PRACTICE (REGARDLESS OF THE DRILL)

As mentioned earlier when discussing practices, the drills are not as important as the skills and tactics that you, as the coach, are emphasizing. What follows is a summary of teaching points that can be emphasized in your daily practices to help your players improve their scoring abilities.

Get players to bear down in practice. Every time a player takes a shot, he should be trying to score. Some players just throw the puck at the net, almost as though they don't even care to score. Shooting drills are really scoring drills for the skaters and save drills for the goalies.

If you miss the net, you can't score and you can't create a rebound opportunity. Remember to look beyond the goalie, finding the white mesh. If the goalie gives nothing, hit him with the shot, especially in the low areas. Today's butterfly goalies often let their stick pop off the ice as they go down, leaving the area between the pads open.

- A shot on net is never a bad play. As New Jersey Devils goalie coach Jacques Caron has often pointed out, goalies love it when they don't have to make saves.

- Release shots quickly and in stride before the goalie can get set. If goalies are given enough time to set up for a save, they usually make it.

- On rebound shots, look to get the puck up into the top part of the net. Most of the time, goalies are down after making the first save. Even when the goalie is completely out of position in practice and the scorer can just slide it into the net, get the players to shoot the puck in the air anyway. How often have we seen a scoring chance thwarted by a goalie who dives in desperation, making a save he couldn't have made if only the shooter had gone upstairs with the shot.

- Take the puck to the net whenever you can. Avoid hanging around on the perimeter. Most goals are scored within a few feet of the net.

- Go to the net as hard and as fast as possible without the puck when it becomes clear that the play is headed that way.

- After going to the net without the puck, stop in front of it. Avoid going for a skate in the corner. Goals are seldom scored from the corner.

- Emphasize screens and deflections in all drills.

For Defensemen

- Emphasize to defensemen the hierarchy of keys to shooting from the point.

- Get the shot through. To do this, defensemen have to have their head up and may have to move laterally to create a clear shooting lane to the net.

- Get the shot in the air unless there is a clear lane for a deflection. Ankle to knee height is the ideal level. A shot on the ice often becomes a quick breakout for the opponent.

- Get the shot on net. If you have to miss the net to get it through, try to miss to the short side so that the puck doesn't come flying around the boards for the opposing winger to break out with it.

There you have it! What we just looked at will serve as a basis for a variety of drilling activities you will find in the next chapter of this book. Let me conclude this section on offensive zone skills and strategies by noting that this is one area of the ice where coaches will allow players to show their creativity. After all, defensive and neutral zone coverages tend to be rather regimented, so players often look forward to being more instinctual at the offensive end of the ice. As coach, remember that not everyone can be a game breaker, but when you have that type of player, you must allow them some flexibility to show their stuff. Remember, it takes all kinds of personalities and playing types to ice a successful team.

Chapter 13

OFFENSIVE ZONE DRILLING

In the previous chapter, we began looking at some offensive zone drills, primarily within the context of forechecking and gaining the zone. This chapter includes a set of drills you can use to develop other skill sets in the offensive zone—skills such as goal scoring, learning to protect the puck while pressured, one-timed shooting, and cycling. Keep in mind that drills alone do not guarantee that players will improve. Rather, it is the proper execution of skills and tactics that will foster improvement, and that, in part, is your job as coach!

GOAL-SCORING DRILLS

Fake and Shoot Forehand or Backhand

Place three sets of three cones in three lanes in front of the net. The cones should be roughly three to five feet apart in a triangular formation. The sets of cones on the sides are placed about 15 feet from the net. The set in the middle is placed about 20-25 feet from the net. Players are positioned in three lanes at the red line (figures 13.1 a-c). One player at a time skates at full speed, carrying the puck directly at the apex of the cone formation, fakes to one side, and slides to the other for a shot. Which side the player skates to dictates whether it's a forehand or backhand shot. The fakes and lateral movement change the angle and force the goalie to move. Players rotate from lane to lane.

a

b

c

Figure 13.1   (*a*) Fake, (*b*) shoot forehand, and (*c*) backhand.

Three Shot Types Off the Rush

Players take three fundamental forehand shot types off the initial rush. The first type is to come down the wing on the forehand side (right-hand shooter skating down the right wing) and blast a shot. The second is to come down off the wing and shoot from the side in a manner similar to Mark Messiers. The third is to skate down off the wing, fake wide, and cut quickly to the middle on the forehand for a quick-release forehand shot. Joe Sakic is one of the best players at executing this type of shot. In this drill, players line up on the side boards in the neutral zone, come across the ice, take a pass, and then head down the wing to take one of the three shot types described earlier. Another sequence players can practice in this drill format is to come down the wing, fake the shot, take another stride, and then shoot (see photo below).

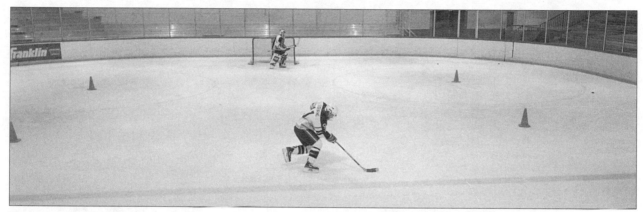

Three shot types off rush.

Shooting With Feet Moving Under Pressure

For this drill, two cones are positioned at the blue line a bit farther apart than the dots. Players in the inside lines have the pucks. On the whistle, the player from the inside line goes first, carrying the puck across the front of the cone so that he is in the wide lane (figure 13.2). The player from the board-side line cuts across the front of the cone toward the middle of the ice after the puck carrier passes and puts checking pressure on the shooter.

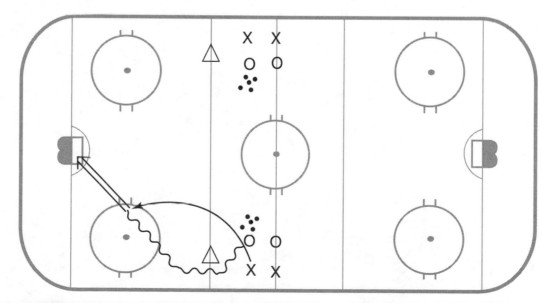

Figure 13.2
Shooting under pressure.

2 v 0 Stiff Stick and One-Timed Shots

Players form two lines on the half wall in an end zone. They skate out into the neutral zone and cross, changing lanes for the attack. One pass is made inside the blue line for either a one-timed shot for a shooter on his off wing or a stiff-stick shot for a player coming down on his strong side (figure 13.3). For a one-timed shot, the shooter will have to pivot to backward in order to face the passer and position himself for the shot. The key to the stiff-stick shot is to tightly squeeze the top hand and slide the bottom hand down the shaft a bit.

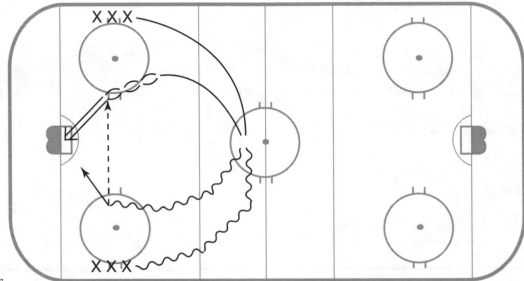

Figure 13.3
2 v 0 stiff stick
and one-time shots.

Catch and Shoot Drill With Stuff

Players are positioned at the red line. Each player skates down the wing, receives a pass, and gets off a quick shot (figure 13.4). After shooting and playing the rebound, if it lies close to the front of the net, the player skates behind the net, receives a second pass, and walks out to the front for a stuff shot.

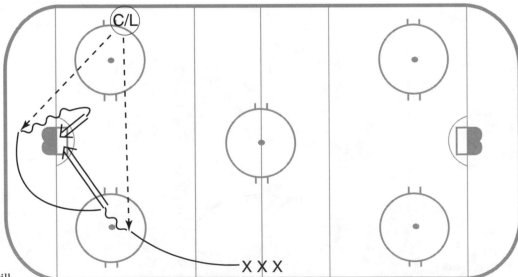

Figure 13.4
Catch and shoot drill.

Walkouts or Wraparounds

We covered this drill in the section pertaining to goalies playing close to the net. It's a great drill for shooters too. Shooters are positioned in each corner. Cones are placed in front of the net to limit the space the shooter has in that area (figure 13.5 a-b). The shooter must skate with the puck along the goal line extended. This forces the goalie to hold his position, not knowing whether the shooter will come out front or go behind the net. The shooter has the option of walking in front or faking a move to the front and going around behind, emerging on the other side for a wraparound shot.

a

b

Figure 13.5   (*a*) Walkouts, (*b*) wraparounds.

As mentioned in the section on scoring goals in chapter 12, it is often difficult to score unless players are driving to the net and distracting or screening the goalie, constantly on the lookout for rebounds and deflections. The next several drills involve these types of conditions. I can't emphasize enough how important this is to improving your team's ability to score, especially against quality goalkeepers.

Drive Drill

Players are positioned on diagonally opposite sides of the ice at the blue lines. The first player takes off across the ice without a puck. The next player in line carries the puck and makes a pass to the first player, who by now is traveling down the wide lane (figure 13.6). The first player accepts the pass and skates down the wing for a shot. The player must hit the net with the shot. The player who made the pass flies down the middle lane looking for a rebound.

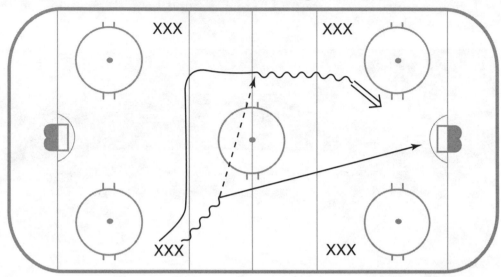

Figure 13.6
Drive drill.

Drive Drill 2 v 1

This version of the drive drill begins with a pass from the first forward to a defenseman positioned inside the blue line, who then passes to the second forward off the wall. Meanwhile, a second defenseman waits in the neutral zone to play the attack (figure 13.7). The defender is not at all concerned with the puck, allowing the forward in the wide lane to shoot it. The defenseman plays only the forward driving to the net through the middle lane. The forward driving wide with the puck must shoot before reaching the face-off dot. The forward driving to the net through the middle lane must try to get free of the checking defenseman to play the rebound.

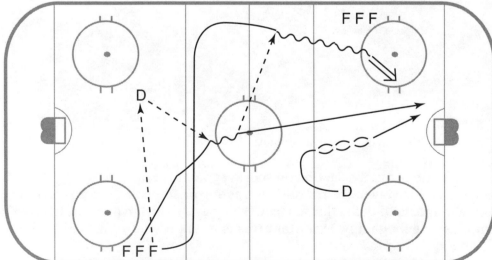

Figure 13.7
Drive drill 2 v 1.

2 v 2 Shooting Under Pressure

This drill has the same format as the shooting under pressure with feet moving drill diagramed earlier except that a defenseman and another forward are added on the weak side. The inside forward cuts in front of the cone with the puck, skating down the wide lane for a shot while being chased (figure 13.8). The forward on the weak side drives to the net without the puck.

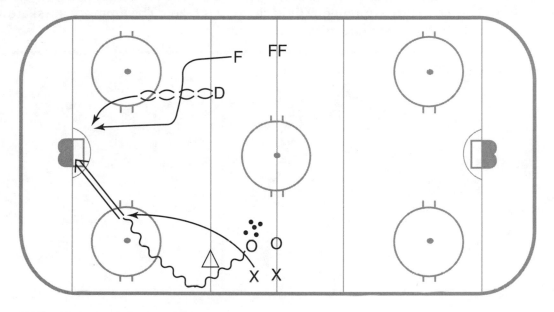

Figure 13.8   2 v 2 shooting under pressure.

Three Lanes, Shot, Screened Shot

This is a simple drill for teaching and reinforcing screening of the goaltender. The drill starts with three lines of players at center ice and can be initiated from either of the three lanes. The first player in a line skates toward the net and takes a shot, playing the rebound if it is nearby. The next player from the same line skates with a second puck for a shot through a screen established by the first shooter (figure 13.9). The sequence is repeated with the other lines.

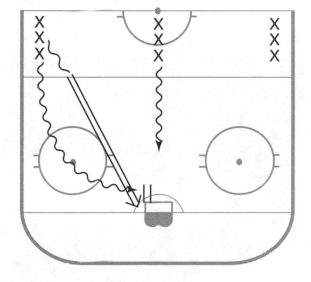

Figure 13.9   Three lanes, shot, screened shot.

Moving Screen Drill

Players form a line along the wall on each side near the top of the circle. The first player in line on one side skates across the ice, around the cone, and in for a shot (figure 13.10). After taking the shot, the player may play a rebound if the puck is nearby, then must remain near the side of the net. The next player skates with the puck from the other line, around a cone, and heads in for a shot. Just before the shot comes, the player to the side of the net skates across in front of the goalie, obstructing his vision momentarily as the shot is taken. The timing of the skate across the front is critical. Both players now play the rebound.

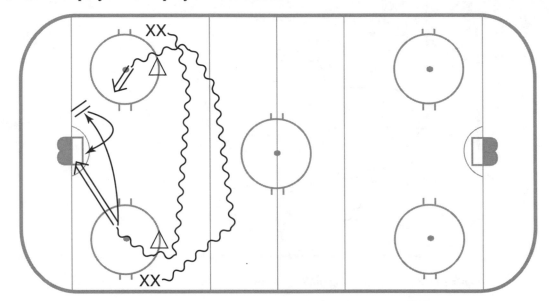

Figure 13.10 Moving screen drill.

1 v 0 and 1 v 1 Roof the Puck Rebound Simulation

A coach is positioned in the slot, about 15 feet from the net, with several pucks. The shooter faces the coach with his back to the net. The coach tosses a puck to the side of the shooter, who must

a

Figure 13.11   (*a*) 1 v 0, (*b*) 1 v 1 roof the puck rebound.

b

get to it and then get it to the top of the net quickly. Subsequent pucks are tossed out to alternating sides. Later, add a defender with his stick turned over so that the blade is in the top hand and the knob of the stick is on the ice. The defender provides resistance by bumping and slashing the shooter, making it tough for him to score. The defender is not allowed to go for the puck at first. As your scorers become more proficient, allow the defenders to go for the puck with their knobs. See figure 13.11 a-b.

Stationary Head on Screen and Deflection Drill

Position three defensemen at the point, each with a pile of pucks. A forward should establish a screen in front of each defenseman and execute a deflection as each takes a turn shooting the puck (figure 13.12). Make sure that the forwards are at least six or seven feet from the top of the crease. If the deflection comes too close to the goalie, he should smother it. The biggest mistake forwards tend to make is trying to tip a puck while too close to the net.

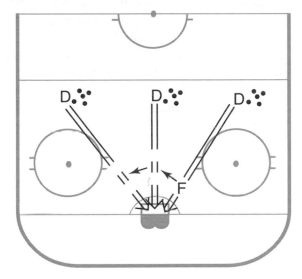

Figure 13.12   Stationary head on screen and deflection drill.

Deflections While Moving

A forward skates under control in a figure-of-eight pattern between the end zone face-off dots. A defenseman is positioned at the blue line in the middle of the ice with a pile of pucks. As the forward comes through the slot, a defenseman at the point fires a wrist shot in the air for the forward to deflect (figure 13.13). If there is a rebound, the forward plays it before continuing the figure-of-eight skate in preparation for the next point shot and deflection.

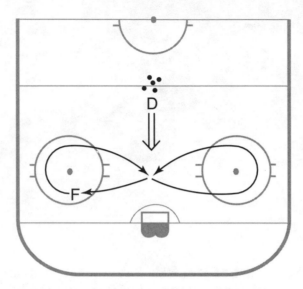

Figure 13.13   Deflections while moving.

Five-Shot Drill

In this exercise, the shooter will have five shots of various types. The drill begins with a shooter coming down the wing for a shot, choosing any of the three shot types previously discussed for shooting off the wing (figure 13.14 a-e). After shooting and going for the rebound, if nearby, the shooter goes to the goal line extended, 10 to 15 feet from the net, gets a pass from the coach, and walks to the net for shot. The player then goes to the slot for a pass from the coach for either a catch and shoot or one-timer, depending on which hand the player shoots with. After taking that shot, the player pauses, then drives to the far post for a cross-ice pass from the coach on the back door. After another pause, the player goes behind the net, receives a final pass, and coming out on either side, tries to stuff the puck on the goalie.

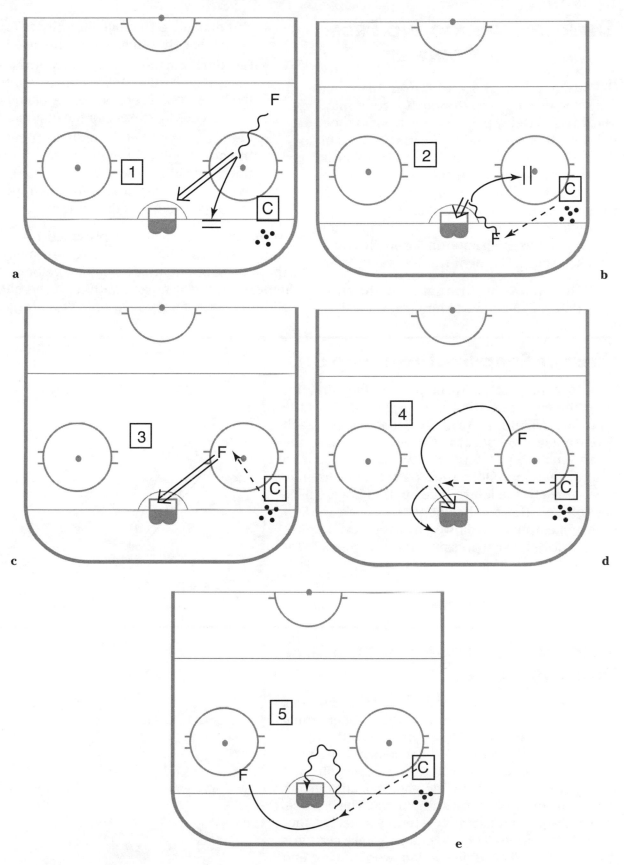

Figure 13.14 Five shot drill.

DEFENSEMEN SHOOTING FROM THE POINT

Defensemen who shoot well from the point are vital to successful offensive zone play. Many teams today pack the low front of their net with all five defenders inside the tops of the circles. This means that when the puck is being controlled in the offensive zone, the only outlets are at the points. In chapter 12, the section on Points of Emphasis for Scoring in Practice included a hierarchy of important keys for defensemen shooting from the point. It makes sense to repeat these here:

- Get the shot through. To do this, defensemen have to have their head up

and may have to move laterally to create a clear shooting lane to the net.

- Get the shot in the air unless there is a clear lane for a deflection. Ankle to knee height is the ideal level. A shot on the ice often becomes a quick breakout for the opponent.

- Get the shot on net. If you have to miss the net to get it through, try to miss to the short side so the puck doesn't come flying around the boards for the opposing winger to break out with it.

The following drills are provided to help you develop the ability of your defensemen to shoot from the point. Remember, velocity is important, but it means nothing if the shot either doesn't get through or isn't on target.

Wrist or Snap Shot Two-Step Drill

This is a nice little warm-up shooting drill for defensemen where they are spread out near the blue line (figure 13.15). The coach gives each defenseman two passes. On the first pass, the defenseman steps laterally to the right and takes a wrist or snap shot. On the next pass, the defenseman must move to the left to take another shot. Quickness of execution and height of the shot are the first points of emphasis, followed by accuracy. Because there is no defensive pressure, there's no excuse for missing the net. Right?

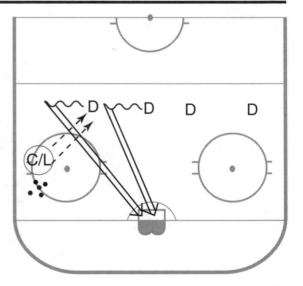

Figure 13.15 Snap shot two-step drill.

Wrist or Snap Shot Two-Step Drill Under Pressure

Two defensemen are positioned inside the blue line, even with the face-off dots. The other defensemen (with pucks) are in two lines just below the top of the circles (figure 13.16). A defenseman with a puck passes to the defenseman at the opposite point and then sprints toward the defenseman inside out, outside in, or directly in a straight line. The defenseman at the point must move laterally to get the shot to the net or shoot it very quickly to make certain it gets through. The defenseman who passes and

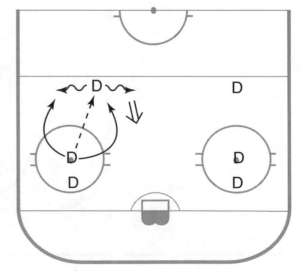

Figure 13.16 Snap shot two-step drill under pressure.

races out should try to block the shot, at least with the stick. After passing, the player goes to the shooting line, and after shooting, the shooter skates to the passing line.

Point Shot and Backdoor Shooting Drill

Pucks and defensemen are lined up in the corners. The drill begins with a pass from the corner to the point (figure 13.17). The defenseman at the point takes a shot from there and then heads to the net, receiving a cross-ice pass for a backdoor shot.

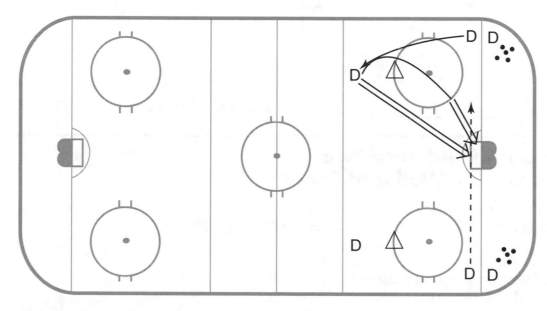

Figure 13.17   Point shot and backdoor shooting drill.

Walking the Line Drill Series

Defensemen are in line outside the blue line near the face-off dots. Pucks are at the tops of the circles (figure 13.18a-c). A defenseman skates forward toward a puck, retrieves it while immediately pivoting to backward, and continues skating backward in possession of the puck to the blue

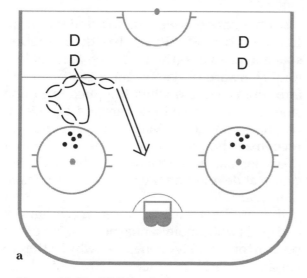 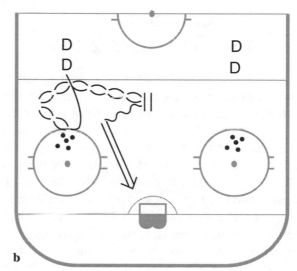

a   b

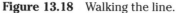

Figure 13.18   Walking the line.

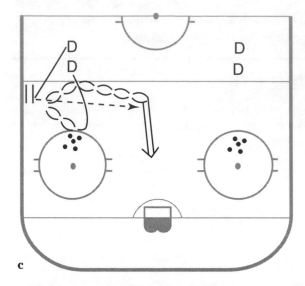

line and then across it for a shot from inside the dots. The next drill in the series is to walk the line, fake the shot, stop, and take two steps laterally in the opposite direction before shooting. Part three in the series involves passing the puck to the next defenseman in line, then receiving a return pass across the blue line for a shot, possibly a one-timer.

Figure 13.18   Walking the line, *continued*.

Trap a Rimmed Puck Two Steps Off the Wall and Shoot

Defensemen are positioned at the end zone dots, one at each point. The defenseman at the end of the line tosses a puck off the backboards, retrieves it, then rings it up the near wall (figure 13.19). The defenseman at the blue line goes from the neutral zone dot to the puck, collects it off the wall, takes two steps to the middle, then shoots.

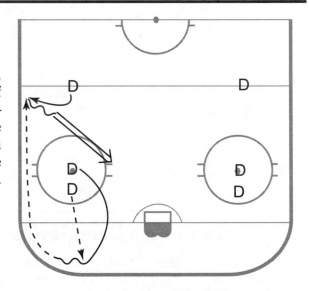

Figure 13.19   Trapped puck two steps off wall and shoot.

GRINDING IN THE OFFENSIVE ZONE

One of the most difficult ways to score goals is to maintain possession of the puck in the attacking zone for a length of time and find a way to get a good shot. One reason this is difficult is that the opponent is already in good defensive position. Another reason is that the defenders recognize the danger involved when the puck is in their defensive zone, so the mental disposition of those defenders is intense, determined, and usually conservative. Unlike offense generated from the neutral and defensive zones, there is no opportunity for outnumbering the opponent

on a change of possession, so there will be no transition opportunities. Also, the operating space available to the attacking team is limited. There are 10 skaters and a goalie packed into one zone, and when the puck is to one side, there are often 10 skaters and a goalie on only half of one zone. Finally, opposing coaches recognize the importance of playing well in their defensive zone and usually work diligently at developing the coverage abilities of their team.

If it's so difficult to generate scoring chances and goals while maintaining possession of the puck in the offensive zone, then why bother to emphasize and practice this phase of the game? It's simply that good teams won't allow your team many transition opportunities or get caught out of position to allow you odd-man rushes. If you want to score at even strength, you had better be able to generate offense in this phase of the game. Also, if your team is good on the offensive zone grinds, it controls the puck, and if your team has the puck, the other team can't score. Finally, even if your team can't score on the grinds, good execution of offensive zone play skills and tactics often leads to opponents taking penalties, and the resulting power play gives your team a chance to score.

Within the limited space available while operating in the offensive zone, there are three soft areas where the puck can be sent in order to buy time or generate a shot. Figures 13.20 through 13.22 illustrate the three soft areas.

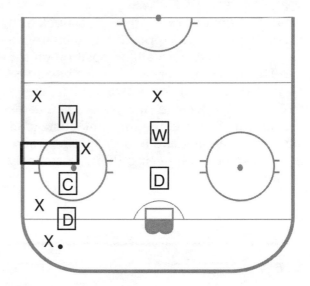

Figure 13.20 The seam in the defensive formation between the low defenders and the winger covering the point.

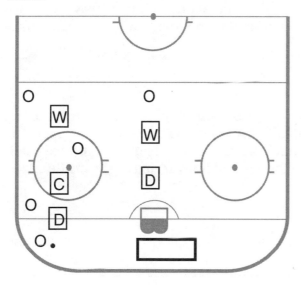

Figure 13.21 The area behind the net.

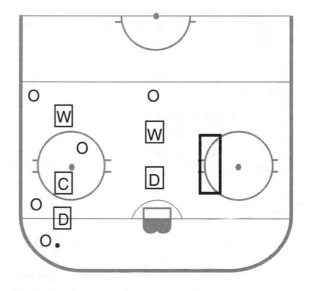

Figure 13.22 The back-side of the attacking zone.

PUCK PROTECTION AND CLOSE SUPPORT

Except for finishing the play with a good shot at the net and possibly a goal, the most important tactical skill is the ability of forwards to protect the puck. The play options we've just looked at won't work without good puck-protection skills. Without puck-protection skills and a determined attitude to keep the puck from the opponent, and equal determination to get the puck to the net somehow, there is little chance for success on the offensive zone grinds. Good puck protection must be combined with close support in the offensive zone. Even the best players in the game usually can't do it alone, at least not consistently. If the player with the puck has a teammate close by, a short pass or simply locking up the checker and leaving the puck for that teammate works well. Close support means that quick little 2 v 1 situations can be effective.

Finally, after a player protects a puck and makes a play to a supporting teammate, he must move quickly to a new position on the ice. This is often referred to as a give-and-go play. One of the major reasons for failure in any type of offensive hockey is teammates getting caught watching the game instead of supporting it—instead of anticipating where they must go and getting there in a timely fashion!

BASIC TECHNIQUES AND TEACHING PROGRESSIONS FOR EFFECTIVE PUCK PROTECTION

The fundamental principle of puck protection is to keep the body between the checker and the puck. Also of vital importance is to stay on the inside edges of the skates as much as possible to promote maximum balance and strength. To teach this skill, use the following simple progression of 1 v 1 drills.

Step 1

Instruct the puck carrier to remain somewhat stationary with the puck in front of the body in any open area of the ice, with feet shoulder-width or perhaps slightly wider apart. Good knee and ankle flexion are required. The puck protector is not allowed to touch the puck with the stick. He must move his body and use his stick to keep a checker from taking the puck away. The puck protector will be forced to spin to keep the puck away from the opponent. In spinning, the puck protector should use the inside edges of the skates.

Step 2

Again, the puck carrier remains in a somewhat stationary position. He is now allowed to control the puck with his stick at times while trying to maintain his body position on the checker. Any time he feels the opponent is thrusting toward the puck, he can spin and push it subtly to a new position, or he can whack the opponent's stick with his own, all while turning on the inside edges.

Step 3

Finally, instruct the puck carrier to bring the 1 v 1 battle over to the boards. Stress inside-edge turns.

DRILLS TO PRACTICE PUCK PROTECTION

Three Zones Puck Protection

Players are paired off, with an equal or near-equal number of pairs in each of three zones, away from the boards. On the coach's whistle, the players in zone 1 protect the puck against an opponent. This should be done for 10-15 seconds. On the next whistle, the players in zone 2 protect the puck while the players in zones 1 and 3 rest. On the next whistle, the players in zone 3 activate. On the next whistle, the players in zone 1 go back to work, switching roles between checker and puck protector. After several rounds of this type of puck protection, move the players over to the boards and practice battles from there with the same work-to-rest ratio.

Get Off the Wall Game

Two players conduct a 1 v 1 battle along the boards (figure 13.23). The puck protector must try to get off the wall and advance the puck into the middle of the ice, even with the face-off dots. The playing area along the wall should be no larger than 15 feet per pair of combatants. The players count the number of times they can get to the middle in each 15-second repetition. The player with the most points wins.

Figure 13.23   Get off the wall game.

Chairman of the Boards Drill

The puck is chipped in the corner and two players compete for possession (figure 13.24). The offensive player receives a point if he can protect the puck and get a shot on goal. The defender gets a point if he can get possession of the puck and throw it out of the zone off the boards or glass.

Figure 13.24   Chairman of the boards drill.

The next phase of development involves learning how to provide support on the offensive zone grinds. While one player is busy trying to protect the puck, a teammate must get over to him quickly to create numerical superiority and improve the chances of maintaining possession of the puck. Getting a supporting player near the puck offensively before the opponent gets a defender into the play is a major element of success on offensive zone grinds. Another important element is the use of verbal communication. Verbal communication is very important to the puck carrier. In games, the puck carrier is under tremendous pressure, and if teammates are telling him what to do with the puck, he is more likely to execute a good play. What follows are some simple drills to develop this tactic among your players.

2 v 0 Cycling

This introductory support drill begins with the puck being chipped into a corner. The first player in line retrieves and rolls up the wall with the puck (figure 13.25). This effort is supported by the next player in line, who follows in the first player's wake, ready for a pass. The first player throws the puck off the boards to the second player, then continues to the net for a pass and a shot. You can make players execute more than one pass off the boards before the pass to the net for a shot. It is important to throw the puck off the boards and avoid a direct pass. In game situations, defenders are usually chasing the puck carrier from the inside, so it's important for players to get in the habit of using the wall to pass the puck on grinds.

Figure 13.25   2 v 0 cycling.

This drill has several variations.

1.   **2 v 0 scissors cycling.** The format for this drill is the same as the 2 v 0 cycling drill except that the support player now moves in the opposite direction of the puck carrier for a pass off the boards and subsequent attack on the net.

2.   **2 v 1 cycling or scissors cycling.** This drill has the same format as the preceding two drills except that a defender is added. The defender must attack the puck carrier aggressively, not playing it as a soft 2 v 1. Remember, you want to teach the attacking players to give and go, so aggressive pressure from the defender is required.

3.   **2 v 2 cycling or scissors cycling.** Use the same drill format as in the previous exercises but simply add a second defender. At first, you may choose to have the defenders turn their sticks over to improve the prospects for success by the attackers.

4.   **3 v 0 cycling or scissors cycling.** Maintaining the same drill format, simply add a third attacker to the offensive zone cycle (figure 13.26). The attackers must make at least two passes back along the boards before taking a shot.

Once you are satisfied with the execution of passes using the three-player cycling rotation, simply add defenders to the drill, beginning with one defender and progressing to three. To improve success in the initial learning phase, you may want to have the defenders turn their sticks over.

Figure 13.26   3 v 0 scissors cycling.

Cycles vs. 1, 2, or 3 Defenders (Three Pucks)

Using the previous drill format, a coach dumps the puck in for a unit of three to cycle against one defender. After a shot is achieved, the coach blows the whistle, throws in a second puck, and sends a second defender. After a shot is achieved or the defenders clear the puck out of the zone, the coach blows the whistle, throws in the final puck, and sends a third defender.

3 v 3 Low With Two Point Players

This is one of my favorite drills for practicing the offensive zone grinds because it gives offensive players the opportunity to pass the puck to the point for a shot and go to the net for screens, deflections, and rebounds. The point players must remain out near the blue line. When a pass is made out to point, these defensemen must snap the shot off quickly.

3 v 3 low with two point players.

OFFENSE GENERATED FROM BEHIND THE NET AND DOT PLAYS

In recent years, no professional hockey player put more pressure on defenses than Wayne Gretzky did by simply getting control of the puck behind the net in the attacking zone and making plays from that area. Why is controlling the puck and making a play from behind the net such an effective offensive zone play tactic? The reasons are as follows:

- The defending team must look to the puck, so at times they are unable to see other attackers who are operating in front of the net.
- It is often difficult to predict which side of the net the pass out or attempted stuff shot will come from.
- The goalie must look behind the net for the puck, and he too cannot see the attackers in front of him.
- The goalie must remain deep in the net until the puck is passed to the front, so

Figure 13.27   Dot concept.

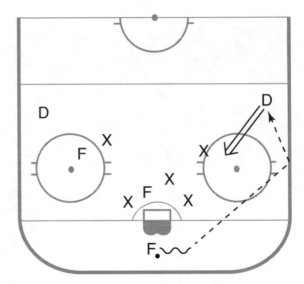

Figure 13.28   Defenseman stays out near blue line.

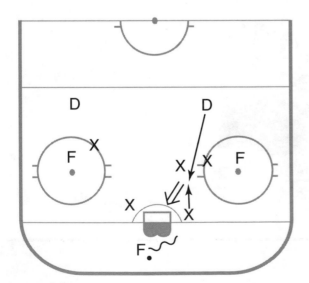

Figure 13.29   Forwards widen, defenseman down the middle.

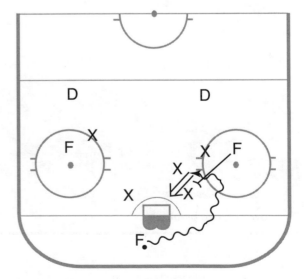

Figure 13.30   Taking puck to front for shot.

he is often unable to challenge the shooter by telescoping out to cut the angle, thereby leaving much of the net exposed.

Getting a player to control the puck behind the opponent's net is only half the formula for success in this scenario. The other half involves the other two forwards and possibly a defenseman finding ways to get open for a shot. This is where the dot concept becomes a useful tactic (figure 13.27). When the puck is controlled behind the net, the defending team tends to collapse its defensive formation tightly toward the net. If all the other attackers go directly to the net in the middle of the ice, they've succeeded in creating traffic around the goalie but probably won't be open for a pass. What works well most of the time is for one of the other attacking forwards to go to the front of the net, attracting coverage and being disruptive to the defenders, while the other forward widens out and moves toward a face-off dot for a pass.

It is a good idea for defensemen to stay wide and remain out toward the blue line initially (figure 13.28). This gives the player with the puck behind the net an additional pass option if nothing is open at the dot or directly at the net.

Another play option is to widen out both forwards toward the dots and slide a defenseman right down the middle of the slot to the front of the net for a shot (figure 13.29). This play is a little risky but can be effective.

The most obvious play options from behind the net involve jamming the net and the opposing defenders around the net and having the puck carrier take the puck out to the front for a shot (figure 13.30). This may involve some form of pick, which, if subtly executed, will not result in a penalty.

DRILLS FOR DEVELOPING OFFENSE FROM BEHIND THE NET

2 v 0 Strong-Side Dot Play

Position players in line along the boards (figure 13.31). The first player carries the puck behind the net, and the second player follows, heading for the strong-side dot. The puck carrier makes a pass to the dot for the second attacker to shoot.

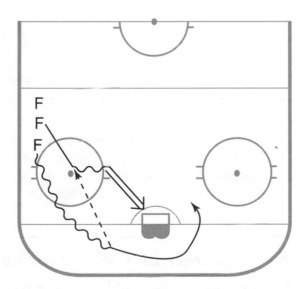

Figure 13.31   2 v 0 strong-side dot play.

2 v 0 Weak-Side Dot Play

Players are in line along the boards on both sides of the rink. The player with the puck carries it behind the net and comes out the other side (figure 13.32). A teammate comes from the other boards to the dot for a pass and shot.

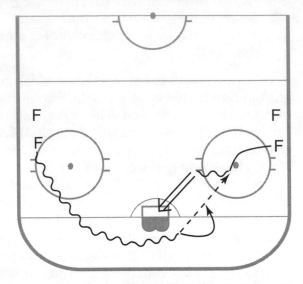

Figure 13.32   2 v 0 weak-side dot play.

3 v 0 Dot Play and Wraparound Options

Players line up on the boards on both sides of the rink. The first player carries the puck behind the net (figure 13.33). He has the option of passing to either of the support players, who have gone to the dots for a pass and possible shot. The puck carrier can also take the front for a wraparound shot.

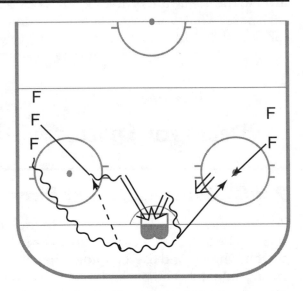

Figure 13.33   3 v 0 dot play and wraparound options.

Once your players are accustomed to recognizing and executing the various options without resistance, add defenders to the above drills, with sticks turned over initially, and then finally run the plays live. The next few drills involve behind-the-net offense against three and then five defenders.

5 v 3 Defenders With Sticks Turned Over

The drill format is to create a 3 v 3 down low starting behind the net. The player with the puck behind the net has the option of sending it up to the defenseman at the blue line for a point shot or running the play where the forwards widen out to the dots and a defenseman sneaks down the middle for a shot. In a 5 v 5 version of this drill, the puck begins behind the net with the offensive players executing any of the play options described earlier.

OFFENSIVE DRILLS COMBINING INITIAL ATTACKS AND OFFENSIVE ZONE PLAY TACTICS

The next three drills involve an initial attack from the neutral zone, culminating with offensive zone play tactics and shots using second and third pucks. Using the following drills as a guide, you can easily create your own to fit the offensive objectives of your team.

D to D to W (Three) Shots

This drill begins with forwards positioned along the boards in the neutral zone at the blue lines. Two defensemen slide out and take a pass from one of the forwards, following up with a D-to-D pass and then passing to the posted forward. The forward who started the drill comes across to provide support, takes a pass from the posted forward, and comes down wing for the shot. Extra pucks are placed in the corner. After the first shot, the shooter retrieves the puck and passes it to the defenseman for a second shot from the point for a tip, screen, or rebound. After the point shot, the forward who didn't get a shot on the rush retrieves the puck and rolls around the top of the circle for a shot (figure 13.34).

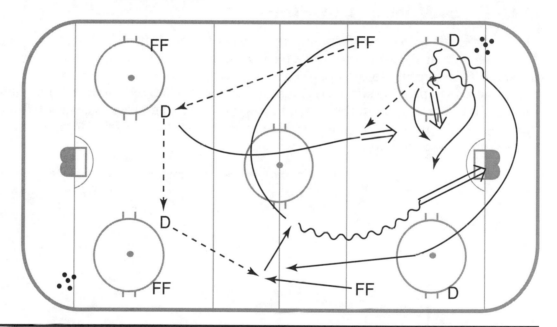

Figure 13.34
D to D to W
three shots.

D to D to W With Stuff

This drill begins with forwards positioned along the boards in the neutral zone at the blue lines. Two defensemen slide out and take a pass from one of the forwards, following up with a D-to-D pass and then passing to the posted forward. The forward who started the drill comes across to provide support, takes a pass from the posted forward, and comes down wing for the shot. After the shot, the coach blows the whistle and throws a second puck to the back boards. One of the forwards retrieves the puck and makes a pass behind the net to the other forward, who comes out to the front for a stuff or wraparound shot (figure 13.5).

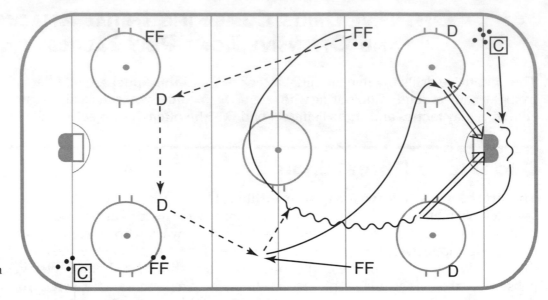

Figure 13.35
D to D to W with
stuff.

D to D to W With Dot Play

This drill begins with forwards positioned along the boards in the neutral zone at the blue lines. Two defensemen slide out and take a pass from one of the forwards, following up with a D-to-D pass and then passing to the posted forward (figure 13.36). The forward who started the drill comes across to provide support, takes a pass from the posted forward, and comes down wing for the shot. After the shot, the coach blows the whistle and tosses a puck behind the net. The puck is picked up behind net, and the other forward goes to one of the dots for a pass from behind the net and a second shot.

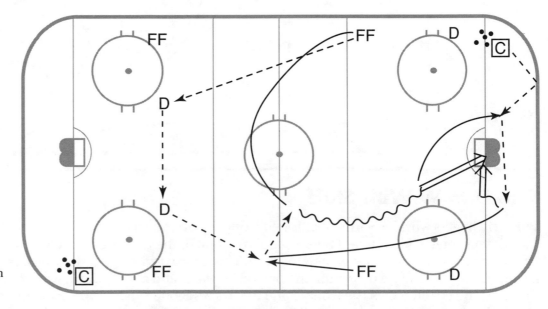

Figure 13.36
D to D to W with
dot.

OFFENSIVE ZONE FACE-OFFS

When a draw is won in the offensive zone, it usually means a shot on goal—possibly a scoring chance or a goal. If the draw is lost, it becomes an opportunity to forecheck and, if successful, get the puck back in the attacking zone for a chance to grind the opponent. Having a few face-off plays designed to generate a scoring chance or perhaps a goal can make the difference in a tight hockey game. Perhaps your team is overmatched skillwise but has good draw men so that you can get a goal or two off this situation. Regardless, it's an important phase of the game that must be attended to.

Forechecking Off a Lost Draw

There are only a couple of things to make your players aware of when forechecking off a lost draw in the attacking zone.

• Wings have to be intense off the drop of the puck. Often the opposing defensemen are asleep, and if the wings are intense, they can tie up the opponent or strip the puck right away. After all, the wings are only a few feet from the opponent at the time the puck is dropped.

• Opponents are usually predictable about how they will break out off a won draw. For example, the opponent may like to ring the puck to the weak side every time they win a draw cleanly. You can easily adjust from the bench or between periods to take this away from the opponent and force them to do something they are not comfortable with.

Face-Off Plays From a Won Draw

The objective of your team is to win the draw and find a way to get a shot on net. To do this, your center must win the draw, either cleanly or with help from the wingers. Most of the time, the shot from the point man is the best play because of its simplicity. To achieve this, you usually need a blockout from a winger on the opposing winger so your defenseman has time to shoot the puck.

The following is a series of face-off plays you may choose to use in the attacking zone to try to generate a shot and possibly a scoring chance.

Draw to Point for Shot or Flip-Flop Defensemen for One-Timer

The simplest and probably the most effective face-off play is to get the puck back to the point for a shot or flip-flop the defensemen, then make a D-to-D pass for a one-timer. Besides getting a blockout from the inside winger, it is important for the center to spin off to the inside so he can deflect the shot or be in position for a rebound. The board defenseman should also be driving to the net.

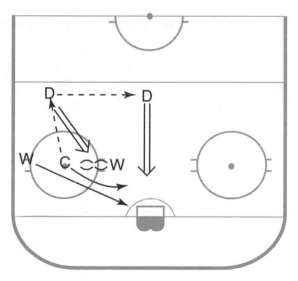

Figure 13.37   Point for shot or flip-flop.

Slot Formation One-Timer for Winger

Slide a defenseman down the wall and put the right winger in the slot. The center draws the puck back to the right winger for a one-timer, with the left winger blocking out (figure 13.38).

Figure 13.38   One-timer for winger.

Behind the Net Off Slot Formation

The board defenseman moves up for the draw. The center bumps the puck to the defenseman. The defenseman throws the puck along the boards, where the wing retrieves it. The center slips to the front of the net for the shot. This play is used if the opponent does not cover the boards in an effort to counter the slot formation (figure 13.39).

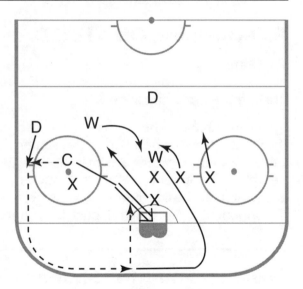

Figure 13.39   Behind the net formation.

Double-Wing Shoot Off Draw

Both wings line up on the net side of the face-off circle. The center tries to shoot the puck at or toward the front of the net. The two wings crash the net, looking for a rebound or loose puck (figure 13.40).

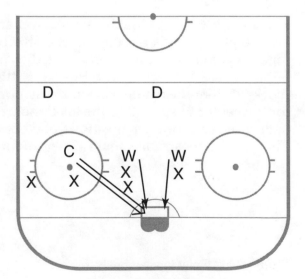

Figure 13.40   Double-wing shoot off draw.

Double-Wing Defenseman Slot

The defensemen come up to cover the boards and the slot area. The center draws the puck to the slot defenseman for a quick shot (figure 13.41).

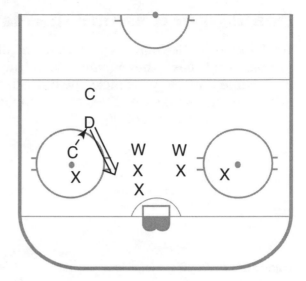

Figure 13.41   Double-wing defenseman shot.

Double-Wing One-Timer

The inside winger slides out of the formation, positioning himself for a pass and one-timed shot (figure 13.42).

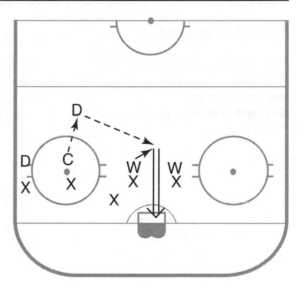

Figure 13.42   Double-wing one-timer.

Double-Wing Slip-Through by Center

Because both wings are up on the inside hash mark and the board defenseman is also up, the opponent is unlikely to have anyone in a second line of defense behind their center. Thus, the center attempts to slip the puck through, go to the net, then shoot. The center is supported by the wingers going to the net (figure 13.43).

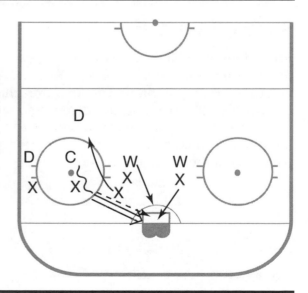

Figure 13.43   Double-wing slip through.

Double-Wing Behind the Net

We looked at this play earlier under a different format. In this case, the outside wing retrieves the puck while the near wing picks the other opposing defenseman. The center slides across the front to receive a pass and shoot (figure 13.44).

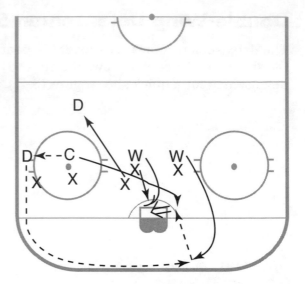

Figure 13.44   Double wing behind the net.

V-Formation

The wings are flip-flopped and off the line, creating a V-formation. The center can draw the puck to either wing for a one-timed shot. This play is particularly effective if the inside wing can get the puck (figure 13.45).

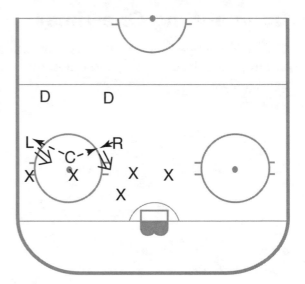

Figure 13.45   V-formation.

Shock Face-Off

The wings both line up as defensemen and the defensemen line up in the wing positions. All four must anticipate the draw. The forwards charge as the puck is dropped and the defensemen retreat. The center tries to tie up the opponent so that the puck lies behind him and one of the onrushing wings can shoot it (figure 13.46).

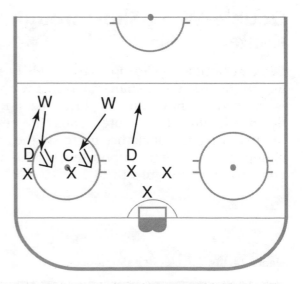

Figure 13.46   Shock face-off.

Part 6

COACHING IN GAMES

Chapter
14

SPECIAL
TEAMS PLAY

All other elements being equal, the outcome of a game can often be changed by quality execution in the area of special teams. If your team has an effective power play, you will be able to score or at least create positive momentum by generating scoring chances. If your power play is solid, your opponent will be concerned about taking foolish penalties, resulting in tentative play due to a fear of being too aggressive. In my first season as head high school coach at Bellows Free Academy, we scored a power play goal in double overtime to win the state championship. We had been effective in scoring timely goals all season long, so when we were awarded this power play, there was a confidence apparent on the faces of our players. We knew the game was over and that we were about to win. Take note of the statement regarding confidence showing on players' faces, as we will revisit that notion in greater detail later in this chapter.

On the flip side of the special teams coin, effective penalty killing can also be a momentum builder. A well-executed penalty kill often frustrates the opponent and lifts your players. Furthermore, it allows your players to play aggressively at even strength, unconcerned about crossing the line accidentally with physical play. Scoring a shorthanded goal is one of the most elating plays for your team and deflating events for the opponent.

Finally, unique special teams situations, such as a 4 v 4 or 3 v 3, afford both teams more open space to conduct offensive activities. Obviously, these situations represent an advantage for the more skilled players. If you have highly skilled athletes, these situations can be taken advantage of in ways similar to the power play. The Edmonton Oilers of the mid-1980s are a classic example. They were so good at scoring in 4 v 4 situations, the NHL actually changed the rules for a time so that coincidental minor penalties were served without manpower loss to the teams, and play continued with five skaters a side. Of course, few teams have players the caliber of Gretzky, Kurri, Coffey, Anderson, and Messier to throw out on the ice in a 4 v 4. If you don't possess any of those types of players, your team had better be schooled defensively and not allow the opponent to score.

Being able to score in the waning seconds of a game or holding a lead in those final moments when the goalie has been replaced by an extra attacker is crucial. Nothing is more disheartening than controlling a game for nearly its entirety before giving up a goal with a few seconds remaining on the clock. Nothing is more elating than scoring a goal with your goalie on the bench to send the game into overtime. One of the most exciting situations I've ever been associated with occurred in the 1994 Stanley Cup playoffs when Valeri Zelepukin scored in the closing seconds to send game seven of the Eastern Conference finals into overtime against the New York Rangers. The Devils lost this game in double overtime on a Stephane Matteau goal, but it didn't seem that we would lose at the time Zelepukin's shot crossed the line.

In summary, the many special teams situations that occur during a game must be understood, drilled, and perfected in practice. This chapter will assist you in achieving those goals.

Understanding the Mental Elements of the Power Play

Power plays rarely work unless players have confidence in their ability to execute plays common to special teams play. A player afraid to make a mistake lacks the confidence required to execute effectively. Remember that even great power plays fail to score most of the time. A great power play at the high school or junior levels should score about 30 percent of the time, probably 5 to 10 percent less than teams at the professional levels. This means that 70 to 80 percent of the time the power play fails to score, so it is important for a coach to constantly strive to help players develop and maintain confidence. You should always be looking for ways to measure success on the power play by identifying executable outcomes other than just scoring goals. Your team may do everything right on the power play but fail because of the efforts of one opponent, the goalie. If the players feel excessive pressure from the coach to score during power plays, I guarantee that matters will get worse rather than improve. Ask yourself these questions when analyzing your team's performance on the power play:

- Did we win the face-offs while on the power play?
- Did we win the battles for loose pucks in the offensive zone?
- Did we have good support for the puck, and did we execute passes and shots at the right time?
- Did we get our shots on net?
- Did we get traffic in front of their goalie and compete for rebounds?
- Did we generate scoring chances on our power play?
- Did we enter the zone smoothly or dump and recover the puck where appropriate?

By addressing these questions and sharing the results with your players, you will avoid some of the unnecessary anxiety that can result from not scoring on the power play. Simply stated, if your power play executes these elements well, your team will score its share of power play goals. Even if your team doesn't score, it will be able to create positive momentum for the period immediately after the power play expires.

Another psychological factor is the tendency for players on the power play to relax because they are aware the opponent has less than a full complement of players. To be effective on the power play, players on the ice actually have to be more intense and determined to execute, because the opponent almost always increases its intensity while defending shorthanded. This notion can be effectively summarized with one statement: "Never, ever, allow yourselves to be outworked by the opposing penalty killers." Although work is thought of as being a physical function, in this case, it is far more closely associated with the mental side of preparation and play.

Execution and Time

Most power plays have a time limit of two minutes or less. To use an academic analogy, it's like taking a timed exam in school. If the student doesn't finish in the allotted time, the incomplete portions of the exam are marked incorrect. Proper execution of tactical skill and combination play concepts saves time that will be required for the end result, a shot at the net and hopefully a goal. Some of you will be coaching in high school leagues with 15-minute periods and only 90 seconds for the power play. Quality execution is important to any power play in any league, but becomes even more so as the time allowed for the power play is further limited.

Assessing Talent

To develop a high-functioning special teams complement, you must first assess the talent level of your players, determining what types of skills they can bring to the power play. If you have players with well-developed hockey sense and passing skills, you might want to work the puck around for high-quality shots from the prime scoring area. If you have a defenseman or perhaps a forward with a big slap shot, you may want to shoot the puck from the point with traffic in front. Likewise, if you have physically dominating forwards who can take punishment in front of the net and get their sticks on shots for deflections or score on rebounds, your power play should look to get the puck to the front of the net while taking advantage of this physical superiority.

Coaches commonly use forwards to play the point positions on the power play. If your team doesn't have defensemen who are skilled enough to make plays, get shots through from the point, or advance the puck intelligently on the power play breakout, I highly recommend trying at least one forward on the point. If your defensemen are adequately skilled to perform the offensive duties inherent in the power play, then use them. By utilizing defensemen, you reduce the risk of shorthanded goals being scored against your team.

As you consider the talent of your players, be mindful of both right- and left-handed shooters on your roster. Usually, right-handed shots work from the left side of the power play formation and left-handed shots off the right side Having players positioned on their "off wing" allows them the chance to take one-timed shots, an important consideration in determining basic formations and the play options associated with them for individual special teams units.

Be careful what you ask your players to execute on the power play. Coaches often want their teams to execute plays on the power play that are too far beyond their talent level. This can lead to player frustration. The power play can be frustrating enough because, as noted earlier, even if a team has a great power play, it fails to score 70 to 75 percent of the time. Certainly, you want to challenge players to improve, asking them to try things that can result in further development. Determining what is appropriate for your team and when to apply it is more of an art than a science, however. There simply is no exact formula for solving this dilemma.

ADVANCED SKILLS AND THEIR TACTICAL APPLICATION FOR SUCCESS ON THE POWER PLAY

There are several skills that can be helpful to use in a power play situation.

One-Timed Shooting

Being able to shoot the puck off the pass without stopping it is the ultimate in quick-release shooting and is very much like hitting a baseball. However, unlike the pitcher and hitter in baseball, in hockey, the passer wants to pass the puck so that it's easy for the shooter to hit it with force. The goaltender defending against the shot has only a minimum amount of time to get into position and get set for the shot. The difficulty in executing a one-timer revolves around accuracy. The player shooting the puck must be checking where the net is before the pass comes (orientation), so that both mind and body know how to align for an accurate shot when the puck finally arrives. Unlike other shot types, the shooter must look at the puck/pass to execute the one-timer, just as a hitter must watch the baseball.

The shooter or potential one-timed shooter can't do the job unless the passer does his first. To use another sports analogy, it's much like kicking a field goal in football. Before worrying about how the kicker will hit the shot through the uprights, a good snap and hold must be executed. In hockey, a good pass on a line between the skates of the shooter must occur for a good one-timed shot to result.

When practicing one-timers with the power play in mind, set up the drill so that players are shooting from areas where they seem to take shots from during a game. For example, if you have a defenseman who shoots one-timers from the midpoint, that's a good place to take practice from. If you have a forward who tends to take one-timers from the top of the circle off a pass from the middle, then practice shots from that spot. In figure 14.1a-b, all three players are practicing one-timed shots from

Figure 14.1 One-time shots from three different areas.

three different areas, including the midpoint and the tops of the circles on each side.

One-Touch Passing

One-touch passing involves receiving a pass from a teammate and immediately passing the puck back to that player or to another player. The player does no stick handling after receiving the pass. To execute this type of pass, a player has to read the situation before receiving the pass, thereby knowing where to locate the next pass. One-touch passing coincides with the rapid puck movement principle, which will be discussed later. Being able to move the puck quickly affords an opponent very little time to adjust position to keep your team from getting a good shot.

There is one more point to make regarding one-touch passing, and it relates to what is commonly known as "false information." When a player has control of the puck and focuses for too long on the player who is going to receive a pass, the pass is often disrupted or intercepted. Players should be taught to look off their intended pass at times to confuse the defenders. There aren't many players who can do this well, even at the NHL level, yet it's really not that difficult to learn. Other forms of false information include fake passes and fake shots.

Screens, Deflections, and Rebounds

Screens, deflections, and rebounds were discussed at length in chapter 12, so they will receive only cursory mention here. The key is to remember that successful goalies stop pucks that they can see and are generally better at making the first save than they are at making the second save off a rebound. In addition, virtually all goalies have difficulty with properly executed deflections. Remember, as well, that often the only shot penalty killers will allow enough time and space for your team to execute is the point shot, which may include a one-timer. Good screens and players skilled at deflections or scoring on rebounds are rendered ineffective if the point

shots don't get through to the net. Again, look back at the offensive zone chapter for more detailed descriptions.

Puck Protection and Retrieval

There are times on the power play when the puck must be protected from defenders attacking aggressively. The ability to protect the puck until an open teammate is available is important to keeping the play alive. If the puck is lost to the penalty killers, a long skate is required to retrieve the puck and get it back into the offensive zone, severely limiting the time available to score on the power play. Getting loose pucks is also important. By winning the races and subsequent battles for loose pucks in the attacking zone, your team increases its offensive zone control time, improving the odds of scoring. The key idea is to outnumber the opponent in the area of the puck while combining that with superior physical determination. Once again, refer to the section on puck protection in chapter 13 for details on how to develop these abilities in your athletes.

OFFENSIVE CONCEPTS CRUCIAL TO POWER PLAY SUCCESS

The following concepts represent a foundation for any successful power play. Given adequate skill, the application of these concepts at the appropriate times will lead to success on the power play.

Taking What They Give: Reading the Defense

The ability to read what's available based on the position and tactics of the opponent is a critical component of success on the power play. The most common mistake players make is trying to force their favorite plays when the opponent has these options well covered. Another related issue is the ability to read the defense before getting the puck. If the penalty killers are well trained, a very limited amount of time is available to make the next play once a pass has been received. If the power play personnel aren't aware of the defenders and the options available before touching the puck, a play option often evaporates before the play can be made. You must teach your players to not only read the defense, but also to have the necessary discipline to take away their space while executing the options your defenders allow.

Support

Support, the most important concept in hockey, is equally important to success on the power play. The player with the puck should have at least two play options: one pass option with a shot option or two pass options. The responsibility for creating these options falls to the players without the puck, so those players must move to get open. One common problem with a struggling power play is that players want to get to a spot where they like to operate and not move from this general area. Given the amount of pressure applied by modern penalty killers, this doesn't work. Players must be taught to both move without the puck and improvise when checking pressure is intense. The concept of supporting the player in possession of the puck supercedes any system formation responsibilities.

Numerical Superiority (Creating 2 v 1s)

Because of the manpower advantage, there will always be the potential to create small-area 2 v 1s, isolating opponents in the attempt to create shot opportunities. To do this, your team must have more players in the area of the puck than the penalty killers have. Players should be taught the concept of using support to create these numerical advantages in the area of the puck and, once created, to take full advantage of the isolated opponent by executing a quick play.

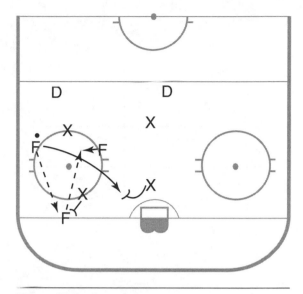

Figure 14.2   Give and go.

Give and Go

The next principle for the power play is the simple give and go, something that relates closely to support and the notion of creating 2 v 1s. The give and go implies motion, and motion is very important on the power play. When players move without the puck, they force the opponent to cover, and even if the cutting player isn't open for the pass, someone else will be! After all, your team does have more players on the ice than the opponent. In figure 14.2, notice how the player on the half wall has made a pass to a teammate on the goal line extended and then cut to the net. If it's open going to the net, the player who now has the puck on the goal line can feed the pass for a shot. See how the cutting player is being picked up by the opponent's net front defenseman so that the third forward can be open in the slot on the puck side because of the space created by the forward cutting from the half wall.

Controlling the Middle and Attacking the Seams

The box, or 2-2 formation, is the basic formation most teams use to kill penalties (figure 14.3a-b). From this formation, the penalty killers will rotate out to attack the puck, but it

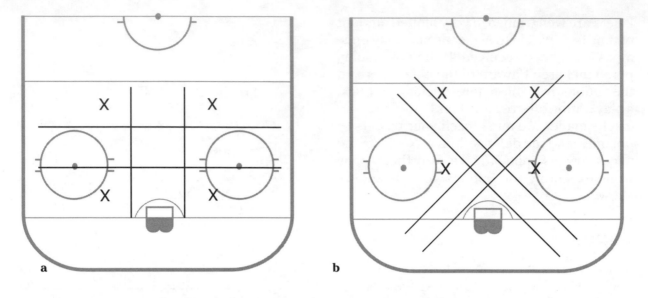

Figure 14.3   Box formation.

is without question the most common alignment the power play will encounter. Therefore, it is important that your players try to attack the seams or lanes through this formation.

The first step in being able to attack the seams is for the point player to get the middle. There is a natural seam from the midpoint through to the net. This seam allows the defensemen to create a 2 v 1 near the blue line against one of the penalty-killing forwards on the other team (figure 14.4). Another natural

seam exists between the penalty-killing forward and defenseman on the puck side. The power play forward on the half wall can attack this seam by putting pressure on the defenders, creating a 2 v 1 low against the opposing defensemen (figure 14.5).

Whenever I introduce the power play to a new group of players at the start of a season, the first thing I do is to place four cones on the ice in the box formation. I then explain the principle of attacking the seams and getting

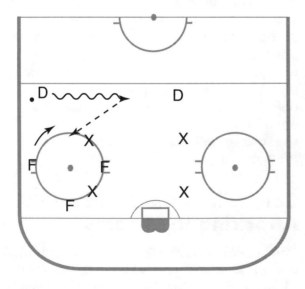

Figure 14.4   2 v 1 near blue line.

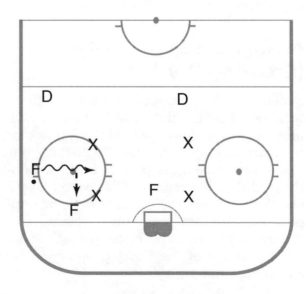

Figure 14.5   2 v 1 low.

the middle of the ice, along with the principles of support, creating 2 v 1's, and so on. I find this to be an excellent method of developing the cognitive foundation needed by players.

Overlapping

Overlapping means that one player will skate through an area of the ice either with or without the puck for the purpose of clearing that area of defenders. Once the space is cleared, a teammate can skate into that free space for a possible scoring opportunity. This principle is commonly applied on power play breakouts.

The principle of overlapping is applied in the attacking zone every time there is any type of cycling in the corners. It can also be used effectively on set plays in the attacking zone, particularly when the opponent has stopped using aggressive pressure tactics. In a recent Stanley Cup playoff game, Brett Hull scored a beautiful goal on a one-timed shot as Dallas used an overlap with Darryl Sydor coming down from the left point to the net. Hull skated from the net front toward Sydor's position at the point. The Colorado forward had skated down to the net with Sydor, leaving that area open for Hull to receive a pass from Mike Modano for the shot. Figure 14.6 illustrates this play.

Stretching the Defense

The principle of stretching out the defensive formations of the opponent is applied both on the breakout and in the attacking zone while on the power play. On the breakout, it is common to deploy one or two forwards in the neutral zone to force the opposing defensemen back, leaving space in front of these positions to be used by the players carrying and passing the puck up ice from the defensive zone. Whether or not you play with a center red line for two-line passes will have a bearing on where you might position the players whose job is to stretch the defense on the breakout. Figure 14.7 illustrates a power play breakout employing two stretch men at the attacking blue line for the purpose of keeping both

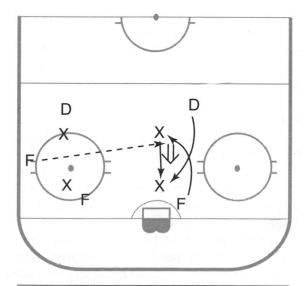

Figure 14.6   Overlap play.

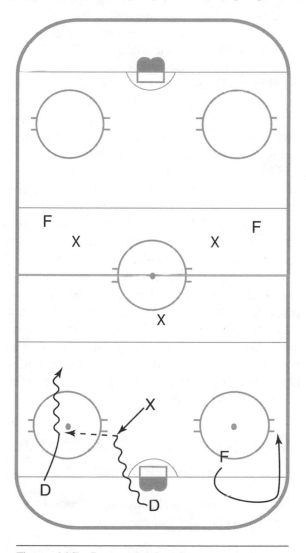

Figure 14.7   Power play breakout.

defensemen back. This type of play is best used in a high school situation where there is no center red line for two-line passes.

Please note how the forward and two defensemen bringing up the puck have a 3 v 2 against the penalty-killing forwards and two zones of space in which to execute any type of passes dictated by the positioning and pressure applied by those forwards. If the opponent does not honor the stretch men at the attacking blue line, a long pass up to either of them can result in an outnumbered chance off the initial entry.

If you are coaching with a center red line, it makes sense to deploy stretching forwards in the center-ice area. This allows the players with the puck one and a half zones of space to advance the puck, generating speed in the process. As the play moves to the first blue line, the stretching players can now advance, skating to the attacking blue line.

Stretching also occurs when the power play team has possession of the puck in the attacking zone and is achieved through sound positioning. Having attacking players at all three levels of the attacking zone—low near the net, in the middle of the zone, and high out toward the blue line—increases the space the penalty killers must defend. A common mistake made by teams on the power play occurs when their point players start to creep down 15-20 feet from the blue line. This limits the space the penalty killers must defend and reduces the time for the power play team to shoot the puck or make a pass. Working the puck from low to high and high to low can have the effect of stretching out the defensive formation. This allows the puck to find its way to the middle of the zone for a shot, provided the defending formation of penalty killers does not move as a cohesive unit.

ANATOMY OF A SUCCESSFUL POWER PLAY

There are two fundamental phases to any power play:

- Breakout or neutral zone regroup followed by a successful entry or quality

dump-in that is retrieved for offensive zone possession
- Play in the offensive zone that includes getting loose pucks and face-offs, as well as the more obvious elements of passing, shooting, play recognition, and execution

Entering the Attacking Zone: Breakouts and Regroups

A team must first and foremost have the ability to gain the offensive zone efficiently as described earlier. If it does, it has two attack options: (1) try to score off the initial entry, or (2) set up in the attacking zone and try to score on the subsequent offensive zone play. Without efficient entries, neither option is possible.

The first play concept described in this chapter was simply to "take what they give." If the opponent lines up four across at their defensive blue line, they make it difficult to carry the puck into the attacking zone, but they give you the opportunity to dump the puck in and get it back. If they forecheck aggressively, perhaps they give you the entry and, with quality execution of the breakout or regroup, a chance to score off the rush. Get your players to read the defense and be prepared and disciplined enough to take what is given.

Speed and Timing

All of the basic offensive concepts apply to breakouts and regroups resulting in successful entries into the attacking zone: support, outnumbering the opponent in the area of the puck, creating 2 v 1s, overlapping, stretching, and so on. Add to this the element of raw speed. When all of these principles are applied in conjunction with skating speed, the prospects for success are enhanced. However, speed alone is not enough! Players must know when to increase speed by reading the play and darting to the open space at precisely the right time.

A player attacking the offensive blue line in possession of the puck skating at high speed has a greater chance of helping to generate a chance off the rush or successfully control the puck in the attacking zone than one who moves slowly and deliberately. Speed creates pressure on the defenders, quite often forcing them to back off toward the net, giving your team the lines.

Timing is a concept that is as difficult to describe as it is to develop. We all know what timing is and that it is important, but isolating it and drilling it can be a challenge. There are drills that can be used to introduce timing to players, but as it pertains to the power play, it will be best for you to design your own drills based on your team's power play breakout and regroup patterns. When I talk to players about timing, I tell them to read the defense first, identifying where the open areas will be. Second, read the level of possession the puck carrier has and the amount of defensive pressure being faced. Being open when a puck-carrying teammate has no chance to deliver the pass due to pressure is useless. Thus, players must control their skating speed, conserve spaces on the ice, and accelerate to top speed at just the right moment.

If you want to achieve speed and enhance your team's chances of a successful entry, get the puck to your best player with speed at an early stage of your breakout. The other players on the ice can then support him in a timely and intelligent manner to produce the intended results.

Most teams generate speed on the power play breakout by having the defenseman stop behind the net, allowing a forward to swing into an open corner while the other defenseman swings on the opposite side of the ice. If you have a defenseman with great speed going back to pick up the puck behind the net, get them to skate with the puck immediately rather than stop, coming out from behind the net with speed. This is a tactic that Paul Coffey employed successfully in his prime.

The First Pass

Whatever breakout is used, the first pass must be executed cleanly. If it is too far ahead of or behind the receiver, or if the receiver fumbles the pass, the timing of the play is destroyed and the penalty killers usually wind up getting the puck and throwing it back down the ice. There are some common mistakes associated with why the first pass doesn't succeed.

- The players supporting the puck carrier get too far up the ice too soon so that the puck carrier has a poor angle, perhaps through an opponent's stick, from which to make the play.
- The players making and receiving the pass are not properly focused because the pressure from the penalty killers is only moderate.
- The puck carrier doesn't read the defending players' positioning properly and tries to force the pass to the wrong player.

The tone of the power play is established by the first breakout pass. Demand quality execution of this pass, particularly in practice, because its execution in games will foster confidence among your players.

Isolating the First Forechecker or Changing the Point of Attack

When the power play breakout is being initiated, the puck carrier has two tactical options to choose from when pressured by an opposing forechecker (figure 14.8). First, the puck carrier can skate directly at the first enemy

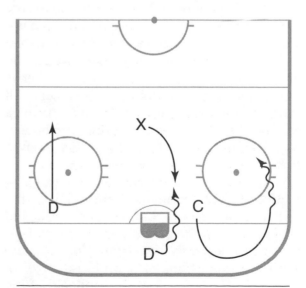

Figure 14.8 Puck carrier skates directly at the first forechecker.

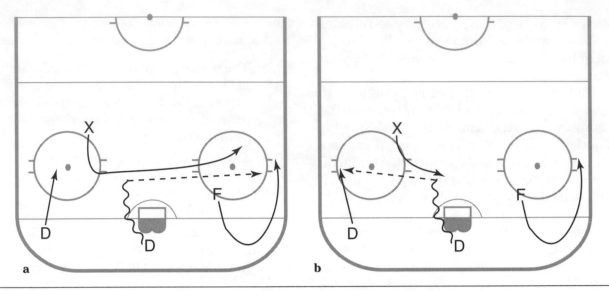

Figure 14.9   (*a*) Incorrect choice, (*b*) correct pass choice.

forechecker, forcing that player to commit and then make a pass.

Notice that the first forechecker in the above diagram has chosen to attack the puck carrier head on. Forecheckers who attack directly rather than utilizing an angle are very easy to beat with the first pass.

If the forechecker comes at the puck carrier utilizing good angling technique, the puck carrier should look to pass the puck back to the side of the ice from which the forechecker started his swing. If the pass is made to the side the forechecker swings toward, that forechecker will be able to continue to the pass receiver and apply pressure there too. Figure 14.9a illustrates the incorrect choice of pass, and figure 14.9b illustrates the correct choice.

Another key to successful execution of the first pass against an angling forechecker is the timing and positioning of the receiver. If the pass receiver is too far ahead of the puck carrier, the skating angle of the forechecker will be in the passing lane. If the pass receiver times the skate correctly, the first pass will be a flat or lateral pass unaffected by the angling tactics of the opponent's first forechecker.

The other tactic that can be employed when initiating the power play breakout is to move the puck early, not attempting to isolate the first forechecker, but rather to change the point of attack so that the opposing forecheckers are forced to react to a new puck position earlier than expected. Figure 14.10

illustrates an example of how this can work against a fairly aggressive 1-1 tandem forecheck employed by the penalty-killing team.

The next section illustrates and briefly explains a few of the breakout patterns and options available to you on the power play. As you look at these, try to envision your own players performing the roles diagramed, imagining how each pattern might work with your team. Also, as you study the patterns, be mindful of the offensive concepts being applied in each phase of each pattern. Remember the first lesson of offensive hockey: *Take what the opponent gives!* Trying to force plays that aren't available because of the opponent's positioning and tactics is like trying to fit the proverbial square peg in a round hole.

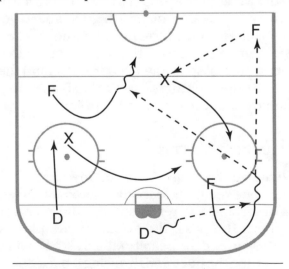

Figure 14.10   Changing attack vs. 1-1 tandem.

BREAKOUT PATTERNS FOR THE POWER PLAY

3-2 Pattern

This pattern features two stretch players at the offensive blue line. The two defensemen and a forward work together to advance the puck up the ice, likely enjoying a 3 v 2 player advantage. The two teammates responsible for stretching are positioned at the offensive blue line, pulling the opposing defensemen back and creating space (figure 14.11). If you have a two-line pass rule in your league, the stretch players would be positioned at the center red line. When it is clear that the puck will be advanced on one side of the ice, the stretch players slide toward the middle to create room for a controlled entry or to create space for a ringed dump-in.

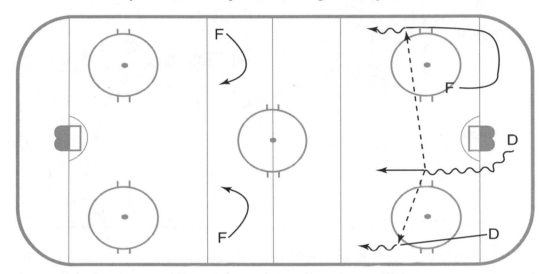

Figure 14.11
3-2 pattern.

If the opponent activates both of its penalty-killing forwards against this type of breakout, a second pass, usually a cross-ice pass board to board, has to be made. To make this kind of pass successfully, it is important that the receiver not be too far up ice. If the receiver is too far ahead of the play, the pass can be intercepted by a defenseman stepping up. Figure 14.12 illustrates the cross-ice pass common with this system, where the three players bringing up the puck are at roughly the same depth, advancing together.

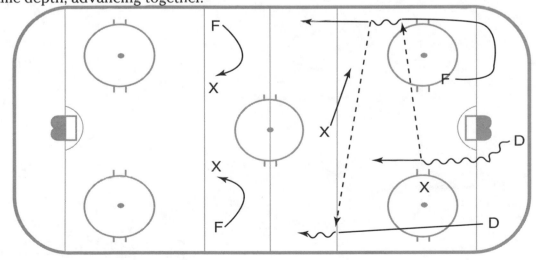

Figure 14.12
Cross-ice pass.

3-1-1 Pattern

This pattern utilizes one stretching forward at the offensive blue line or red line. Two defensemen and a forward will swing deep to bring the puck up ice, with a fourth player skating through the middle to support the puck, generate speed, or clear space for one of the three players advancing the puck. The stretch player will come off the wall as the play enters the neutral zone to create a possible breakaway pass or clear a lane for a ring. Figure 14.13 illustrates the three possible options available to the puck carrier in making the first pass.

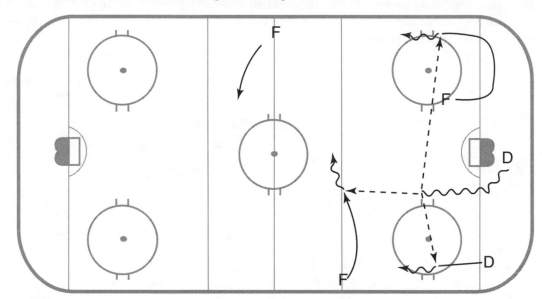

Figure 14.13
3-1-1 pattern.

The next set of figures illustrates the options available after successful completion of the first pass. Figure 14.13 illustrates which options are available to the forward swinging in the corner after receiving the first pass. The forward can bump the puck back to the defenseman who made the first pass, send the puck across to the other defenseman wide on the weak side, pass to the forward supporting in the middle lane, pass to the stretch player at the center red line, or simply carry the puck himself (figure 14.14). The option selected will, as always, be determined solely by the viability of that option based on the opponent's positioning.

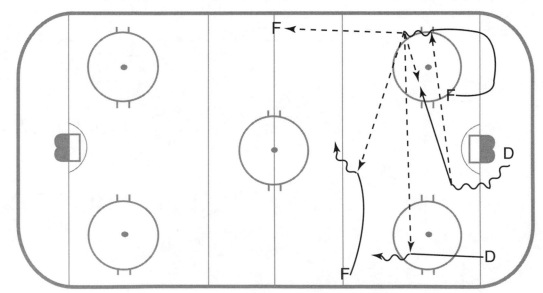

Figure 14.14
Options for forward after receiving pass.

If the first pass goes to the defenseman advancing up the left wing side, the following options become possible: The defenseman may bump the puck back to the defenseman who made the first pass, pass the puck across the ice to the forward who swung in the left wing corner, or pass to the stretch player who has come across the middle to support (figure 14.15).

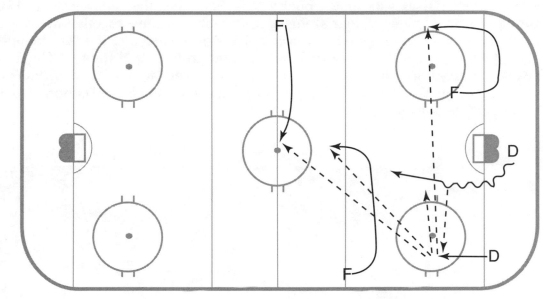

Figure 14.15
Options for first pass to defenseman up left wing.

If the opponent doesn't apply pressure to the puck-carrying defenseman coming up the middle, that defenseman can carry to the red line and ring the puck wide at the rim. Alternatively, an attempt for a breakaway can be made with a penetrating pass through the seam to the stretch player. A final option would be to make a late pass to the other defenseman or forward support player on the advance of the puck (figure 14.16).

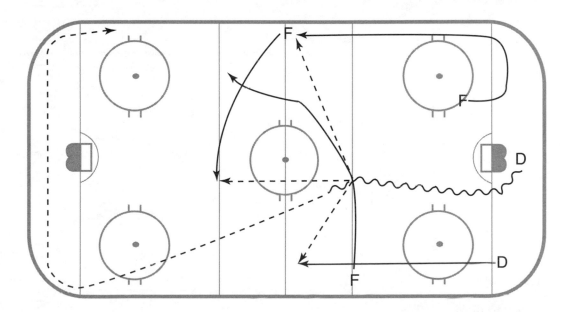

Figure 14.16
Making a late pass.

1-2-2 Deep Double Swing

This pattern utilizes the concepts of speed and timing as the primary weapon, along with overlapping. Two forwards will swing in the corner on one side of the net, and a forward along with the defenseman without the puck will swing on the other side (figure 14.17). To establish the appropriate timing, all four swinging players should come together in the area around the front of the net before beginning the swing. The defenseman with the puck behind the net must allow them to begin the swing and then step out from behind the net. The first two players swinging on each side of the net may advance up the wings, and at a predetermined moment, one or both may break into the middle lane or cut across the middle and continue to opposite sides of the rink, establishing speed (figure 14.18).

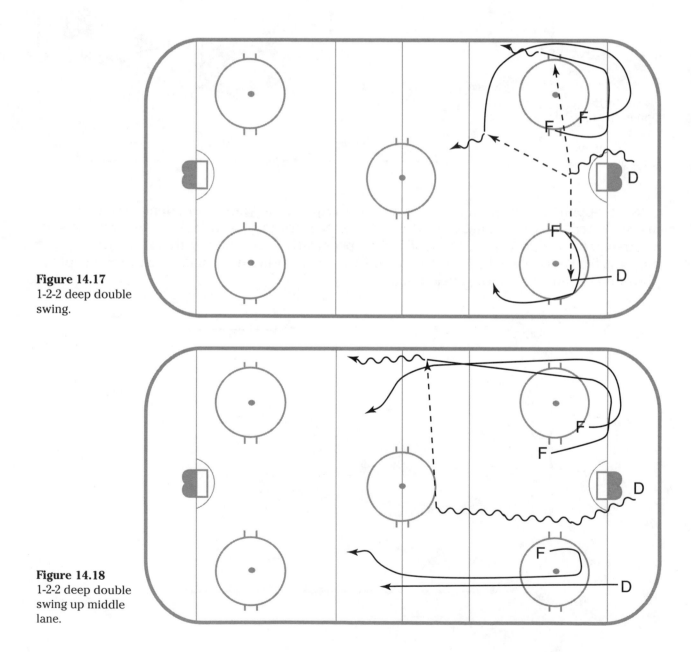

Figure 14.17
1-2-2 deep double swing.

Figure 14.18
1-2-2 deep double swing up middle lane.

1-2-2 Spread

This pattern can be very useful against penalty killers who forecheck deeply, aggressively pursuing the power play player going back for the puck. It can be a very effective pattern when trying to score on the initial entry before setting up any offensive zone patterns. Two players are positioned at the first blue line and two at the far blue line (figure 14.19). When the player going back for the puck retrieves it, it must be passed immediately to one of the two players at the first blue line. This pass traps the opposition's first forechecker, creating at worst a 4 v 3 situation in the neutral zone. Once the pass is received at the first blue line, the two-line pass is eliminated if that rule is in effect in your league. The player receiving the pass at the first blue line can now tip the puck ahead to a teammate at the next blue line or make a cross-ice pass to the teammate positioned parallel.

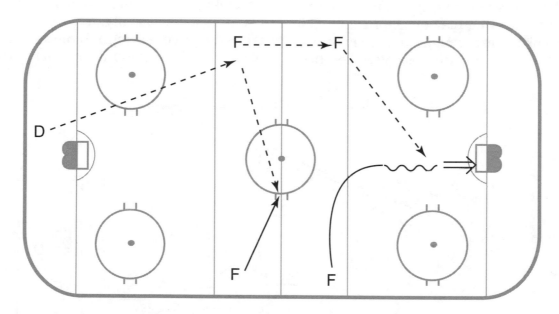

Figure 14.19   1-2-2 spread.

The power play breakout patterns illustrated and explained in previous pages are some of the more common in modern hockey. Each pattern works with proper execution of passing and receiving, support, speed generation, and timing. If properly designed and executed, one power play breakout pattern will be all your team needs to successfully enter the offensive zone or gain the center red line for a dump-in that can be retrieved. Having a second pattern can be useful to confuse opponents or take advantage of their penalty-killing strategy and tactics. The coach must decide whether or not the players are capable of properly executing multiple patterns. High-quality execution of one power play breakout pattern is better than low-quality execution of two or three patterns.

SCORING ON THE INITIAL ENTRY

It can be very difficult to score on the initial entry into the attacking zone if the opponent gets all four players back over the defensive blue line in good position just after the puck crosses into that zone. Most teams forecheck in a manner that guarantees at least three players back at the defensive blue line. The potential for generating a scoring chance usually occurs when one or two of the penalty-killing forwards becomes trapped up ice, attempting to forecheck too aggressively. If one forechecker is trapped, the potential exists for a 4 v 3 scoring play on the rush. If both forecheckers are caught overcommitting, 3 v 2's and 4 v 2's are possible. The other situation that can lead to rush-type scoring chances on the power play occurs when the penalty killers attempt to score a shorthanded goal, miss, and are then caught out of position in transition.

The 4 v 3 situation just inside the attacking zone is the most common one your power play will see. Perhaps the most effective offensive play in this attack situation is to get the puck over to the weak side to a player coming late, with another player driving to the net to clear out the enemy defenseman on that side. Figure 14.20 illustrates this play beginning with the breakout from behind the net. Notice how one of the two forecheckers is caught up ice, leaving only one forechecker back at the blue line at the crucial moment.

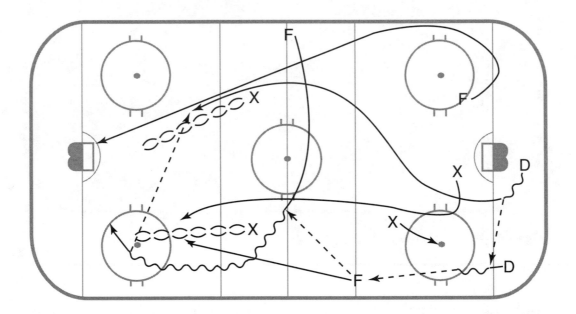

Figure 14.20   Breaking out behind net.

DRILLS FOR PRACTICING POWER PLAY BREAKOUTS

Three Breakouts Into Offensive Zone Play Drill

A unit of five power play skaters breaks out from the defensive zone, advancing the puck through the neutral zone. The coach is positioned at the attacking blue line. The power play unit passes the puck to the coach, who promptly fires it back into the defensive zone for a second breakout. The power play group reforms, breaking out a second time, again passing the puck to the coach at the attacking blue line, who again fires the puck back down the ice for a third breakout. Meanwhile, four penalty killers are standing inside the far blue line waiting for the power play group to arrive with the puck after the third breakout. After the power play unit has set up, a live 5 v 4 scrimmage occurs in the attacking zone. The next power play unit comes out and waits in the neutral zone. Once the puck has been cleared by the penalty killers, the second power play unit will begin its three breakout repetitions, culminating with a 5 v 4 scrimmage in the attacking zone against four penalty killers. Figure 14.21 illustrates breakouts 1 and 2, where the power play unit passes to the coach at the far blue line, who fires the puck back for another breakout. Figure 14.22 illustrates the third breakout, which culminates in a 5 v 4 scrimmage in the attacking zone.

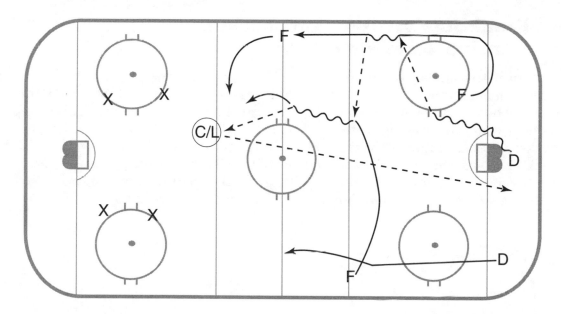

Figure 14.21   Breakouts 1 and 2.

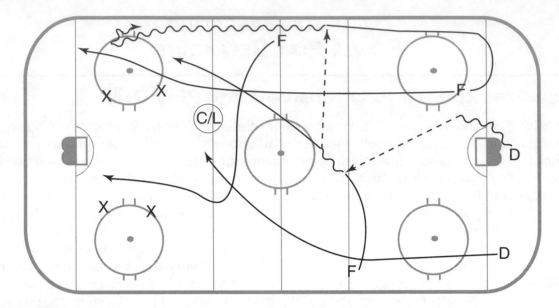

Figure 14.22   Breakout 3.

Three Breakouts vs. Two Forecheckers Into Offensive Zone Play Drill

This drill format is similar to the previous drill in which the power play unit executes three breakouts, culminating with a pass to the coach at the far blue line on the first two. The difference is simply that two penalty-killing forecheckers are used against the power play. The two penalty-killing defensemen are waiting in the end zone to play a 5 v 4 live teamed with the two forecheckers after execution of the third breakout. The two penalty-killing forwards who did the forechecking against the three breakouts remain as the killers once the play has entered the end zone for the 5 v 4 scrimmage. Figure 14.23 illustrates the last breakout vs. two forecheckers, which utilizes a ringed dump-in followed by the 5 v 4 end zone scrimmage.

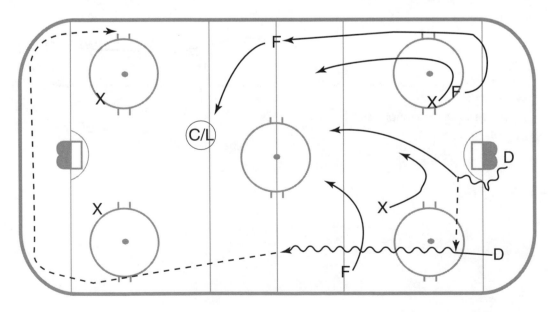

Figure 14.23   Offensive zone play.

Three Breakouts vs. Four Defenders Into Offensive Zone Play Drill

Again, this drill uses the same format as in the previous two drills, only now the breakouts are executed against an entire penalty-killing unit, with the third puck played out as a 5 v 4 scrimmage in the attacking zone. If the power play unit can advance the puck to the neutral zone, they pass it to the coach for a dump back down the ice and subsequent breakout repetition. If the penalty-killing team disrupts the play, they send the puck back down the ice.

NEUTRAL ZONE REGROUPING ON THE POWER PLAY

Often during power plays, the penalty killers are able to clear the puck outside the blue line into the neutral zone. It is wise to have an organized plan for reentry to the attacking zone without having to retreat deep toward your own net to form a new attack. Time and energy are precious on the power play, so the sooner and more efficiently the puck gets back into the attacking zone, the better your team's chances for success.

As with any offensive strategy, your players must recognize what the opponent gives them and attempt to exploit what is available rather than force a play with limited prospects for success. In the case of neutral zone regroups on the power play, the most common play available and the easiest to execute is the dump-in.

The same principles discussed in the section on power play breakouts continue to apply to neutral zone regrouping. It is important to generate speed, support the puck in a timely fashion, try to get the puck to your top player, and so on. However, the space you have to work with—the relatively small space the penalty killers have to defend—is a limiting factor. You can always increase the offensive space available to generate speed by backing up farther. What you forfeit by choosing this strategy is a measure of time. However, if you are up against an aggressive group of penalty killers, it may be prudent to back up, getting them to overcommit, and then break back into the attacking zone in possession of the puck.

D to D to Posted Forward or Forward Swinging in Middle Lane

After the puck has been chipped out to the neutral zone, the puck-retrieving defenseman simply fires a pass across to the other defense-man. This allows time for the forwards to clear out of

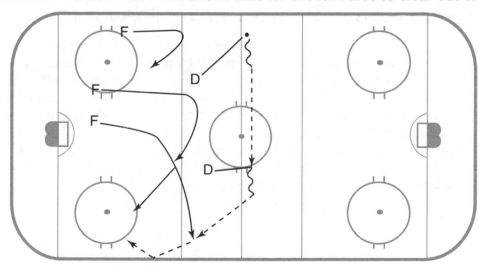

Figure 14.24
D to D to forward.

the attacking zone and get to support positions for the next pass. The defense-man receiving the pass from a partner has at least two pass options: one to the posted winger and the other to the forward swinging through the middle (figure 14.24). In most instances, the forward in the middle will likely have limited space to do anything with the puck after receiving the pass. A pass to the posted wing leaves that player with the options of carrying the puck over the blue line, making a direct pass to the swinging forward, or chipping the puck off the boards behind the defenders to be retrieved by the swinging forward from the middle lane.

D to D Then Ring

A D-to-D pass on this play creates time for the forwards to clear out of the attacking zone and get into position for a possible pass or to create speed to retrieve a dump-in (figure 14.25). The key is that the forwards recognize that the defenseman intends to get to the red line and dump the puck. Once they have done so, the forwards must pick up skating speed, coming toward their own net or across the ice to be utilized when trying to recapture the puck in the attacking zone.

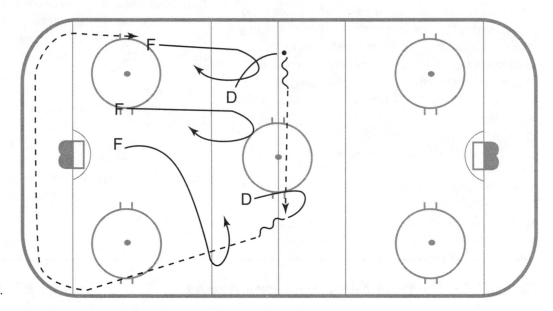

Figure 14.25
D to D then ring.

Long Regroup With Swinging Forward

If the puck is chipped out farther into the neutral zone, or if the desired play is to try to utilize space for speed creation and carry the puck back to the attacking zone, a long regroup with a forward swinging in support of the two defensemen can be an effective strategy (figure 14.26). The skating patterns for the forwards now become similar to those your team would use on a power play breakout initiated from the defensive zone. In this example, the defenseman goes back for the puck and makes a pass to the other defenseman. Meanwhile, a forward swings back deep. One of the other two forwards can post up while the second of the remaining two forwards skates through the middle lane. The posted-up forward can remain just outside the attacking blue line, thereby acting as a stretch player.

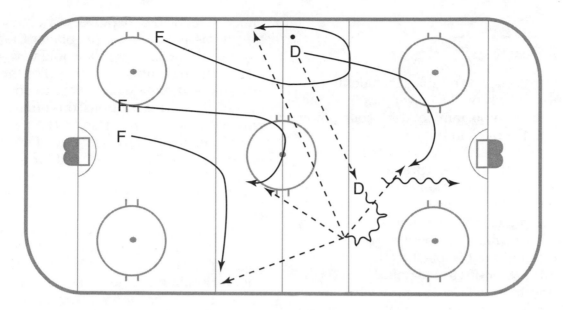

Figure 14.26   Long regroup with swinging forward.

To practice this situation, use the drill designs and progressions from the previous section on power play breakouts. Remember, a neutral zone regroup is nothing more than a spatially shortened version of a breakout.

OFFENSIVE ZONE PLAY ON THE POWER PLAY

Now the real fun begins! Some of the prettiest scoring plays in the game often occur during this phase of a power play, which is hockey's equivalent of the half-court offense in basketball. Players working, thinking, moving, creating, and generally executing plays as one can be a beautiful thing to watch and even more fun for a coach to help develop. However, the reality of play conditions in this situation in modern hockey seldom affords a power play unit the time and space needed to execute a "beautiful goal." More often than not, goals are scored on rebounds off a point shot or shot from the half wall or off a point shot that gets to the net through a well-established screen. There is greater opportunity to score a goal by deflecting a shot off a teammate, or even an opponent, than there is to score "the perfect goal."

The reality of modern hockey is that players are better coached on how to play defense in general and how to kill off power plays in particular. When my coaching career was in its infancy at Bellows Free Academy, teams stood in a box formation and allowed our skilled players all the time and space needed to pick the opponent apart. Now, teams use rotating pressure, make intelligent use of their sticks to block off passing and shooting lanes, and go down to block shots, all things that make it more difficult to execute on the power play. This brings us back to the phrase you are probably tired of reading: "Take what the opponent gives you." If a point shot is all the penalty killers give, then take it while making certain the forwards get traffic in front of the goalie and go hard for rebounds. If the penalty killers give you time to make a fancy play, by all means, make the pretty play.

Quarterback and Point of Attack

Similar to the notion of giving the puck to your best player early on the power play breakout, it is equally important to start your power play with the puck in the hands of your best player once control is gained in the offensive zone. Where that player's primary position on the ice will be is a decision you and the player must make. Most power plays at the high school and junior hockey levels have a nifty forward who likes to operate from the half wall, distributing the puck to the other two forwards low or out to the point. If this is the case, the half wall is the primary point of attack, and the forward operating from that location is your quarterback. You may have a defenseman who is a skilled passer and playmaker act as quarterback on the power play from the blue line. You may want to use a forward at the point, having that player quarterback from the blue line. It is also possible to quarterback the power play from the goal line extended or even from behind the enemy net. You and your players must decide where to direct your power play from based on their skills, how well each sees the ice, and their ability to execute plays from different locations.

If you play a particular opponent several times during a season, they will learn your team's power play tendencies and try to deny your favorite play options from a particular point of attack. When this happens, you have two options. Either allow another player to handle the puck as the quarterback from a different position on the ice or allow your quarterback to operate from a different position on the ice using a different set of play options from the new point of attack.

Rapid Puck Movement Principle

Moving the puck quickly, using one-touch passes where possible, and generally not taking time to dribble the puck two or three times before making the next pass is a very effective tactic on the power play. Each time the puck is moved to another player, the point of attack is changed and a whole new set of angles and pass options evolve. For the penalty killers attempting to rotate to cover the new angles and play options, this often causes confusion. A slow reaction to the pass or a mistake in position by only one of the opponents may be all that is needed for a scoring chance to occur. As coaches, we cannot overemphasize the importance of the previous statement.

To be able to execute the rapid puck movement principle, players must first be aware of support and have good anticipation instincts and work habits. It's much easier to stand still in a particular spot and wait for teammates to get you the puck than it is to work to get open through play reading and skating. Unfortunately, players who won't move and work cooperatively with teammates to keep the puck moving and under control become better killers of the power play than your opponents can ever be.

I suspect that by now many of you are thinking about how lengthy this chapter on special teams has been and are wondering when I'm going to give you all the Xs and Os for a variety of power play formations. Well, I will admit to being "thorough" as opposed to "excessive" in this chapter, perhaps exhaustively so. Believe me when I say that I would have preferred to be more cursory, as that would have meant less work for your humble author! However, I'm convinced that understanding all of the aforementioned principles is vital to success on the power play. My stubborn conviction on this matter has led to an increase in your electric bill and a reduction in your sleep time. However, I can sleep comfortably knowing that you are prepared to do a solid job developing your power play. Yes, you are now ready for the Xs and Os that follow on the next several pages.

Power Play Formations and Options

There are only so many ways to deploy five skaters inside one zone. The next several pages explain and illustrate many of the power play formations common in today's game. Unfortunately, the diagrams offer only a static view of the power play. Only briefly during a power play will all five of the attackers and the four penalty killers be in exactly these spots. The formations you decide to implement should be influenced by the abilities of the players you have, what these players do well, and as always, what the opposing penalty killers make available for your team to exploit. Well-coached teams also have the ability to change formation as the situation dictates. For example, switching from an overload to an umbrella or 1-3-1 because the point player has been able to walk the puck to the middle.

Also keep in mind the tactics and principles discussed above as you wade through the following formations. No power play formation or the play options inherent in that formation can work without quality execution of fundamental skills or principles of play.

Umbrella Formation

The umbrella formation is designed so that the point of attack is at the point position in the middle of the ice (figure 14.27). The player at the top of the umbrella formation is usually the quarterback, but not always. The player at the top of the formation may be at that location so that they can get a pass for a one-timer from the middle of the ice. The umbrella formation is designed to create 2 v 1s high, toward the blue line initially. Its purpose is to get shots from the midpoint or from the tops of the circles on the flanks. The two low forwards move around in front of and slightly to the sides of the net to create traffic in front of the goalie or provide a pass option for teammates operating near the blue line.

Figure 14.28 illustrates a few of the simple play options common to this formation, simple passes and shots from either the midpoint or from the flanks. Keep in mind that players working the top of the umbrella have to take right-handed shots on the left side or left-handed shots on the right if you wish to utilize the one-timed shot option.

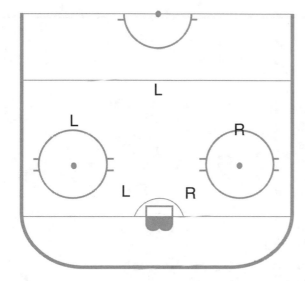

Figure 14.27   Umbrella formation.

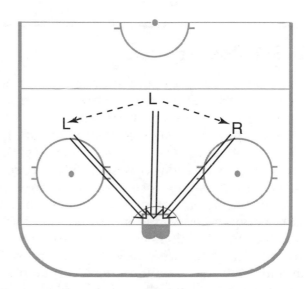

Figure 14.28   Passing and shooting from midpoint and flanks.

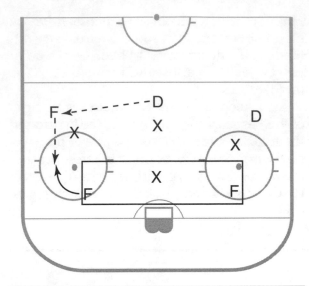

Figure 14.29   Diamond penalty killing formation.

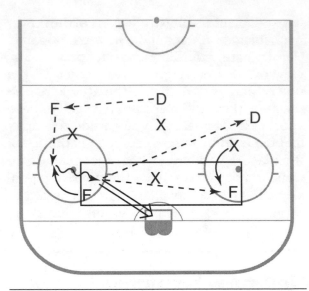

Figure 14.30   2 v 1 pass or shoot.

Penalty-killing teams that are well coached will eventually use a diamond-type formation to check the simple passing and shooting plays diagramed earlier. When this occurs, the 2 v 1 isolation sought exists near the net rather than at the blue line area. Power play personnel must recognize this and work the puck down low, taking advantage of the 2 v 1 in front of the net while taking what the defenders give. The puck can get to the net either through a shot from one of the three players at the top or via a pass. Figure 14.29 illustrates the diamond penalty-killing formation along with a pass made to one of the forwards down low.

Once the puck has rotated to a low forward, that player may be able to attack the net quickly, creating a 2 v 1 and the option to pass across or shoot. The third option would be to hit the defenseman on the backside of the formation, particularly if the player guarding the backside collapses to the net to negate the net front 2 v 1 (figure 14.30).

1-3-1 Power Play

The 1-3-1 power play formation is nothing more than a slight variation of the umbrella where one of the two low forwards moves from the side of the net into the slot. The preferred point of attack remains at the top of the formation, just as with the umbrella. Having a player positioned in the center of the penalty-killing formation puts more pressure on the defenders due to the existence of a more complicated and less obvious set of potential 2 v 1s for the killers to cover. To execute all of the options effectively, exerting the maximum amount of pressure on the killers, certain players have to shoot either right- or left-handed, as figure 14.31 illustrates.

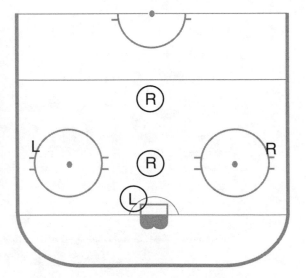

Figure 14.31   1-3-1 power play.

Equally important is the movement required, especially by players on the wings, to open up seams to accept passes or get shots (figure 14.32 and 14.33 a–b). I tell those players that they must imagine being on a ladder, moving up or down depending on the situation, based on puck position, level of puck possession, and positioning of the penalty killers.

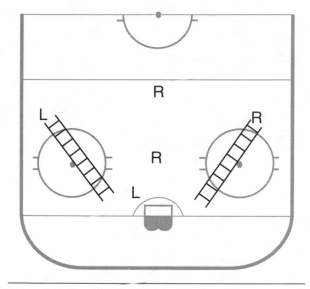

Figure 14.32 Open up seams.

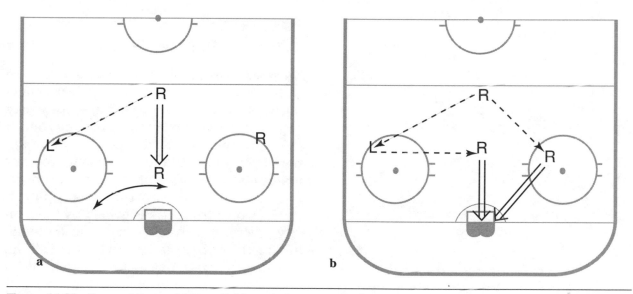

Figure 14.33 Some of the options available with this type of power play.

Overload

The power play formation known as overload is the most commonly used alignment in hockey. It features three players on the puck side of the ice and two players on the weak side. The point of attack is at the half wall and allows the quarterback operating from that position to work 2 v 1s either high or low (figure 14.34a–c). The quarterback on the half wall must recognize immediately whether to work high or low based on checking pressure. Alternatively, if the defenders are inclined

to play a more static box, the player at the half wall can isolate an opposing player by attacking that player directly to create the desired 2 v 1. If the quarterback makes the play to the point, the following options are possible.

Running the down-low options as diagramed above will not work if the opposing penalty killers all collapse toward the net. When the puck gets to the player operating at the goal line extended, and that player reads a collapsing penalty-killing formation, the puck has to be moved back out to the point. Quite

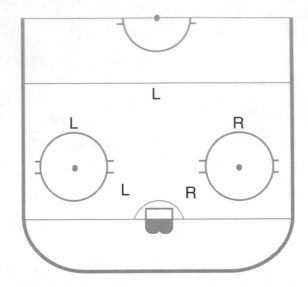

Figure 14.34 *(a)*   High 2 v 1.

Figure 14.34 *(b)*   Low 2 v 1.

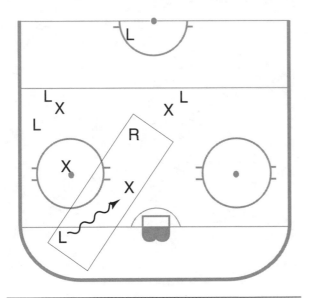

Figure 14.34 *(c)*   Low 2 v 1.

often players try to force down-low options when the opponent has all four of its killers low, resulting in a 4 v 3 numerical advantage for the penalty killers. My experience has been that young forwards are reluctant to throw the puck back to the point once they get it near the net. They prefer to force passes into tight defensive formations, hoping the play will work despite the positioning of the penalty killers. This is an example of "hope" becoming the enemy of efficient execution.

Face-Offs and the Power Play

Face-offs, particularly those in the offensive zone, are very important to the overall effectiveness of the power play. Often a power play begins with a face-off in the attacking zone. If the power play team wins possession of the puck off the draw, they get the chance to work it around for an attempt at the net or might even try to score on a set face-off play. If possession of the puck is gained by the penalty killers, it normally results in an icing, forcing the power play group to skate all the way back to their own end to regroup. Valuable power play time, usually in the range of 15-20 seconds, is lost as the result of a single icing, and energy must be expended to get the puck back to the attacking zone.

The top priority must always be to win possession of the puck either off a clean face-off or a second effort by the center. Next, all players must be alert and intense, ready to help out on any loose pucks. If the draw is lost cleanly, that same intensity is required in quick forechecking efforts to stop the clearing attempt by the penalty killers.

Most of the time, the penalty killers will try to ice the puck by sending it to the weak side using a hard ring to a penalty-killing forward or a soft chip to a forward in the corner, who in turn can ice the puck. Knowing that a hard ring is one of the typical face-off plays penalty killers use to ice the puck dictates that the middle point should widen out on the draw, ensuring time to get to the boards to try to keep the ring in the attacking zone.

The forward on the line nearest the net knows that the penalty-killing forward may go to the corner for a chip; therefore, the net front power play forward must move with the penalty-killing forward if the face-off is lost.

There are two reasons for trying to score off a set face-off play while on the power play. First, when a face-off is won cleanly, the opponent usually has only two players positioned inside the prime scoring area, ready to defend. Typically, one of their defensemen is on the boards, and the forward taking the draw is tied up on the face-off dot. If the puck can be moved quickly from the face-off dot to the prime scoring area before the penalty killers can all establish more desirable positions, the chances of scoring off the draw improve. Second, if the opponent is well schooled in their defensive zone penalty-killing tactics and strategy, the best chances to score may come immediately after a face-off win.

Which are the best face-off plays available for scoring off the draw? The answer is two-fold. First, it depends on your personnel. If you have someone operating at the point with a big shot, a setup for a one-timer in the high slot is a strong option. If you have a wing who is a good shooter, setting up that player for a one-timed shot off the draw is a good bet. In addition, several of the offensive zone face-off plays discussed earlier can be adapted for use on the power play.

This first play involves winning the draw back to the board-side point player. The board wing and the middle point player must both be right-hand shots. The board wing comes across and pivots to backward while the mid-point defenseman widens out, also pivoting to backward. The board-side defenseman moves across the ice with the puck and has the option of passing to either the wing or the point defenseman for a one-timed shot. The center and net-side wing head for the net, tying up both opposing defensemen. This

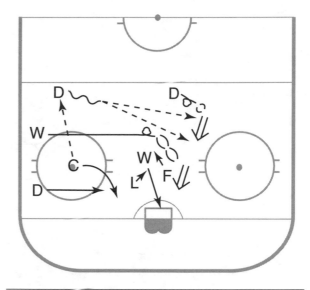

Figure 14.35   Draw back to board-side player.

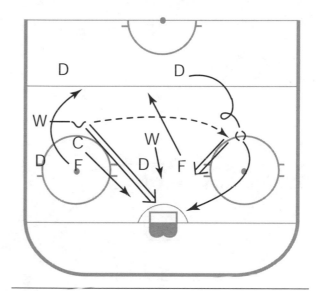

Figure 14.36   Middle defenseman open for one-timer shot.

creates a 2 v 1 problem for the penalty-killing forward heading out to the point. If that forward goes out too high, the winger will be open in the slot for a one-timer. If the forward goes out slowly, taking away the pass to the winger, then the middle defenseman is open for the one-timed shot (figures 14.35 and 14.36).

Another favorite of mine involves putting a left-handed shooting forward on the wall for the draw with a right-handed shooting defenseman at the middle point. The center tries to win the draw to a position directly

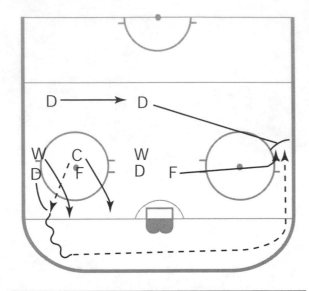

Figure 14.37   Forechecking off lost draw.

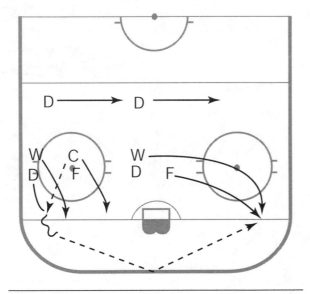

Figure 14.38   Forechecking off lost draw.

behind the face-off dot. The board wing comes across and skates with the puck toward the prime scoring area. Meanwhile, the middle point player widens out and then skates toward the net for a pass, possibly pivoting to skating backward. The wing with the puck has the option of shooting or making a pass to the defenseman sneaking down from the point for a shot. If the wing chooses to shoot, the defenseman continues toward the net looking for a rebound. If you lose a power play draw, figures 14.37 and 14.38 display how to cover and keep the puck alive.

5 v 3 Power Plays

A 5 v 3 power play opportunity is an enormous momentum-building scenario, particularly in a close game. Scoring a goal in this situation builds momentum for the power play unit, while a kill by the opponent creates colossal confidence. The players must understand the significance of this situation and be prepared to execute with the appropriate intensity and commitment to a successful outcome. A long 5 v 3 power play early in a game can set a mental tone for the entire game. A 5 v 3 later in the game can put your team over the top or fuel the opponent's confidence and energy level. Failure to score in this situation can be overcome, but don't underestimate the psychological and game-altering value of scoring with a two-player advantage.

If properly executed, a 5 v 3 power play lasting one minute or more should result in a goal being scored—unless the opposing goalie plays the situation like a Dominic Hasek or Martin Brodeur! If your team generates several great scoring chances and forces the opposing goalie to make great saves, failure to score is less psychologically painful, though it may still enhance the confidence of the opponent.

What are the penalty-killing formations and tactics likely to be encountered by the power play? The answer is fairly simple, as there are really only two ways to deploy three players in formation: either a triangle with apex high or an inverted triangle with apex low (figures 14.39 and 14.40).

The amount of pressure your team faces is likely to vary with each opponent. If the opponent is well coached, their players will not move outside the dots to apply pressure unless the puck is loose. They will change formation automatically between the standard triangle and inverted triangle based on puck position. I have seen teams successfully kill off 5 v 3 power plays with very aggressive pressure outside the dots and tops of the circles. However, with only three defenders, that tactic leaves a lot of open ice for two players to cover if one penalty killer is easily

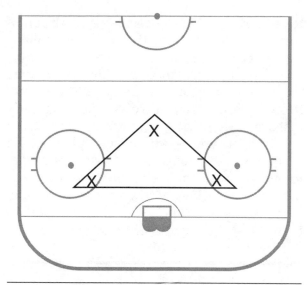

Figure 14.39 Triangle with apex high.

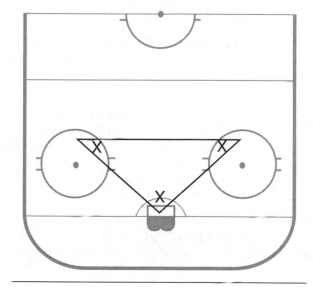

Figure 14.40 Inverted triangle, apex low.

beaten with a pass outside of the prime scoring area.

Patience

Here's a great quote for you to consider: "Genius is but a greater aptitude for patience." Pretty deep for a hockey coach, right? But if you want to look very smart over time, begin by practicing patience on the bench and finish by preaching it to your players! This is especially true and meaningful during a long 5 v 3 situation. Patience means moving the puck around rapidly, attempting to tire the

opposing penalty killers. The ideal shot on any 5 v 3 power play is a one-timed shot off a pass across the ice or diagonally from low to high or high to low. This means that the opposing goalie will have to move laterally or out to establish optimum position for making a save. As noted in the section on scoring goals in chapter 12, the likelihood of a shot eluding the goalie improves dramatically the more distance the goalie is forced to move.

Sometimes on a 5 v 3 the opponent's penalty killers play the situation poorly and a great one-timer chance occurs early. By all means, teach your players to take that shot. Patience is important, but not as important as taking advantage of what the opponent gives, the overriding principle for success in any power play situation.

Understand that when playing at home, it will be more difficult for players to display patience. The parents and fans will be screaming for your team to shoot the puck. Some players don't hear those comments coming from the crowd or, if they do, aren't affected by it. Others are influenced by it and will shoot at the wrong time or become nervous, limiting their effectiveness.

Breakouts and Regroups

There is no need to add any new patterns for the 5 v 3 power play situation. What you use for 5 v 4 situations will do nicely. However, following the principle of getting the puck to your best puck handler with speed is very wise in this scenario. There's nothing worse than a failed entry resulting in a clear by the opponent while enjoying a 5 v 3.

The other idea to stress is support. Often the players without the puck fail to give adequate support because they don't feel the urgency normally felt in a 5 v 4, assuming the opponent will be less aggressive. Even having your best player in possession of the puck with speed doesn't ensure a successful entry if the opponent tries to hold the defensive blue line with good execution.

The goal of any 5 v 3 breakout or regroup is to carry the puck into the attacking zone if at all possible, avoiding the dump-in. This is a fairly safe strategy most of the time, and successful entries in possession of the puck usually mean more time to set up the end zone play.

OFFENSIVE ZONE FORMATIONS AND OPTIONS FOR THE 5 V 3 POWER PLAY

Once your team is set up in the attacking zone, the formation and options you choose

to employ should be determined by the abilities of the players. Keep this principle in mind as you read along. Remain aware that even on a 5 v 3, your players must be able to take what the opponent gives, so perhaps the formations and options you would like to employ just aren't there. As you continue to read, try to visualize your own players playing the positions and executing the play options diagramed. If you can't envision any of these formations working with your personnel, design your own 5 v 3 power play to take advantage of the playing attributes of your people.

2-1-2 Formation

This is perhaps the most popular power play formation used in 5 v 3 situations. Its primary option is to get the puck low after drawing a penalty killer or two out to the point and then make a pass to the slot or a cross-ice pass to the weak side for a one-timed shot (figure 14.41a). The two point players should quarterback this situation, making a few passes at the point and gradually moving to positions somewhere around the tops of the circles. Unlike a 5 v 4 power play, where it is advisable to keep the point men high to stretch the defensive formation, in this case, the points must move lower to create the type of play options and shots desired. If the points stay out near the blue line, the penalty killers usually won't move and will simply allow the shot to be taken from out high (figure 14.41b). Notice how the following diagrams use Rs to represent right-hand shots and Ls for lefties. This will be very important to the potential effectiveness of the play options diagramed, not only for one-timed shots, but also to facilitate more desirable passing angles.

What happens when the left-handed player to the goalie's left gets the puck from the defenseman and the opponent quickly rotates to cover the two pass options to the slot and backdoor? The answer is simple: Send the puck back to the point, followed by a few more crisp

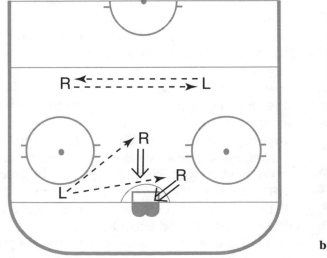
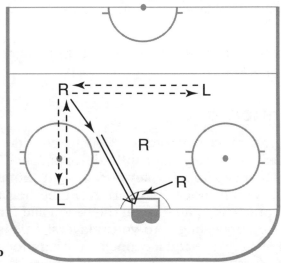

Figure 14.41 2-1-2 formation.

passes. After a period of time passing the puck out high, the defensemen move down, threatening to shoot, and the play can be attempted again. Now, that's patience! What if the primary options still won't materialize? If the desired option is not open, it means that the defenders have collapsed, denying the play options nearer the net. In keeping with the principle of taking what the opponent gives, we arrive at the secondary option, which is to bump the puck back to the defenseman, who walks into a one-timer from inside the top of the circle.

You've probably noticed that to this point the diagrams have illustrated only plays to a goalie's left side. You can also work the other side of the ice in this situation, but when the puck comes to the goal line, that player has only two pass options that involve one-timed shots: the backdoor pass across and the bump back to the defenseman walking into a pass (figures 14.42 and 14.43).

You can also be creative with more advanced tactics such as switching positions low to create shot opportunities. Timing is the key to this type of play and can be very effective if the players possess the required sense of timing.

If you have two defensemen with big shots from the point and the ability to shoot one-timers, it could be effective to move them to their off-wing sides and allow them to bomb one-timers from the point with screens estab-

lished in front of the opposing goalie. The disadvantage of deploying the point men in this way is that the passing angle to a forward down low becomes more difficult, as the puck must travel through the inside of the defending formation.

When this type of shooting 5 v 3 power play is used, the defending team usually uses an inverted triangle, aggressively fronting the points with two players. That leaves a 3 v 1 low if the puck gets through, but as mentioned earlier, the pass or shot must get through the interior of the defensive formation, and good stick work by the opponent can confound this strategy.

The way to combat this type of inverted triangle two-point pressure is to adjust on the ice by changing the formation to an umbrella or 1-3-1, as discussed previously. Umbrella and 1-3-1 power plays allow you to create a 3 v 2 situation up high and leave a 2 v 1 low. Having three players to work against two opponents high will make it easier to create passing lanes to get the puck low and take advantage of the 2 v 1. Also, a variety of one-timers are available high so that if you have players who can shoot the puck, it can be very effective, especially when using the remaining two players low for screens, deflections, and rebounds. There are three one-timer options high. If the opponent becomes overly aggressive, the puck can be passed low for a quick play that produces several other options.

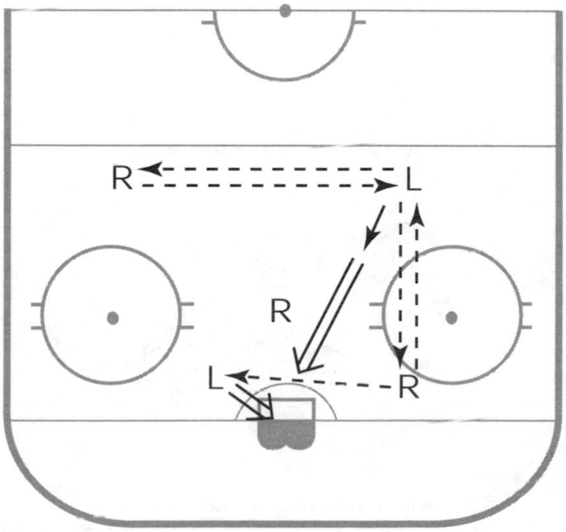

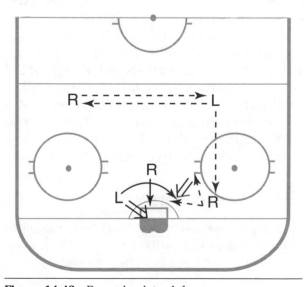

Figure 14.42 Back door pass across.

Figure 14.43 Bump back to defenseman.

Notice how the play develops, beginning at the opposing goalie's left and moving first to the middle and then to the other side. Notice also that after starting with two players high, the penalty killers sag toward the net once the puck is passed low. This means that there will be a limited amount of time to make a play for a one-timed shot. If the chances of successfully executing the play are poor, the player with the puck low must pass it back out high for a shot.

4 v 3 Power Plays

The 4 v 3 power play is similar to the 5 v 3 in all phases, from breakouts and regroups through to the play options available once the puck is under control in the attacking zone. Large areas of open ice are available to retain control of the puck and to make plays that result in successful entries and the creation of scoring chances.

As with 5 v 3 power plays, the concepts of taking what the opponent gives and patience are vital to success in the 4 v 3 situation. This situation represents a huge opportunity to score a goal and is probably as important a momentum builder as the 5 v 3 power play.

There are two common formations for deploying players in 4 v 3 power play situations. The first is a box or 2-2 formation; the other is a diamond or 1-2-1 formation. The formation chosen should be based on both the abilities of your personnel and the defensive scheme of your opponent. Basically, the opposition can deploy its defenders in only one of two ways: a triangle or an inverted triangle. If the opponent plays with a standard triangle formation, the 2-2 formation is easily executed. If the opponent uses an inverted triangle formation, the diamond 4 v 3 power play deployment is the easiest to execute.

2-2 Formation

The 2-2 formation is designed to create shot opportunities high with some traffic in front of the opposing goalie. The two shooters up high must work the puck between them to

create an open shot. Depending on available personnel, you may have one-timer options at your disposal.

The two players high must have patience, moving the puck between them while creeping forward toward the net (figure 14.44). Taking a shot from above the tops of the circles is not your primary objective. The players out high should be able to create a shot opportunity from slightly below the tops of the circles to increase your scoring chances. If the opponent is positioned in an inverted triangle formation, there are two options (figure 14.45). First, the point players can switch to their regular sides, right-hand shot on the

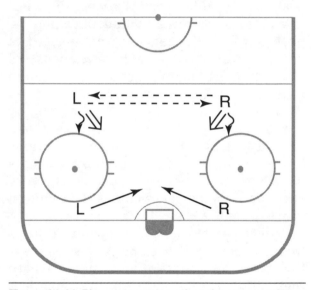

Figure 14.44 Players moving puck as they approach net.

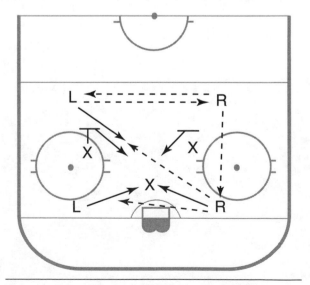

Figure 14.45 Low plays for 2-2 power play formation

right side and left-hand shot on the left. This creates an easier pass to a player low for a quick 2 v 1 at the net. The second option is to slide into a diamond formation.

1-2-1 Diamond Formation

This formation is very effective against inverted triangle defensive formations. It allows for one-timed shots from the point with a screen in front, and it also creates opportunities for seam passes made toward the net (figures 14.46 and 14.47). The role of the player

in front of the enemy net is to screen the opposing goalie and attract the attention of an opposing defender. This allows the players out high to work a 3 v 2 against the two remaining penalty killers (figures 14.48 and 14.49).

POWER PLAY SUMMARY

As with any phase of the game, skill is the single most important element for success on the power play. Players must be able to pass and receive the puck fluidly, handle it with

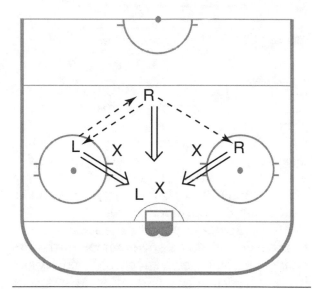

Figure 14.46   1-2-1 diamond—example 1.

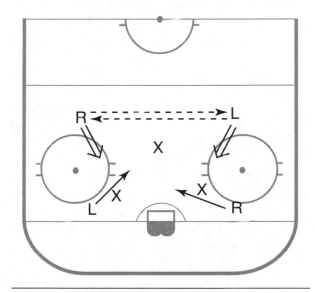

Figure 14.48   1-2-1 vs. penalty killers—1.

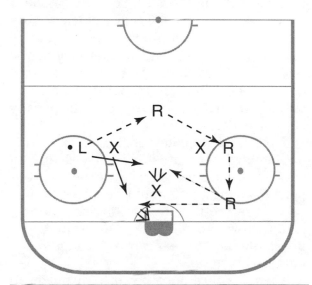

Figure 14.47   1-2-1 diamond—example 2.

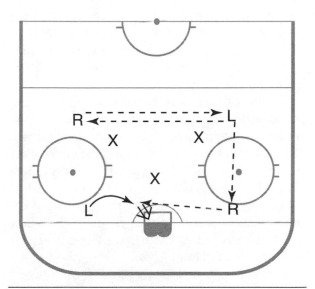

Figure 14.49   1-2-1 vs. penalty killers—2.

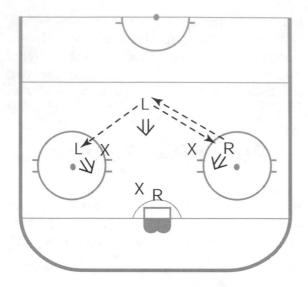

Figure 14.50   1-2-1 vs. penalty killers—3.

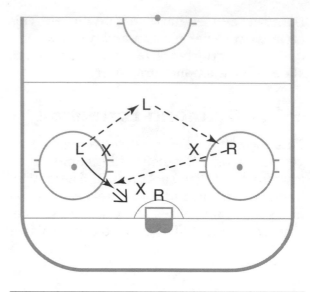

Figure 14.51   1-2-1 vs. penalty killers—3.

grace, shoot, screen, rebound, deflect, and retrieve loose pucks if goals are to be scored. Equally important are the play concepts of support, taking what the opponent gives, out-numbering, give-and-go plays, overlapping, and patience. As coach, your job is to both drill the skill and conceptual elements and assess the abilities of your personnel, giving each player a role that is appropriate to that individual's ability.

PENALTY KILLING

Defending one's goal short-handed is every bit as important as scoring with a man advantage. Indeed, penalty killing can determine the outcome of games as much its counter-part, the power play, can.

Unlike power play tactics, penalty killing prowess is relatively easy to develop because only a small amount of puck skill is required. Most of the technical demands involve skat-ing and stick checking. Penalty killing is less difficult when power plays are very predict-able, making anticipation and defense of the next pass or shot simpler to defend. Even a poor penalty killing team is successful 70 to 75 percent of the time.

Penalty killing also is easier on players mentally because it requires only one to two minutes of focused concentration on stop-ping the opponent from scoring. A short-handed goal is a bonus but should not be the main objective unless your team is trailing late in a game. Thinking almost exclusively in a defensive mode is much less taxing than playing dual roles of trying to score and mak-ing certain the opponent doesn't score.

Although killing penalties is less complex than executing on the power play, it too has its challenges. Sustained, successful penalty kill-ing requires quality goaltending. Mistakes or good power play will occur and therefore result in scoring chances. So, if the goalie is good, the penalty-killing rate of efficiency will be good. The importance of quality goalkeeping while killing penalties cannot be overstated. In fact, the forwards and defensemen killing the penalty can be bru-tally poor; but if the goalie is good, the penalty kill succeeds.

If you have a quality goalie, quick-skating and intelligent forwards, and defensemen with good stick skills who can cover the net, your penalty-killing unit should be successful 90 percent of the time in shutting down oppo-nents' power play, which is outstanding. A penalty-killing success rate exceeding 85 per-cent is very good.

A team with a poor power play needs an effective penalty-killing unit even more. If you can't score on power plays, you'd better make sure the opponent can't score on theirs. The goal is to achieve a positive result when you subtract the number of power-play goals allowed from the number of power-play goals scored. Being ahead in special teams play takes some of the pressure off scoring at even strength. In today's game, scoring at even strength is increasingly difficult because of better goalies and coaches who stress solid defensive play.

If your team has a large disparity between the number of power play opportunities and the number of penalty-killing opportunities, you still can analyze the effectiveness of your special teams' units by adding the penalty-killing percentage to your team's power-play success rate. For example, if your team kills penalties 87 percent of the time and scores 13 percent of the time while on the power play, you have a special teams success rate of 100 percent. This means that your team scores about as often as the opponent. The aim is to be as far above the 100 percent mark as possible.

Goalies

The goalie has two jobs in killing penalties. The first job is to stop the puck from going into the net. The second job is to handle the puck to set up for a defenseman to clear, or clear the puck himself. A goalie who has the ability to fire the puck down the ice after an errant dump-in is a great advantage to a penalty-killing unit, allowing you to employ checking systems and other tactics.

The goalie must work at setting up the puck for the defenseman so that the defenseman can play the puck immediately from the forehand side and clear the puck quickly. Generally it is better for the defenseman to play the puck with ample time to clear it than for the goalie to attempt to clear the puck himself.

If the goalie cannot play the puck either by setting it up or shooting it out, he should provide verbal instructions to the defenseman involved. This communication makes the job of puck retrieval and clear much easier for the defense.

The goalkeeper will benefit from viewing the tendencies of your opponent's power play on videotape. A goalie who knows what to expect can anticipate and move into appropriate position when the puck changes location. However, warn goalies not to anticipate too quickly and instead play one option at a time.

Defensemen

Defensemen on the penalty kill are responsible for stopping the initial entry and zone coverage. The main difference between even-strength and power-play defensive zone coverage is the level of aggressiveness the defensemen should employ. They should not finish checks on the side wall because the distance to the front of the net is too great, which leaves only three teammates to defend the prime scoring area. And, if a defenseman falls down while finishing a check on the side wall, it further delays his return to the prime scoring area. Finishing body checks on the backboards is acceptable because the distance back to the front of the net is shorter.

When killing penalties, a defenseman in front of the net will quite often find that he has two opponents to cover. Defensemen should never be tied up with one opponent, and that is even more important when they're on the penalty kill. Defensemen must use the stick intelligently to block passes, deny passing lanes, and challenge shots for killing penalty success. When a manpower disadvantage exists, the additional yard-and-a-half of defense provided by the stick limits the space for an opponent to operate on a power play.

Shooting the puck out of the zone is another primary skill for defensemen on the penalty kill. A strong wrist shot released quickly to clear the puck out of the defensive zone is a big plus in penalty killing. Too many times in my coaching career an opponent has scored shortly after a botched clearing attempt. Sending the puck down the ice is helpful for the penalty killers because it

- allows you to get fresh penalty killers on the ice,

- fatigues the opponents' power play personnel because they must skate to their defensive zone and back again to the attacking zone,
- frustrates the opposing power play unit, and
- diminishes the effectiveness of the opponent's execution.

Forwards

Forwards play a more diverse role than defensemen and the goalie do during power plays. They are responsible for forechecking the power play as it breaks out of its defensive zone or regroups in the neutral zone. They must also take face-offs, try to win the draws, and allow their team to clear the puck back to the enemy's defensive zone. Nothing kills more time on the penalty kill than face-off wins and subsequent successful icings of the puck.

Forwards also must be able to use their sticks effectively to block off passing lanes and use their sticks and bodies to block shots. The must be able to sag toward their own net to assist the defensemen after a point shot or when the defensemen pressure aggressively leaving the front of the net temporarily. When the defensemen fire the puck up along the boards, they must make a strong play along the wall and chip or fire the puck out of the defensive zone.

Top-level penalty killing forwards are worth their weight in gold. Quite often your most skilled offensive players are also your best penalty killers. Those players tend to have greater pure hockey sense that allows them to anticipate and foil the tactics of the power play unit. Also, an opponent focusing on scoring can sometimes be caught off guard by a short-handed foray by effective penalty killers. And, when an opponent uses forwards at the point positions on the power play, your forwards might have a better chance to score short-handed because your top offensive people are going against forwards playing defense. At times during his career, Jaromir Jagr has killed penalties for those reasons. He is a speedy and dangerous player who can apply his skills defensively while constantly being a threat to score short-handed. His skill has prompted some NHL teams to rethink their use of a forward at the point on the power play.

FORECHECKING

The primary objective of forechecking forwards is to disrupt the opponent's breakout patterns and timing by forcing passes while maintaining a good position on the ice where a rapid recovery to the middle of the ice can be affected. When the opponent is forced to make a pass, he always runs the risk of mishandling the puck—either by turning it over to the penalty killers or creating a disruption of the breakout's timing.

Good forechecking involves the ability to read the opponents' position and their desired play options. The coaching staff can usually assist the penalty killers by scouting the opponent's power-play breakout and informing the players of their patterns. Good forechecking also involves the effective use of steering and angling technique along with skating speed—required tools for successful disruption of the opponent's breakout.

When an opponent successfully advances the puck, the next objective of the penalty-killing forecheckers is to use their speed and angling technique to force the opponent to dump the puck in. On a dump-in, possession of the puck is up for grabs and allows the penalty killing a chance to retrieve it and clear to the enemy's defensive zone.

Effective penalty killers often use an angling technique to drive the puck carrier toward the backhand side. A good puckhandler will recognize this and turn toward the forechecker and thus to the forehand early, but many players won't execute this simple play offensively.

Forechecking also is important when the puck is cleared from the defensive zone into the neutral zone. One of the two penalty-killing forwards should attack the puck carrier quickly and aggressively as the opponent typically has players caught inside the attacking blue line and needs time to regroup to get players on-side and into support positions. The second forward must maintain a position of support for the defensemen near the defensive blue line. The supporting forward should become involved only if the first forechecker has recovered or is about to recover to a position capable of supporting the defensemen.

A forecheck by penalty killers can make opponents feel uncomfortable on the breakout and prevent them from doing what they prefer on the power play. This often leads to misplays and clears before the opposition enters the offensive zone; it results in frustration, confusion, and indecision once they do reach the attacking end.

Forechecking also is used to slow down the top puck carrier on a power play. When Paul Coffee was in his prime, he liked to pick up the puck behind the net without stopping and accelerate up the ice with his phenomenal speed. Good penalty-killing teams chased Coffee down the ice as he went after the puck and, through a combination of pressure and angling, force him to stop behind the net. Once he was stopped, it was more difficult for him to accelerate to top speed on the breakout, thereby reducing the pressure on the penalty killers.

When possible, force the weakest possible player on the opposing team to handle the puck on the power play. And remember, the more time that your penalty killers can chew up outside of your defensive zone, the less time the opponent will have to set up scoring plays.

Chase Forecheck

When the puck is fired down the ice, the nearest penalty-killing forward skates as fast as he can to chase the opposing defenseman going after the puck. Applying maximum pressure down the ice will disrupt the opposition's set breakout pattern. The first forechecker should avoid finishing his check unless he's certain that he can stop the play immediately. Finishing a check after a pass can result in a four man rush against the remaining three defenders.

If the first forechecker can force a poor pass and is about to recover to a solid position in the middle of the ice, the second forward can attack aggressively. If the first forechecker was unsuccessful in disrupting the play and the opponent has control of the puck, the second player should retreat for effective defensive positioning.

One useful ploy in this system: Change the first forechecker on the backcheck. If the first forechecker has been effective, he'll have expended a great deal of energy. By changing on the backcheck, a fresh forward will be on the ice if the puck enters the defensive zone. Players must be awake and ready to change, cheating on the change as much as possible without risking a penalty.

The chase forecheck is ineffective when a forward changes off the clear to the opponent's end. It takes too much time and the opponent will have the chance to set up behind the net to organize the breakout. If your forwards are tired from a long stint in the defensive zone, it's more important to change than to try to chase. It simply means that the next set of penalty killers will have to employ a different system.

Tandem Forecheck (or 1-1-2)

Tandem forechecking is the simplest and most common way to forecheck on the penalty kill. When an opponent stops behind the net, the first penalty killer stops in front while the other forward is positioned behind him in the middle of the ice. The first forward should not be too deep in the attacking zone. Otherwise, one pass to a speedy player swinging deep and skating up the boards will easily beat him. He should start by shading to one side of the ice, steering the play to the desired side. He might steer the puck carrier moving up the middle from behind the net to that player's backhand, or he might steer the play so that the weakest opponent becomes more likely to get the puck.

The second forward's job is to apply pressure to the opponent receiving that first pass taking an inside-out angle. Meanwhile, as the second forechecker jumps the first pass, the first forechecker recovers as rapidly as possible through the middle of the ice to cut off any cross-ice passes and provide support for the defensemen to ensure that they are not outnumbered 3 v 2 at the defensive blue line.

This is a good introductory forechecking system to teach players. It is easy to execute, but it can also be quite easy to defeat if your opponent is skilled and well coached. This system is weak in the stagnant initial positioning of the forecheckers, which makes them vulnerable to speedy breakouts. Opponents often beat it with a pass up the wall to a player coming with speed and then an immediate rink-wide pass.

Swing Tandem Forecheck

The swing tandem is similar to the tandem except that some of the inherent weakness, the inability to deal with opponents' speed, is eliminated because now the first forechecker swings with one of the power-play opponents. As the puck carrier comes up the ice from behind the net, the swinging forechecker can now leave the opponent and double back toward the middle, pressuring the puck carrier into making a pass.

As figure 14.52 illustrates, the puck carrier

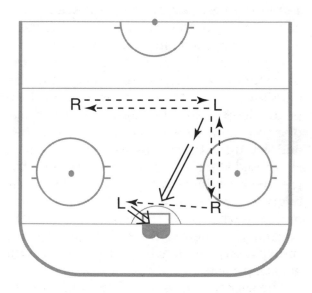

Figure 14.52 Swing tandem forecheck.

is driven to his backhand through angling and steering, as seen in the previous section on tandem forechecking. The difference is the employment of the swing-producing skating speed to counter the opponents' speed on their breakout. Once the first penalty-killing forward has left the opponent with whom he made the original swing, the angle used to attack the puck carrier makes it difficult for a pass back through to the opponent, now left unattended. It should be the first forechecker's goal not to do everything possible with stick position and angling to deny the completion of that pass. Again, the second forechecker attacks the first pass while the first forechecker continues back through the middle.

Adjusting to the Opponent's Breakout Package

Let's assume that you are playing against an opponent with several players who can score on the initial power-play entry to the attacking zone. They also are very good when they have control of the puck inside the attacking zone, but they are not as good when they have to dig it off the boards before setting up their attacking zone power play.

The key to defending this or any other opponent is to decide what you wish to deny and allow the opponent to do. It's impossible to deny an opponent all its options. Yet, teams have certain play tendencies that they will attempt to force even when it's clear that your team does not have those options at their disposal.

Trapping Forechecks

This type of forecheck against a team's power-play breakout allows them to come up the ice uncontested until they reach the neutral ice area, then set a trap and force a play. This reduces the patch of ice your penalty killers must defend to the attacking blue line to the center red line or, as might be the case in high school hockey, to the far or defensive blue line. Trap forechecks present a disadvantage because the opponent is allowed to develop speed and timing without disrupting its pattern from their defensive zone.

Single and Double Traps

Perhaps the best execution of penalty-killing traps I'd ever seen came from the Hamilton Bulldogs of the late 1990s. They used two variations of this system that forced our power-play puck carrier to read quickly and make the appropriate play. If the puck carrier read the wrong variation of the trap and made what he thought was the correct pass, the play was dead.

The first variation occurs when a penalty-killing forward angles down somewhere around the first blue line or just beyond it, forcing the puck carrier into the second forechecker, who steps up to deny the center red line (see figure 14.53).

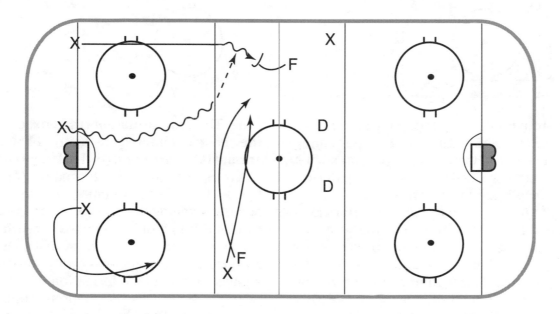

Figure 14.53   Hamilton trap 1.

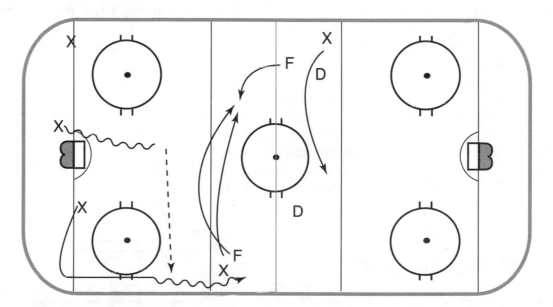

Figure 14.54   Breaking the Hamilton trap.

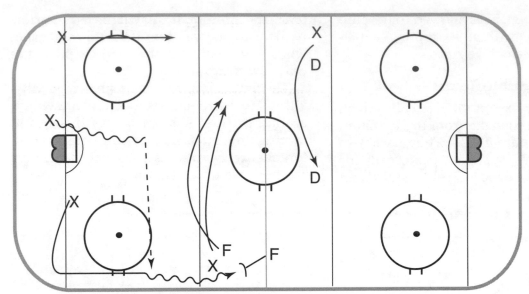

Figure 14.55
Hamilton trap 2.

The trap is also easy enough to break. If the puck carrier cuts toward the oncoming forechecker, the trap is broken. That's what we did, and it worked the first time up the ice, as shown in figure 14.54. At this point Hamilton began to line up both forechecking forwards on the same side of the ice. Now when we made the cut back and pass, our pass receiver coming up the boards was jumped and the play was dead. This is their second variation of the neutral zone trap (see figure 14.55).

Afterward, Hamilton did a good job of mixing up the two variations of their trap and keeping us on our toes as we came up the ice on the power play. These adjustments seem easy for the power-play puck carrier to read, but you'd be surprised at how difficult it can be in the heat of battle.

Hamilton's trap variations made our team uncomfortable coming up the ice and made it difficult for us to gain the attacking zone with control of the puck. Remember, one of the most important principles of forechecking on the penalty kill is to force the opponent to do things they don't like to do, thereby making them uncomfortable and less likely to execute cleanly.

DEFENSIVE ZONE

You can use three fundamental formations while killing penalties inside the defensive zone. The first formation (the box, or 2-2) is the most common (see figure 14.56). The second is the diamond (or 1-2-1, figure 14.57), the third a triangle + 1 formation (or 1-1-2, figure 14.58). Each formation has advantages and disadvantages based on what the opponent is capable of and can execute while on the power play. Keep in mind that these formations are not completely static and that, at a given moment, the formation may not appear the way these formations appear on paper. What follows are three figures illustrating the basic penalty-killing formations.

Regardless of the basic formation you select for your team, what really matters is

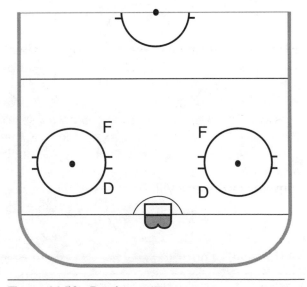

Figure 14.56   Box formation.

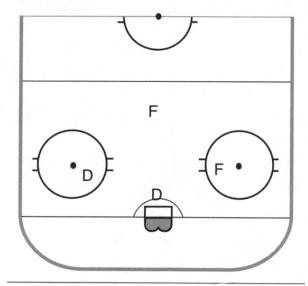

Figure 14.57 Diamond formation.

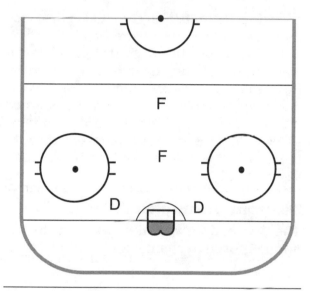

Figure 14.58 Triangle +1 formation.

when and how much pressure to apply against the opposing power play. The best penalty-killing teams in recent years at the professional levels are the most aggressive. In professional hockey, sometimes teams must go back to fairly passive formations because the opponent has complete control of the puck when facing the net and defenders so that mindless pressure will only result in a breakdown and wide-open opportunity. At the high school and junior levels, well-coordinated, intense pressure can be effective regardless of the level of puck control the opponent has because the players just aren't good enough to handle it.

Common Sense and Pressure

No matter what system you employ or what level of pressure you want your players to execute while killing penalties, you must use common sense. For example, whenever the puck is rolling along the sideboards, there should be intense pressure. Whenever an opponent is fumbling the puck, attempting to gain complete control of it, there should be pressure. Any time a puck has entered the zone on a ring, there should be pressure at the point of the puck. Make sure your players understand this principle and recognize it instantly on the ice and react accordingly. It will make your penalty killing more effective.

Box Formation and Three-Point Pressure

Let's assume that the puck has gone to the point. The penalty-killing forward on that side of the ice moves out on the point player with the puck taking an inside-out angle trying to deny a cross-ice pass D to D at the blue and force the puck down the wall. The players must use the stick to try to deny the D-to-D pass. When the puck moves down the wall, the defenseman anticipates it on that side of the ice and immediately applies inside-out pressure. If the puck is passed down to the goal line, the net-front or weak-side

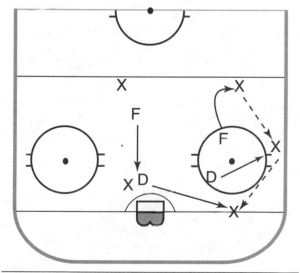

Figure 14.59 Box formation with three-point pressure.

defenseman immediately attacks the opponent on the goal line extended. The weak-side penalty-killing forward slides down to cover the net front. Figure 14.59 illustrates how three-point pressure works.

Remember, for this to work properly, each player applying pressure has to arrive at the pass receiver at the same time as the puck or no more than a fraction of a second after. The sticks must be extended to decrease the distance the defenders must skate before arriving at the point of attack. All four players must think alike and anticipate in harmony. At any point in the sequence, a player can use common sense and not apply pressure if it becomes apparent that too much risk is involved. This is most true for the two defensemen but especially so for the net front defenseman.

U-Maine and Four-Point Pressure

One of the ways to relieve the pressure applied by team's use of a three-point pressure system is to bump the puck behind the net to the other side of the ice. The late University of Maine coach, Shawn Walsh, employed four-point pressure by allowing the weak-side forward (who is already down covering the net front) to attack the opponent's third forward,

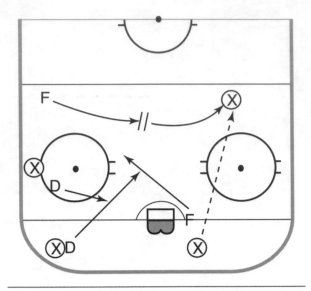

Figure 14.61   Maine four-point pressure.

providing the outlet on the weak side of the ice or behind the net (figure 14.60).

As this occurs, the original strong-side forward who initiated the pressure recovers through the middle and comes across to the new strong side, ready to cover the point on the new puck side. The forward who pressures below the goal line recovers through the ice at the net front to cover the other point (figure 14.61).

Diamond Formation

The diamond formation is a system that is normally used to counter an umbrella or 1-3-

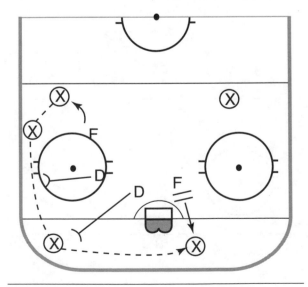

Figure 14.60   Maine four-point pressure.

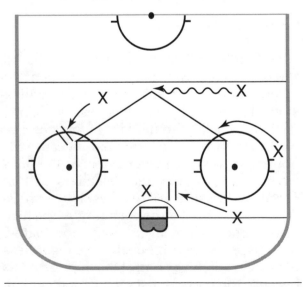

Figure 14.62   Opponent into umbrella formation.

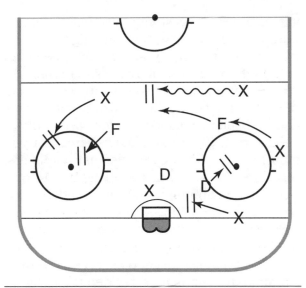

Figure 14.63 Rotating into diamond formation.

1 power play. If you are playing against an opponent with a top defenseman at the point who is smart and skilled enough to get the middle of the ice, your players should be able to recognize this and rotate into a diamond immediately. In an ideal world, you would like your team to deny the opponent the middle and negate the need for a rotation into a diamond penalty killing alignment. However, once in a diamond formation, it becomes more difficult to apply extreme pressure. Figure 14.63 illustrates how an opponent might rotate into an umbrella formation.

NEUTRAL ZONE FACE-OFFS

There isn't much to think about in this situation because the offensive element is, for the most part, eliminated as a viable option. The fundamental mind-set is defensive and should always be so unless it is late in the game and your team trails. The first key is to make sure that the forward not taking the draw is toward the middle of the ice, not along the boards. One of the two defenseman should cover the boards. This allows the defensemen behind the initial line of the formation freedom to react, particularly if the forward gets picked. The defenseman, along the boards on a lost draw, can immediately recover back and toward the middle of the ice to provide support. Ideally, the player taking the draw tries to win

the puck back to the one remaining defenseman who can then clear the puck the length of the ice. On a lost draw, the forward not taking the draw can forecheck passively at first, making sure the teammate taking the draw has had time to assume a reasonable position defensively.

Defensive Zone

In the case of a lost draw, the forward taking the draw should move out toward the strong-side point. The weak-side forward moves out slowly, first checking any seam pass options off the lost draw. One defensemen is on the boards, the other on the hash mark in front of the net. The board defenseman must recover to the front of the net immediately once the possession has been lost to the opponent's point (figure 14.64).

When lining up for the draw, the defensemen should position themselves so that if they win the draw, they can execute a play that results in a clear. Ideally, the defenseman positioned on the wall should be on his forehand. This allows for puck protection and a strong clear if that is the desired play option. Figure 14.65 illustrates a hard ring to the weak side off a won draw.

A slightly different play involves the weak-side forward going down into the corner. On this play, the defenseman on the boards

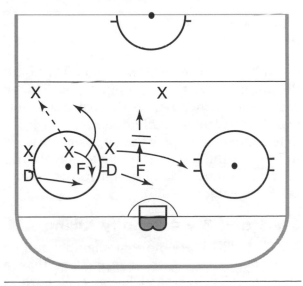

Figure 14.64 Defensive zone draw penalty killing.

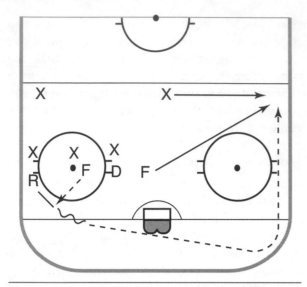

Figure 14.65   Ring on won penalty-killing draw.

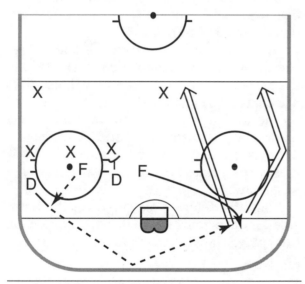

Figure 14.66   Weak-side chip on won penalty-killing draw.

doesn't have to be on his forehand. The board defenseman must simply chip the puck to the weak-side corner where the weak-side forward collects and clears. The net-front defenseman must pick the opposing forward in front of the net so that his teammate has time to execute the clear on retrieving the puck. (See figure 14.66)

3 v 5 and 3 v 4 Penalty Killing

Nothing will create more momentum and be more discouraging to an opponent than a successful 3 v 5 penalty kill, especially early in the game. The most important principle in kill-

ing penalties in this situation is that of limiting the space your team will defend. High-pressure tactics are not usually an effective means of killing off power plays in these situations.

One of the key questions facing coaches in this situation is whether to use two forwards and one defenseman or one forward and two defensemen (figure 14.67). I believe that you must use your top three defensive players, regardless of position. The exception to that would be beginning the kill from a defensive zone draw situation. A good defensive forward can win the draw and allow a clear right off the draw. Obviously, if there's a full-length clear, that player can get off the ice in favor of a teammate who is a better defender (figure 14.68).

You can't do much in the way of forechecking to stop the opponent from gaining the zone other than have a forward in the middle trying to deflect the puck carrier to the outside so that a defenseman can apply some pressure. It is risky to try too hard to deny the blue line because if they are successful in putting the puck by the defenseman playing too aggressively at the blue line, an odd-man attack easily results.

Once the puck is inside the defensive zone, clog up the prime scoring area with sticks and bodies to keep the puck on the perimeter. Regardless, your goalie will be called on to make saves. What's important is making sure the shots come from the side angles and a range greater than the top of the circles. Stick position is important, along with a tight formation. If sticks are properly positioned, the opponent will not be able to make passes through the formation, which will make it easier for the goalie to move back and forth across the net to make saves. The next key is to collapse the formation and attempt to deny any rebound shots once a player takes a shot. Finally, remember that the extended stick creates one and one-half yards of additional defense. If the defenders play with their sticks out when challenging a shot, they have a shorter distance in which to skate. It's difficult to block shots with the body on 3 v 5 penalty kills, but it is much easier to block or at least deflect shots with good stick work.

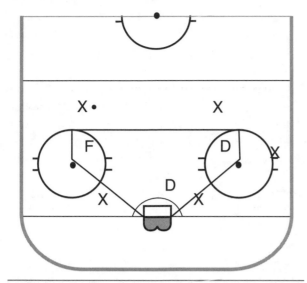

Figure 14.67 5v3 penalty killing formation.

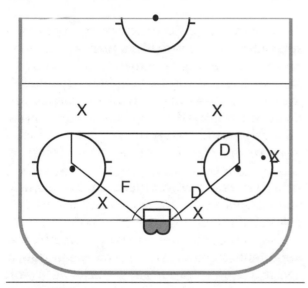

Figure 14.68 5v3 penalty killing formation, not movements.

The formation rule when you are two men short is to have two players facing the puck. If the puck is high, two players are high fronting the puck, and one is low. If the puck is on the right, two players move from the puck on the right side; one player is isolated on the left. Players never leave the area between the dots or an area five feet below the tops of the circles unless they can get the puck, or they are in danger of being unable to recover back to position inside the prime scoring area.

5 v 3 face-offs

In both the neutral zone and defensive zones, it is usually wise to have one defenseman

behind the formation attempting to win back the puck cleanly and then clear the puck the length of the ice. Attempting to gain possession with all three players on the line and opponents exactly opposite on the line of the draw usually allows the opponent to gain possession of the puck.

4 v 4 SITUATIONS

Situations of 4 v 4 afford more open ice and less congestion to the players of both teams than 5 v 5 situations allow. This formation places emphasis on skating speed and overall abilities of the players who are on the ice. Ideally, you will have a group of well-rounded players to employ offensively and defensively in this situation.

4 x 4 in Overtime

In recent years the NHL has explored ways to generate more offense and promote goal scoring. One idea proposed was to change the game so that full-strength play was 4 v 4 rather than 5 v 5. NHL regular-season overtimes are played 4 v 4 rather than 5 v 5 in an effort to increase the likelihood that a deciding goal will be scored in the extra 5-minute period. To placate teams who were not in favor of this rule change and to encourage more attacking hockey in overtime, the NHL agreed to award a point in the standings to each team tied at the end of regulation, then add a point for the team that wins in overtime. Previously, overtimes tended to be cautious affairs; both teams made certain they kept the point for the tie and avoided mistakes that would lead to an overtime loss and zero points in the standings. Most people agree that the change in the overtime rule produced far more exciting overtime sessions than in the past when it was played 5 v 5.

How much time should you spend working on the 4 v 4 situation? If your team averages only one or per game, don't spend too much practice time on this situation. On the other hand, if your team has capable offensive players who effectively use the additional space inherent with this situation, as did the

Edmonton Oilers of the 1980s, 4 v 4 might be as effective a scoring opportunity as a power play. If you have good offensive players, it can be useful to goad an opponent into taking a matching minor penalty. This was one of our tactics at the University of Maine, when we were behind late in a contest. Players like Paul Kariya thrived in the additional space. Conversely, if your team doesn't have people who can score and defend effectively in 4 v 4 situations, avoid these situations as much as possible.

The transition game is the key to offensive and defensive success in 4 v 4 situations. Fewer players on the ice make it easier to outman or to be outmanned on a possession change. A quick counterattack on offense will mean more chances to score. And a fast-forming, effective alignment by all defensive players will reduce opponents' scoring chances.

When I played college hockey, my coaches didn't want us to dump the puck in during 4 v 4 situations. The logic was that you couldn't mount an effective forecheck with only two forwards chasing down the enemy. I agree with that, but I also prefer that the other team have the puck with my team in position to force a low-percentage play than to try to maintain possession and allow them a transition opportunity. And whenever they attempt a low-percentage play, we need to take advantage with a transition and score.

4 v 4 Defensive Play in the Defensive Zone

In 5 v 5 defensive zone coverage, a key rule is to keep one defenseman in front of the net. That rule changes during 4 v 4 play. If the puck is in the corner and two attackers are playing in that area, both defensemen must be involved. The strong-side forward covers the point and the weak-side forward sags towards the front of the net, supporting the actions of the two defensemen while remaining watchful of the opposing defenseman at the midpoint (see figure 14.69).

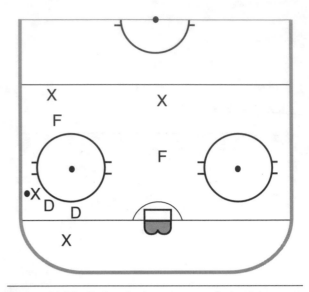

Figure 14.69   Defensive zone coverage 4 v 4.

Generally, defensive zone coverage in 4 v 4 situations looks more like a man-to-man coverage scheme when compared to 5 v 5 play. If the defenseman are playing head up against the enemy forwards, and the forwards are head up against the opposing defensemen, few problems are likely to occur unless someone is beaten cleanly 1 v 1. Anytime a defender is beaten in coverage during a 4 v 4, a 2 v 1 situation exists somewhere on the ice and must be played as specified in chapter 13 on defensive zone.

Use of the stick to restrict passing by the opponent is important to successful coverage. It is equally important to close the gap on an opponent with possession of the puck down low. If an opponent has too much time with the puck, his teammates will be able exchange positions, which can create confusion in coverage.

If an opponent tries to sneak a defenseman down from the point, the defensive forward must sag with him. Problems result when an attacking defenseman sneaks down to the net while an attacking forward replaces him at the point. The defenseman covering in front will be reluctant to go to the point with the enemy forward, so he probably should not. This is the most difficult situation to recognize because the defensive forward must communicate verbally with his defenseman passing the sneaking defenseman off to that defenseman

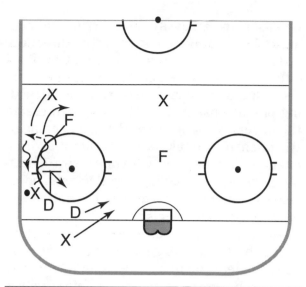

Figure 14.70 4 v 4 defensive zone coverage vs. sneaking defenseman.

and move back toward normal positioning toward the point area (see figure 14.70).

Another way to cover in the defensive zone during 4 v 4 situations is simply to use the rotating pressure discussed in the section on penalty killing.Rotating pressure, often used in penalty-killing situations, maintains pressure on the puck while exchanging positions.

4 v 4 Breakouts

With only two forwards on the ice, players must make adjustments on the breakout. How-

ever, the players on the ice still must fulfill and execute all the roles in 5 v 5 breakouts. For defensemen, the only significant change is that one of the two must look to join the attack as the breakout progresses from the defensive zone into the neutral zone. An attack is much more likely to succeed with three players than with two, making the involvement of one of the defensemen vital.

When a defenseman gets control of the puck and turns up or wheels the net, he must have a forward supporting on the boards ready for a pass. The forward on the weak side must skate across the ice, providing support in the middle lane. As shown in figure 14.71, the net front defenseman is ready to join the attack, filling the wide lane.

The defenseman jumping into the play must read the level of possession and level of checking pressure. If a turnover occurs, that defenseman must be in position to return quickly to a defensive posture. A defenseman's indiscriminate commitment to the attack will likely result in a goal against. Conversely, a defenseman's lack of offensive commitment is unlikely to produce any goals for.

Develop a patterned breakout to use in 4 v 4 situations. Such a pattern will generate speed with support filling all three lanes. As with all patterned or set-up breakouts, timing is key.

Figure 14.72 shows one defenseman stopped behind the net with the puck while the other

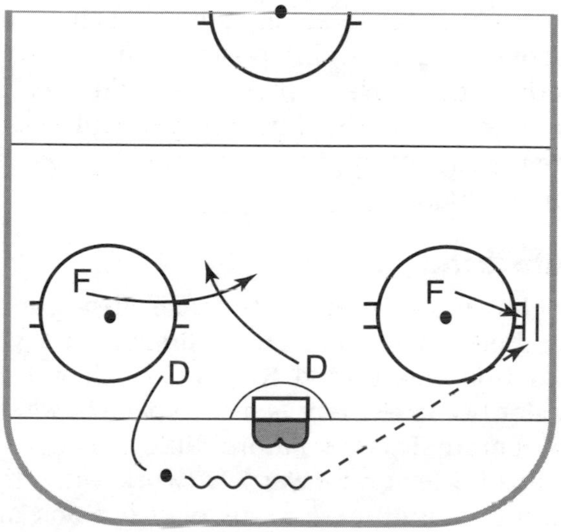

Figure 14.71 Breakout 4 v 4 situation.

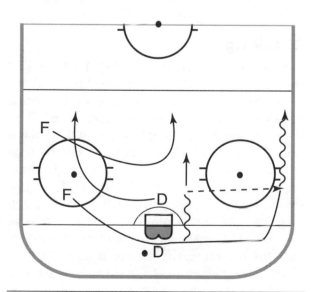

Figure 14.72 Controlled breakout 4 v 4 situation.

defenseman is initially positioned in front of the net. A forward swings behind the net, picking up speed; he can either take the puck or continue up the ice. The other forward is positioned high on the weak side, away from the swinging forward skating behind the net. As the play comes up the ice, the weak-side forward skates through the middle lane, providing support. The other defenseman moves from the net front up ice into the lane vacated by the supporting forward.

You can design many other patterns based on your players' ability and your own creative talents. As you do, remain mindful of the principles of support, creation of speed, and the filling of three lanes in a discriminating manner.

4 v 4 in the Neutral Zone

Follow these steps for forechecking and attacking in the neutral zone.

Forechecking

The first of two basic forechecking options involves steering pressure by one forward against the two enemy defensemen and forming a defensive triangle near the defending blue line. The other option is to forecheck aggressively with both forwards, mirroring the enemy defensemen with your own defensemen playing tight gaps against their forwards.

Attacking

Unless your forwards are much more skilled than the opponent, you will need to involve a defenseman in a support role as the puck crosses the attacking blue line. The defenseman should avoid leading the rush if possible. Ideally, all your players will be able to exchange roles. From experience in coaching high school hockey, I know that few players can handle this, especially forwards getting caught back playing defense as the opponent attacks. As the puck is carried inside the blue line, the forwards must be judicious in their attempts to pass to a defenseman coming up late. A pass to a covered

defenseman can easily result in an odd-man attack by the opponent in the other direction.

The best way to crack defenses in 4 v 4 situations is for forwards to isolate one of the opposing defensemen. Isolating and defeating one defenseman on the rush can create the necessary space to add a defenseman to the offensive attack and generate a scoring chance. Close support with one forward darting between the two enemy defensemen or crossing attacks can work but requires significant skill and precise timing.

To develop such skill and timing, use any 2 v 2 rush attack drill or transition rush drill where defensemen are activated offensively or backcheckers are activated defensively.

4 v 4 in the Offensive Zone

Follow these steps for forechecking and attcking in the offensive zone.

Forechecking

You can accomplish forechecking 4 v 4 with any of the penalty-killing systems described in this chapter. More important, keep a couple of general concepts in mind. First, no forechecker should ever allow the opponent he's zeroed in on to skate past him with or without the puck. This obviously would cause an odd-man attack situation. This is especially true for the second forechecker. Forecheckers must be judicious about finishing body checks, making sure that they can recover to a favorable position after making body contact. Next, players should keep in mind the principle of guarding the middle of the ice and attempt to drive the play toward the boards.

Attacking

Cycling and generation of offense off the grinds are both easier and more difficult in 4 v 4 situations compared to 5 v 5 hockey. It is easier because there is more space in which to operate. It is also more difficult because, with one fewer forward to work with, the possible combinations of play options are limited. Isolating one defender on the grind, creating a 2 v 1 situation similar to that described on the initial attack from the neutral zone, is an excellent tactic. Involving the defensemen, sneaking down from the point, or shooting from the point depending on the actual play situation is a quality weapon. Involving defensemen in the cycles is potentially effective and potentially dangerous should a turnover occur. Again, you, the coach, must accurately assess the abilities of your personnel and decide how much risk you can afford to take offensively.

Perhaps one of the best maneuvers in offensive zone play for 4 v 4 situations is to make use of the space behind the enemy net. As is the case with using this space 5 v 5, it can create enormous difficulties for both the opposing skaters and their goalie. If offensive players can gain full control of the puck behind the net, it makes it far more difficult for the defenders to cover the other three players; it has also been my experience that this is the easiest way to successfully involve your defensemen sneaking down from the point.

Late-Game Tactics

All the work that has gone into building a solid game, with the score close and one goal separating your team and the opponent, can go down the tubes in the last minute or so if your team is not prepared for 6 v 5 and 5 v 6 situations. Let's begin this discussion by dealing with the one-goal-ahead scenario.

When you're playing with the lead late in a game, *simple* and *safe* are the key words. Avoid passes in the middle of the ice unless you're 100 percent certain of completion. The boards and glass become your friends. By all means, if there is a direct pass that your kids can make safely, get them to make it. Controlling the puck is one sure way of avoiding a goal against. Taking icings with enough time to make a play and at least advance the puck to the red line for a dump-in is not a good idea. On the other hand, throwing the puck into the middle, hoping everything will turn out OK, is a less favorable scenario than an icing.

When forechecking, remain relatively aggressive. Remember that the opponent will be pressing mentally to get the equalizer and

that properly applied forechecking pressure can be very effective. It is usually wise to go with a hard 1-2-2, covering the boards initially. Defensemen should not pinch unless they can get the puck uncontested and force it deeper in the attacking zone. All forwards on the forecheck must be certain to beat the opponents back into the play. Body checks are not a good idea deep in the attacking zone during this time of the game because these can cause a player to get tied up, perhaps fall down, or just simply get beaten back up the ice.

Once the opponent pulls the goalie, your players should try to get to the red line before attempting any empty-net shots. This takes the possibility of icing and subsequent face-off in the defensive zone out of the mix.

If a face-off occurs deep in your end, it is usually wise to have both defensemen in front of the net on the draw (figure 14.73). Have the near wing cover the boards and swim through the blockout to get to the strong-side point man. The weak-side forward has to cover the midpoint but must check the slot area first for any sneak face-off plays where an opposing forward pops out for a one-timed shot. It is also wise to have on the ice two centers or two players capable of winning the draw in case one gets thrown out.

Most of the time, the player taking the draw should try to send the puck back toward the

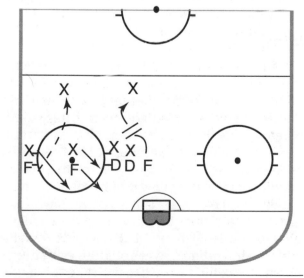

Figure 14.73 Defensive zone face-off versus six attackers.

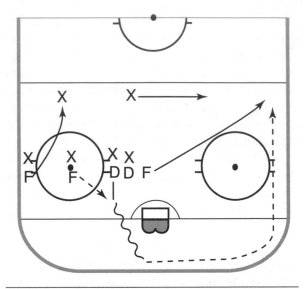

Figure 14.74   Defensive zone face-off breakout play versus six attackers.

goalie. In figure 14.74, the inside defenseman will pick up the puck and ring it to the weak side. The weak-side forward knows that the D is going to send the puck hard and must get to the wall quickly. Given this particular draw to the goalie's left, it would be ideal to have a right-shot defenseman because he will be on his forehand when ringing the puck. The weak-side wing has to be firm on the wall and make sure the puck gets out.

If and when the opponent does get the puck in the attacking zone, the wings must collapse to help out the defensemen and low forward around the net while remaining aware of the positioning of the opponent's point men. Remember that the opponent will have a 4 v 3 advantage down low in this situation, so help from the wings is essential. The goalie is an important part of the mental puzzle also. He has to know when to freeze the puck and when to keep it alive when that situation presents itself. For example, if only 3 seconds remain when the puck comes to the goalie, keeping it alive by giving it to his defenseman or sending it to the corner is a better play than giving the opponent a chance at another face-off. On the other hand, if 15 seconds remain and the defending players on the ice are tired, maybe freezing the puck to call timeout or get fresh players on the ice is the correct play.

Attacking After Pulling the Goalie

When you're down by a goal, roughly how much time should remain on the clock before you look to call the goalie to the bench in favor of an extra attacker? I prefer to wait until 90 to 60 seconds remain. The ideal time to pull the goalie is when there is an offensive zone face-off. It allows time for you and your team to organize, and use your time out to discuss what you will do on the draw and its aftermath.

The first objective in the 6 v 5 is to get control of the puck low in the attacking zone, preferably behind the net. If you can achieve that, position two forwards inside the dots but not too close to the net, and place the fourth forward directly in front of the goalie.

From this setup, your players simply take whatever is available. The player behind the net with the puck can begin to move out, preferably to his forehand, and look for one of the other three forwards moving to openings. The defensemen should stay out high in most cases because the opponents will likely collapse all five of their defenders near their net. Your defensemen must understand that if they get the puck at the point and wish to shoot, they must get it all the way to the net. Otherwise it is better to fire it down along the boards and start all over again.

The key is getting the puck to the net. It will be difficult to make a fancy play, so a shot on goal that produces a rebound is a great play.

6 v 5 FACE-OFFS

The beauty of a 6 v 5 face-off play in the attacking zone is that you can win the draw back to the point, and all opposing players can be blocked out easily so that your defensemen have time to run a play and get the puck to the net. Here are a couple of simple 6 v 5 face-off plays to stoke your creative fires. The first illustrates a simple one-timed shot from the point (see figure 14.75). The second play shows the board-side defenseman walk the line to set up a shot, or a one-timer from either side of the zone (see figure 14.76).

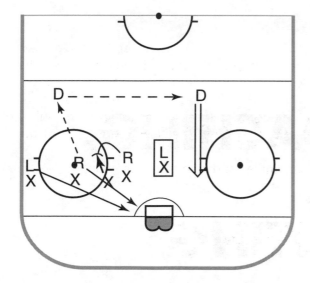
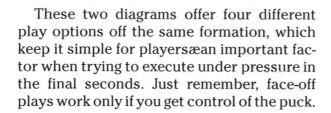

Figure 14.75   6 v 5 offensive zone face-off (a).

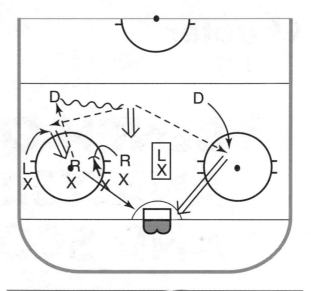

Figure 14.76   6 v 5 offensive zone faceoff (b).

These two diagrams offer four different play options off the same formation, which keep it simple for playersæan important factor when trying to execute under pressure in the final seconds. Just remember, face-off plays work only if you get control of the puck.

Everything I've shown you in this chapter on the power play works on paper. In games, it only works if the skill, the conceptual understanding, the ability to read, and the timing are in sync. And sometimes, it still doesn't work, even though everything is in sync! Remember that even the very best power plays fail at least 70 percent of the time, and this can result in frustration for your players. It will be even more frustrating for them if the coach demonstrates or acts out this frustration as well. Players who lack confidence or are afraid of failure on the power play rarely execute at the optimum level. So, coach, keep them up and optimistic about their power play potential.

Chapter 15

BENCH COACHING, ANALYSIS, AND SCOUTING

Finally, we come to the last section of the book! No serious coach should overlook the information contained in this chapter. For all of the skills you may possess as a coach, understanding the key elements of bench management, analysis, and scouting may mean the difference between winning and losing. What follows are some personal reflections about important people and events that have shaped these aspects of my own coaching life.

THE LOCKER ROOM BEFORE THE GAME

When I think about pregame meetings with the team, I immediately recall my time with Coach Jacques Lemaire. Coach Lemaire was a master of what to say to a team before any game. Jacques had a rather unique way of planning what to say to his players. He loved to sit out in the sun, smoke a cigar, and "give it a good think." It's tough to find the sun sometimes in places like Buffalo and Winnipeg in midwinter, but if it was out, Jacques was out. He had his pen and paper, writing down ideas while trying to predict how the players would react to his comments. He would talk to the players briefly before each game, no more than 5-10 minutes, but probably had spent between one and two hours minimum preparing his remarks. He was brilliant as the coach of the Stanley Cup champion New Jersey Devils, and I often wonder how successful he would be if he were coaching a team in Florida or Phoenix with all that sun!

When I lived in Vermont, there was an old saying Vermonters liked to use that over the years I grew to love: "The hay is in the barn." When the players get to the rink, they like to fiddle with their sticks, get treatment from the trainer where appropriate, chitchat with teammates, listen to music—generally, they want to relax with their personal preparation routines. Pregame meetings are necessary in most cases but should be as brief as possible, preferably 10 minutes or less. But coaches, most of the hay should already be tucked away safely in the barn by the time the players arrive.

If you have the facilities, you might want to show a few video clips that support your pregame message, or you might want to show a highlight tape with music dubbed over the video. Remember that more is not always necessarily better, and sometimes less is best!

You might say a few things about the opponent at a pregame meeting, but be careful not to talk too much about them. What your team does is much more important than what the opposition does. You might want to have the opponent's lineup on the board early so that the players can look at whom they are playing against prior to the meeting. If you want certain matchups to start the game, you may wish to post these on the board adjacent to their lineup. You might leave a few copies of a scouting report laying around for your people to read prior to the meeting.

I've always liked to talk about keys to victory—that is, three or four things that the team must focus on and achieve to succeed in the game. Some coaches call these individual game goals. Keeping it simple while avoiding elaborate explanations is vital to communicating your keys effectively.

Common sense should be your guide in deciding what to say to your charges before the game. If they look to be asleep, there's nothing wrong with a bit of fire and brimstone. If they look nervous, telling them why they will be successful and why they don't need to worry is a wise approach. Just read your players and all will be well.

THE BENCH

The decisions a coach makes on the bench during a game and the adjustments made in the locker room between periods can be the

Before the game keep players relaxed but upbeat.

difference between winning and losing. Basketball is well known as a game where the coaches can be decisive participants while fulfilling their responsibilities from the bench. In basketball, the coach not only determines who is on the floor and which substitutes enter the game under a given set of circumstances, but can also call the defensive and offensive plays the team will attempt to execute each time down the floor. Calling plays from the bench in hockey is unrealistic because the game is too fast and possession of the puck is too precarious to allow this type of direction from the bench.

Bench coaching for hockey involves two significant elements. First, the coach must endeavor to have the right people on the ice based on the situation in the game and the ability of the players the opposing coach has sent out. Second, the coach is responsible, at least in part, for the emotional condition of the players.

Having the right people on the ice at the right time is common sense. Making certain that it happens is sometimes difficult to achieve. As the coach, the more you can prepare prior to the game regarding how you will use your personnel in various situations against specific opponents, the better your chances of achieving the desired matchups. If possible, knowing the patterns of player deployment used by the opposing coach can help you predict which players will be sent out against your team.

One of the most important things to know in advance is which players the opponent will use on their special teams and who they are likely to come back with once full-strength play has resumed. Knowing the opponent's pattern in this area makes the transition from power plays and penalty kills much smoother when matchups are important in a game.

I always carry a card out to the bench that includes our lineup, the opponent's lineup, predetermined matchups, our power play, penalty-killing, and 4 v 4 units, and 6 v 5 and 5 v 6 units for late in the game. Any other information pertinent to the particular game or opponent is also included. In the heat of the moment, the brain can sometimes go blank.

Having information right in front of me on a card makes it easier to refocus. During the game, I also use the card to record any information I deem important for between-period analysis and discussions with the team or individual players. On your card, you might include some blank rink diagrams that can be used on the bench to explain situations to the players. If you don't have any blank diagrams on your card, it's a good idea to bring a dry-erase board to the bench so any explanations that require diagrams can be made effectively.

In basketball, substitutions only occur during whistles. In hockey, players can be substituted for both during stoppages of play and while play progresses. Substitution while the game is in progress is usually called "changing on the fly." This somewhat unique element of the game can lead to temporary matchups that are either favorable or unfavorable to your team. Again, if you are well prepared as to the patterns of the opposing coach, you may be able to get a favorable matchup or avoid an unfavorable one. If the opposing coach is sharp, there will be moments during any game when you have the wrong people on the ice at the wrong time. Conversely, the same will happen to your opposite number.

During stoppages of play, the visiting team must change first, allowing the home team to create the desired matchup. Thus, it is always easier to play the matchup game at home than it is on the road. To maintain matchups, it is important to win the face-off that initiates play. If that face-off is lost, the opponent will be able to dictate where the puck will go and then change the players they have on the ice.

Having worked with Jacques Lemaire in New Jersey, I had seen how his unwavering commitment to getting the matchups he favored was part of the reason for our success in winning the 1995 Stanley Cup. During my coaching tenure at Bellows Free Academy, I was seldom concerned with matchups. At the University of Maine, they weren't important either because often our third-line players were as good as the top line of the opponent. In my first experience behind the bench in Albany, we did not have a clear-cut advantage in personnel, so I had to be somewhat concerned.

A few years ago, while coaching in Albany, head coach John Cunniff had to travel to Vancouver for a meeting regarding the U.S. Olympic Team. He was forced to miss a game against Hershey, then coached by Bob Hartley, who would go on to become the head coach of the Colorado Avalanche in the NHL. I became the acting head coach in Cunny's absence. In the four seasons I worked in the AHL, Bob Hartley was one of the shrewdest bench coaches in the league. He was a master at getting the matchups that favored his team, even when playing on the road. He was adept at slowing down the game so that he could rest his top players and get them on the ice for more shifts. Many coaches in the league were frustrated by some of Coach Hartley's tactics, believing that they were not consistent with the unwritten codes of the game. But Coach Hartley had to be respected because he would use whatever tactics were available to give his team the best possible chance of winning.

From analysis of previous games against Hershey, we knew what coach Hartley's desired matchups would likely be. From this, I prepared our plan for matchups prior to the game. We were the home team, so it should not have been a problem matching our personnel against theirs because we would always have last change. But there was one thing I hadn't counted on—his centers were excellent at winning draws. So at every stoppage of play I was able to get the desired matchup, but 5 to 15 seconds after the drop of the puck, Hartley had changed the line and achieved the matchup he wanted. As a result of his strategy, my only option was to call the players on the ice to come off and substitute them for the players I wanted against the current group of Hershey players. We tried this for a while, but his team was so disciplined that they immediately got the puck deep into our zone and would change again.

As the game moved along I could see that my preoccupation with matchups was not yielding any positive results; in fact, it was disrupting the flow of the game. We had gotten behind and needed to score a couple of goals to get back into the game. I could have been stubborn and forced our players to keep changing, but instead I decided to try to increase the tempo of the game by just rolling our lines, no longer concerning myself with matchups. Because we weren't winning face-offs, and because we fell behind early, the game plan for matchups had to be scrapped midway through the game. We lost this game, but I learned a valuable lesson regarding matchups.

The Physical Bench and Basics of Bench Coaching

Before the game, you, an assistant coach, or the trainer should inspect the bench area to determine how player positioning and movement will occur during the game in the smoothest, most efficient manner. Knowing where you and your staff will stand during the game and making sure you can see well from that position is important. Knowing in advance any potential difficulties associated with your bench area might eliminate problems once the game begins.

Where your players sit on the bench is very important. Defensemen should always be at the end of the bench nearest your team's net. Lengthening the skate from the bench to the net front might leave just enough time for the opponent to score while your fresh players are still scrambling into position. If there are doors, the spare goalkeeper or trainer should be assigned to manage them. Players going on the ice should go over the boards, while returning players can come through the door.

There are several schools of thought as to how players should be positioned while sitting on the bench. Some coaches feel that lines and defense pairs should sit together, shoulder to shoulder. In this way, it is easier to communicate to them when their next turn is coming up, and they can communicate with each other on how to approach the next shift. Other coaches feel that it is easier for players to get on the ice quickly if they are not sitting side by side and possibly getting in each other's way when hustling out on a line change. In my opinion, the defensemen should never be positioned shoulder to shoulder with the partner they will head out onto the ice with on the next shift. If your forwards get tangled up getting out onto the ice, it's not great, but you can live with it; if your defensemen get tangled up, it becomes a much more serious problem.

If you are concerned with matchups and your opposite number is also trying to figure out which players you will throw out next, be careful how loudly you speak to your players. Some coaches like to tap the shoulders of the next players up. That helps ensure that players know when their turn is coming, but it can give away your intentions to the opposing coach. Once you have told the next group of players that they are up, each player should call out which player currently on the ice they will be replacing. This simple exercise conducted by the players helps avoid that terrible penalty called "too many men on the ice." When this penalty occurs, it is usually because two players each think that they are changing for the same teammate. The most frequent cause of having too many men on the ice is players not staying alert on the bench. Players are responsible for being alert, but an active coach can help keep them sharp.

Another basic situation occurs when there is a delayed penalty on your opponent and the goalkeeper comes to the bench for a sixth attacker. As coach, you have two options. The first and traditional option is to designate the center of the next line up to replace the goalie. If you wish, it could be the next right wing or the next left wing. The other option is to call the name of a player who is on the bench, indicating that he or she will replace the goalie. Personally, I recommend the next-center-up method because it eliminates confusion and ensures a quick and smooth change without hesitation.

Who's Playing Well

You may have prepared a desired list of matchups for a particular game, but as the game progresses, you find that certain players on your team aren't performing to their usual standards. Perhaps certain players on the opposing team are playing better than you'd expected. When these situations occur, you must be prepared to alter your plans. Also, when a line or a defense pair is playing well, it is often a good idea to get them out on the ice more frequently. Many coaches play two, three, or four lines regularly and seldom vary the pattern of how they come out onto the ice. I've found that it's best to get the players who are playing well out there more frequently and scrap the notion of just sending out the next line up in the rotation. This is also a good motivational tool for your team. Your players will quickly figure out that when they play well, they play more. Those who aren't playing well get the message that if they want to play more, they will have to elevate their performance.

Emotion and Bench Coaching

How you talk to players on the bench—your demeanor when things go well and when they go poorly—has an effect on the players. Perhaps the best thing a coach can do on the bench is to encourage and exhort rather than criticize. Certainly, there are times when corrections must be made. How you say something is as important as what you say.

Some head coaches avoid talking to players about tactics and specific game situations while on the bench, leaving this to the assistant coaches. This practice makes sense because a head coach can sometimes lose focus while giving directions about how a certain situation should have been played or what to do in the future and make mistakes regarding matchups, a more crucial area of responsibility on the bench.

If you have a quality assistant or two to work with you on the bench, it might be wise to let one of them assume responsibility for changing the defensemen and talking to those players while you, as head coach, manage the forwards. As an assistant coach in Albany, I was responsible for the defensemen. While I was at Maine, head coach Shawn Walsh handled the defensemen and I managed the forwards. Some coaches handle all the

Coach making a point on the bench.

changes. You simply have to find out what works best for you and your team.

Big Picture/Little Picture

To be effective as a bench coach, you must be able to recognize what is actually happening on the ice. As a young coach in St. Albans, Vermont, I made many mistakes on the bench, not because I wasn't paying attention, but because I didn't understand what to look for. At times I would be looking so intently for a specific detail of our team's play that I would miss the big picture.

There are five fundamental big-picture items. First, how hard is your team working? Second, how well are your players executing simple hockey plays such as moving the puck quickly stick-to-stick, movement away from the puck, and defensive reads and reactions? Third, who's playing well for you tonight? Fourth, what is the other team doing that either creates difficulty for your team or that you can take advantage of, and who is playing well or poorly for them? Fifth, especially on the road, pay attention to which players your opposite number wants on the ice against your various lines. Somewhere between the midpoint and the end of the first period, the answers to these questions should be evident. From this analysis, many of the little-picture items—forechecking patterns, power play alignments, face-off plays—that you may wish to attend to will be clearer and their importance to the game correctly prioritized.

Bench Coaching on the Road

The opposing coach has the last change, so on any face-off your opponent will dictate the matchup. The most important thing to consider is face-offs in the defensive zone. Avoid putting your weakest defensive line out for a draw in your own end. Ideally, you should have two lines that you have confidence in so that if the opponent sends out its top line, you are relatively safe. You should have at least one pair of defensemen, preferably two, that you feel completely safe having on the ice.

The most important element of matchups is selecting the right defensemen to go against the opposing forwards. Many times TV commentators talk about forward line matchups, but it is the defensemen versus the forwards that is the most critical and also the easiest to maintain during the course of a hockey game. If you can get both the right forward line and the right defensive combination out on the ice against the desired opposing players, you've done one heck of a job—or the other team's coach hasn't!

A Few Ideas to Consider

One way to gain advantage over your opponent when at home is to get fresh players out when the opposing coach has failed to change players on a face-off in their defensive end of the rink. If your team can win the draw and maintain possession of the puck, you improve your chances of scoring.

When playing against a team whose coach is very concerned with line matchups and stubborn about maintaining them, you can gain advantage by playing the lines that will keep the opposition's top people off the ice. This can work particularly well when your team is ahead.

Whenever there is an important face-off, especially in the defensive zone, it is appropriate to have two centers or two forwards who are good at winning draws in the face-off circle. If one gets thrown out, you have a backup. If the draw is won and the puck is advanced, you can change one of these players for another. Make sure all your players know the various responsibilities defensively on draws. If you assign a player who's normally a wing to take a draw, be sure he knows to stay with the opposing center and not run out to point if he loses the draw. That would leave a 3 v 2 in front of your net.

A vital statistic that one of your players or coaches should track for you during each game is face-off wins and losses. It's very important to know who your best draw players are and against whom they are winning draws for late in the game, when draws may become more critical.

Many coaches like to have balance on their forward lines and with their defense pairs, a practice I recommend in most cases. However, it's good to load up a line or two with your top forwards and have them working together at different times during a game. This can keep the opposing coach off balance.

Sometimes it is a good idea to save this strategic option for late in the game, perhaps with the score tied. It can have a disruptive effect on the opposing coaching staff and force them to think hard about how to counter it without the benefit of any between-period lull. Along these lines, you might want to pair your top two offensive defensemen and play them as much as possible with your top forward line.

A Final Comment About Bench Coaching

In the final analysis, bench coaching is all about using common sense. And yes, I too know the old adage that says "you can't legislate common sense!" However, if you are prepared, relaxed, and can view the big picture clearly, it will be easy to apply common sense to all situations and take the appropriate course of action. I've provided you with some guidelines for bench coaching, but you will undoubtedly develop more of your own while moving forward in your career. Remember that it is the players on the ice who are the show, not the coach on the bench. Mindful of all this, you are sure to be a terrific bench coach.

BETWEEN PERIODS

The first order of business after the period ends is to make sure your players are settled, trying to relax, and that water is available. Next, consult with your staff about what happened in the previous period, assessing the big-picture items first followed by any little-picture concerns. Once this has been accomplished, you should choose one to three items to present to the team. If you ask the players to focus on too many elements of the game, the tendency will be to confuse rather than clarify what's important for success in the next period.

Sometimes you might have an individual player who is struggling and may need some personal attention. This should be handled by an assistant coach prior to the head coach entering the locker room for the between-period talk. The head coach should wait to enter the room until two to three minutes before the players need to get ready to go on the ice, and the talk should be clear and brief.

These are only guidelines that I have found to work well with most teams over my career. There may be circumstances that require deviations from this model. For example, if your team was sleeping through the first period, playing without passion, you might want to shake them up immediately after the period ends, before they have a chance to relax. Obviously, if they were too relaxed in the first period, waking them up in the locker room right away can't hurt. Occasionally, an outburst of negative emotion from the head coach can be a good thing. Just like bench coaching, common sense should always be your guide in the locker room between periods.

POSTGAME

I have always liked to say something to the team after a game to provide some closure. However, I've worked with coaches who didn't like to say anything after a game. They simply made comments about the game the following day at practice. I truly believe that giving a postgame talk is a matter of personal preference, and you should do what you feel is appropriate at the time. One thing is certain, though. If you're not sure what you should say, don't say anything until you've had a chance to review the tape of the game. No damage was ever caused by saying nothing. Saying the wrong things after a game, particularly after an emotional loss, can create problems far more acute than the loss itself.

FILM BREAKDOWNS

The most common method of breaking down a game tape is by noting the scoring chances created by both teams during the contest. While watching the game and recording chances for and against, all other elements of the team's performance can be scrutinized. Remember when we talked about big-picture/little-picture items as they pertained to bench coaching? I like to look for big-picture items

while breaking down a film, as well as to look at the various micromoments that are chances for and against, or power play breakouts, penalty-killing forechecks, face-offs, and so on.

You can capture whatever statistics you wish off the film, but the statistics you keep should be ones that you and your staff consider important to your team's success. Keeping a basketful of statistics that you won't use is a waste of precious time.

You can use your scoring chance statistics to evaluate your players' and your team's performance. Scoring chances can be categorized by type (e.g., rush or initial entry chances, neutral zone counterattacks, forechecking, face-offs, power play, and penalty-killing chances). If your team is allowing numerous neutral zone counterattack chances in a game, it can signal an alarm for you and your staff as to what you may need to focus on in upcoming practices. You can also evaluate the performance of individual athletes by giving them a scoring chance plus/minus rating at the end of each game. I recommend that you develop your own based on your specific circumstances.

The most important use of video is to reinforce, teach, and motivate your players. When players execute effectively, take the time to edit out these positive examples to show the team or individual. If a player is having problems with a portion of his game, show him clips of how he is performing in those areas, and if possible, find a clip where the player executes properly, distinguishing between the correct and incorrect performances. Players love to watch themselves succeed, so one of the most fun uses of video is to create highlight tapes and dub music onto them.

When you are home watching movies on television, don't hesitate to tape them so that you can take out funny or inspiring clips that you can use to reinforce a message. While coaching with the U.S. National Junior Team in 2000 at the World Junior Championships in Russia, we made effective use of this technique to drive home messages about competitiveness and intensity.

Another good use of this technology is to videotape college or NHL games on television. When you find examples of college or pro teams and players executing skills and tactics the way you want your players to perform, showing them the clips will drive the message home in the minds of your charges.

Whatever you show, keep the following in mind:

- The shorter the better.
- Positive is better than negative.

PRESCOUTING OPPONENTS

Before telling you what I like to look for when prescouting an upcoming opponent, let me reiterate: The most important thing is what your team does, not what the opponent does. Knowing what you are up against is certainly very important, but you can paralyze your players with too much information and scare the hell out of them by building up an opponent too much.

First, scrutinize the opponent's lines and defense pairs, along with their top goalie. Figure out who their top players are and how the coach uses them in all situations. Second, figure out what makes them tick. What do they do when they are playing well that results in pressure being applied to the other team? How do they score their goals, and how do they give up goals and chances? What are their weaknesses, especially with their goalie? These are big-picture items, and you should never return from a scouting trip with questions in your mind about these areas.

As you are determining the big-picture ele-

ments, you can also take note of how they forecheck, how they cover in their own end, what they do on face-offs, on the power play, in penalty-killing situations, and so on. It's not brain surgery, so keep it simple.

SOME FINAL COMMENTS

There you have it! When I began writing this book, I never envisioned that it would be this broad in scope. But looking back, I believe that I've been able to touch on most of the important components that make up coaching hockey successfully. The introduction indicated that this book is designed for coaches at the high school/junior levels of play, and that is true. However, I hope that many of the philosophical aspects contained in these pages will have meaning for coaches at all levels of play.

Finally, whether you are coaching at the squirt level or in the NHL, the vast majority of problems we all face are basically the same. It's just that the context is different or the language may be more sophisticated! As such, we have a fraternity that is shared across divisions, across genders, and beyond geographical boundaries as well. I hope that you share your own insights with other coaches so that, as a group, we can continue to improve to the betterment of our players, ourselves, and our game.

All the best as your career unfolds, and here's hoping that your enjoyment of the game will grow as a result of having read these pages.

As always . . . "Keep your stick on the ice!!"

RESOURCES

The following books, manuals, and videos will assist coaches in virtually all aspects of the game. Any of these titles will provide you with useful hockey information.

BOOKS

Blatherwick, Jack. *Over Speed: Skill Training for Hockey*. USA Hockey.

Brown, N. and Vern Stenlund. 1997. *Hockey Drills for Scoring*. Champaign, IL: Human Kinetics.

Cady, Steve, and Vern Stenlund. 1998. *High Performance Skating for Hockey*. Champaign, IL: Human Kinetics.

Chambers, Dave. 1997. Coaching: The Art and Science. Toronto: Key Porter Books.

Chambers, Dave. 1995. *The Incredible Hockey Drill Book*. New York, NY: McGraw-Hill, NTC/Contemporary Publishing Company.

Chu, Donald. 1998. *Jumping into Plyometrics*. Champaign, IL: Human Kinetics.

Daccord, Brian. 1998. *Hockey Goal-tending*. Champaign, IL: Human Kinetics.

Davidson, John. 2000. *Hockey for Dummies*. New York, NY: Wiley Publishers, Inc.

Gwozdecky, G. and Vern Stenlund. 1999. *Hockey Drills for Passing and Receiving*. Champaign, IL: Human Kinetics.

Percival, Lloyd. 1999. *The Hockey Handbook*. Toronto: Firefly Books.

Stenlund, Vern. 1996. *Hockey Drills for Puck Control*. Champaign, IL: Human Kinetics.

Twist, Peter. 1996. *Complete Conditioning for Ice Hockey*. Champaign, IL: Human Kinetics.

Young, Ian. 1998. *Behind the Mask*. Vancouver: Polstar Book Publishers.

MANUALS

The USA Coach's Drill Book

The BCAHA Coach's Drill Book (British Columbia, Canada)

Lloyd Percival's Total Conditioning for Hockey by Lloyd Percival

Finnish Dryland Training Manual

Johnston and Renney. *40 of the Best: Canadian National Team Drill Manual.*

VIDEOS

Note: Search the following website for information on these products: **www.usahockey.com**

Entire USA Hockey Series

Gold in the Net, Volumes 1-5

High Performance Skating for Hockey. Human Kinetics, 1997.

Deking with Dave King

Defensive Concepts with George Kingston

Face-Offs with Guy Charron

Breakouts with Dave Siciliano

MISCELLANEOUS

The Off-Ice Officials Handbook

Officials Development Guide

Referee-in-Chief Handbook

The Hockey Administrators Handbook

Score! An Administrative Manual for All Sports

Parents in Hockey (video)

Stretching/Emergency Action Plan (video)

The Game of Her Life

INDEX

Note: The letters *f* and *t* after page numbers indicate figures/photos and tables, respectively.

A

aggressive forechecking drills
    hard 1-2-2 120-121*f*
    left wing lock 122
    2-3 pick a side 121*f*
    weak wing lock 122*f*
alignment of players in defensive
    zone 51-52
aspirations, players' 18-19
assessment of athletes 24-25*t*
athletic talent 37
attentiveness of players 4

B

backchecking through neutral zone
    basic concepts of 87
    breakout 5 v 0 into 3 v 3 attack 88*f*
    1 v 1 defense 88-89
    2 v 2 communication and decision
        drill 87*f*
    2 v 2 situation 89*f*-90
bench coaching
    basics 215-216
    big picture items 217
    common sense for 218
    emotion and 216-217
    player positioning on physical
        bench 215-216
    on the road 217-218
    significant elements of 213-214
    strategy ideas 218
    who's playing well 216
Benoit, Mr. 127
Blatherwick, Dr. Jack 34
Bob Johnson backward acceleration
    1 v 1 drill 90*f*, 91
books/resources 221-222
Bowman, Scotty 7
bread and butter drill 60*f*
bus trips 26

C

Canadian olympic 1 v 1 drill 91*f*
Caron, Jacques 130
centers
    breakout drills for wings and
        centers 70*f*-72*f*
    in defensive zone drills 68
    role of 55
chairman of the boards drill 147*f*
coach
    as leader 6-8
    in locker room before game 212-213
    roles of 2

    as teacher 3-6
    as technician 8
coaching, bench
    basics 215-216
    big picture items 217
    common sense for 218
    emotion and 216-217
    on the road 217-218
    player positioning on physical
        bench 215-216
    significant elements of 213-214
    strategy ideas 218
    who's playing well 216
coaching clinics 37, 38
coaching foundations. *See also*
    bench coaching
    characteristics of coach 2-8
    communication 15-18
    motivation 18-22
    purpose and philosophy 9-14
coaching in games. *See* special teams
    play
coaching tips. *See also* bench coaching
    between periods 218-219
    film breakdowns 219-220
    giving feedback 16-17
    postgame comments 219
    pregame speeches 22
    prescouting opponents 220
Coffee, Paul 197
communication tips
    dictatorial versus cooperative
        style 15-16
    giving feedback 16-17
    nonverbal signals 17-18
    postgame comments 219
    pregame speeches 22
Complete Conditioning for Ice Hockey 34
conditioning 33-34
Contingency Theory 7-8
criticism 16-17
Cunniff, John 215
Cunny 2 v 2 conditioner 93*f*
curl shooting drill 99*f*

D

defensemen
    communication drill for goalies
        and 63-64*f*
    and neutral zone offensive play
        101*f*-102*f*
    in 1 v 1 defense 88-89
    on penalty kill 195-196

    pinching by 119
    positional guidelines for 54-55*f*
    and scoring goals 130
    shooting drills for 142*f*-144*f*
    tactical breakout skill drills for
        66*f*-68*f*
    tactical tips for 65
defensemen shooting from the point
    142*f*-144*f*
defensive partner 65
defensive zone drilling
    breakout drills for wings and
        centers 70*f*-72*f*
    breakouts from defensive zone 63-64*f*
    breakouts from defensive zone
        face-offs 74*f*-75*f*
    center or first forward back 68
    controlled breakout plan 76*f*
    coverage after losing face-off 62-63
    defensemen and 65-68*f*
    goalies and 64
    initial drills for teaching coverage
        57*f*-62*f*
    tactical breakout skills for
        defensemen 66*f*-68*f*
    team drill for practicing
        breakouts 73*f*-74*f*
    wings and 69-72*f*
defensive zone play
    goalkeeping 43-51
    importance of 43
defensive zone play without puck
    aligning players 51-52*f*
    positional guidelines 54-55*f*
    2-1-2 defensive zone 52-54
deflecting/redirections drill 50*f*
depth chart 24-25*t*
diagonal shooting drill 99*f*
diagrams, key to x
diamond formation 184*f*, 202-203*f*
dot drill for goalies 47*f*
drills and practices
    conditioning and 33-34
    cool-down period 31, 32
    high-tempo practices 32-33
    planning 29-31
    warm-up 31
drills for defensive zone coverage
    (initial drills). *See also*
        defensive zone drilling
    5 v 5 defensive zone coverage
        conditioner 61
    5 v 5 defensive zone coverage

with multiple pucks 61
5 v 2 high forward drill 61*f*
funnel drill 61-62*f*
1 v 1 low drill 57*f*
3 v 3 low drill (bread and butter
    drill) 60*f*
3 v 2 low drill 59*f*-60*f*
2 v 1 low drill 58*f*
2 v 2 low drill 58*f*-59*f*
drills for forechecking practice
aggressive forechecking 120-122*f*
forechecking systems 125*f*-126*f*
steering and angling drills 117*f*-118*f*
trapping forechecks 122-124*f*,
    198-200*f*
2 v 2 dump-in and forecheck drill
    113*f*-115
drills for goalie
deflecting/redirections drill 50*f*
dot drill 47*f*
99 percent drill 46*f*
99 percent drill with second
    attacker 46*f*, 47
drills for neutral zone skills
advanced skills for defensemen
    101*f*-102*f*
advanced skills for forwards 98-100*f*
backchecking 87*f*-90
counterattacks 105-106*f*
defending against odd-man
    attacks 93-94
defending 1 v 1 rushes 90*f*-91*f*
defending 3 v 2 rush situation 95-97*f*
defending 2 v 1 attacks 94*f*-95
defending 2 v 2 attacks 92*f*-93*f*
face-offs and 85
forechecking off lost face-off 86*f*
initial drills 84*f*-85*f*
offensive hockey in neutral zone 97
rapid puck movement 98
regrouping 106-109*f*
support and creating isolation 2 v
    1s 98
width and depth in attack 103-105*f*
drills for practicing power play
    breakouts
three breakouts into offensive
    zone play drill 177*f*, 178*f*
three breakouts vs. four defenders
    into offensive zone play 179
three breakouts vs. two
    forecheckers into offensive
    zone play 178*f*
drills for puck protection practice
chairman of the boards drill 147*f*
cycles vs. 1, 2, or 3 defenders
    (three pucks) 149
get off the wall game 147*f*
3 v 3 low with two point players 149
three zones puck protection 146
2 v 0 cycling 148*f*
drills for scoring goals
catch and shoot drill 134*f*

deflections while moving 140*f*
drive drill 136*f*
drive drill 2 v 1 136*f*
fake and shoot forehand or
    backhand 132*f*
five-shot drill 140-141*f*
moving screen drill 138*f*
1 v 0 and 1 v 1 roof the puck
    rebound simulation 138*f*-139*f*
shooting under pressure 133*f*
stationary head on screen and
    deflection drill 139*f*
three lanes, shot, screened shot 137*f*
three shot types off the rush 133*f*
2 v 0 stiff stick and one-timed
    shots 134*f*
2 v 2 shooting under pressure 137*f*
walkouts or wraparounds 135*f*
Dryden, Ken 79
dump-ins 112-115

E
effort-based goals 20
Emerson, Ralph Waldo 6
enemy forwards, playing against 53-54
enthusiasm 6
equipment checks 30

F
false information 65, 164
false information drill 66*f*
feeder system 35-38
film breakdowns 219-220
flow forechecking drill 126*f*
forechecking
body checking 119
chase forecheck 197
concepts 119-120
defined 111-112
drills for aggressive forechecking
    120-122*f*
drills for forechecking systems
    125*f*-126*f*
drills for fundamental
    forechecking 117*f*-118*f*
dump-ins 112-113
neutral zone 80-82*f*, 85-86*f*
penalty killing and 196-197
skills for 115-117
swing tandem forecheck 198*f*
systems 120
tandem forecheck 197-198
trapping forechecks 122-124*f*,
    198-200*f*
2 v 2 dump-in and forecheck drill
    113*f*-115
forwards
advanced neutral zone offensive
    skills for 98-100*f*
breakout drills for wings 70*f*-72*f*
Mohawk turns by wings 69, 70
penalty-killing 196
playing against enemy forwards
    53-54

role of 55, 69
4 v 4 situations
breakouts 207*f*-208
in defensive zone 206*f*-207*f*
in neutral zone 208
in offensive zone 208-209
in overtime 205-206
funnel drill 61-62*f*

G
game schedule 25-26
game tapes 219-220
Gendron, Red 227*f*
get off the wall game 147*f*
give and go 165*f*
goalkeeper
common mistake of 46
communication drill for
    defensemen and 63-64*f*
deflected shots and 50-51
deflecting/redirections drill 50*f*
dot drill for 47*f*
focus on puck 44
importance of 43-44
in killing penalties 195
99 percent drill for 46*f*
99 percent drill with second
    attacker 46*f*, 47
positioning by 44-47
practice situations for 48-50
teaching points for 64
goal-scoring drills
catch and shoot drill 134*f*
deflections while moving 140*f*
drive drill 136*f*
drive drill 2 v 1 136*f*
fake and shoot forehand or
    backhand 132*f*
five-shot drill 140-141*f*
moving screen drill 138*f*
1 v 0 and 1 v 1 roof the puck
    rebound simulation 138*f*-139*f*
shooting under pressure 133*f*
stationary head on screen and
    deflection drill 139*f*
three lanes, shot, screened shot
    137*f*
three shot types off the rush 133*f*
2 v 0 stiff stick and one-timed
    shots 134*f*
2 v 2 shooting under pressure 137*f*
walkouts or wraparounds 135*f*
goal-setting
effort-based goals 20
performance-based goals 20
performance wheels and 21-22
for season plan 26-27
Gretzky, Wayne 150

H
half-ice drill 125*f*
Hamilton trap 199*f*-200*f*
Hartley, Bob 215
high forwards (wings)

breakout drills for 70f-72f
Mohawk turns by 69, 70
role of 55, 69
teaching points for 69-70
high player or third player 120
high-tempo practices 32-33
Holtz, Lou 3, 17
Hull, Brett 167

I

imagery 32

J

Jagr, Jaromir 196
Johnson, Bob 5, 90

K

Kariya, Paul 206
Knight, Bobby 7

L

leadership 6-8
learning styles 4-6
LeClair, John 11, 37, 127
Lemaire, Jacques 212, 214
Lemaire multiple 1 v 1 91f
Lombardi, Vince 7
low forward/center
    breakout drills for wings and
        centers 70f-72f
    in defensive zone drills 68
    role of 55

M

Maine four-point pressure 202f
Matteau, Stephane 161
mental elements of power play 161-
    162
mental imagery 32
Messiers, Mark 133
Michigan Tech continuous 2 v 2 92f
mistakes
    coach's 4
    correction of 16-17
    goalie's common mistake 46
Modano, Mike 167
Mohawk turns 69, 70
Montreal 2 v 1 95f
motivation
    goal-setting 20-22
    mindset 19-20
    players' aspirations 18-19
    pregame speeches 22

N

neutral zone, defined 40f, 78
neutral zone drilling
    advanced skills for defensemen
        101f-102f
    advanced skills for forwards 98-100f
    backchecking 87f-90
    counterattacks 105-106f
    defending against odd-man
        attacks 93-94
    defending 1 v 1 rushes 90f-91f
    defending 3 v 2 rush situation 95-97f

defending 2 v 1 attacks 94f-95
defending 2 v 2 attacks 92f-93f
face-offs and 85
forechecking off lost face-off 86f
initial drills 84f-85f
offensive hockey in neutral zone 97
rapid puck movement 98
regrouping 106-109f
support and creating isolation 2 v
    1s 98
width and depth in attack 103-105f
neutral zone drills (initial drills)
    angling v 2 defensemen 84f
    5 v 5 neutral zone scrimmage 85
    1 v 1 angling 84f
    trapping 2 v 3 85f
neutral zone forechecking 80-82f, 85-
    86f
neutral zone play
    neutral zone forechecking 80-82f
    Soviet hockey's influence on 78-79
    trapping 79-80
99 percent drill 46f
99 percent drill with second attacker
    46f, 47
nonverbal communication 17-18

O

O'Connor, Coach 5f, 227f, 228
O'Dacre, Paul 33
offensive concepts for power plays
    164-168
offensive zone drilling. *See also* drills
    for forechecking practice
    defensemen shooting from the
        point 142f-144f
    goal-scoring drills 132-141
    grinding in offensive zone 144-145f
    offense generated from behind
        net and dot plays 150f-152f
    offensive drills with initial attacks
        153f-154f
    offensive zone face-offs 155f-158f
    puck protection and close
        support 145-146
    puck protection drills 146-149f
offensive zone skills and strategies
    drills for aggressive forechecking
        120-122f
    drills for forechecking systems
        125f-126f
    drills for fundamental
        forechecking 117f-118f
    forechecking, defined, 111-112
    forechecking concepts 119-120
    forechecking skills 115-117
    how to dump the puck in 112-115
    scoring goals 127-129
    scoring in practice 129-130
    steering and angling 115-117
    steering and angling drills 117, 118f
    trapping forechecks 122-124f,
        198-200f

2 v 2 dump-in and forecheck drill
    113f-115
one-timed shooting 162-164
one-touch passing 164
1 v 1 confrontations 52-53
opponents, prescouting 220
organizational philosophy 10-13
overlapping 167f
overload 185-186f

P

partner communication drill 67f-68
partner options drill 68f
Patton, George 7
Peluso, Mike 112
penalty killing
    defensemen in 195-196
    in defensive zone 200f-203f
    forechecking and 196-200f
    forwards' role in 196
    goalie's role in 195
    importance of 194-195
    neutral zone face-offs and 203f-205
performance-based goals 20
performance wheels 21-22f
philosophy
    organizational 10-13
    playing style 14
pinching 119
pivot, look, forehand drill 66f
planning, season
    athlete assessment 24-25t
    generic ideas for 28
    goals 26-27
    schedule of games 25-26
    start of season 27
players
    aspirations of 18-19
    assessment of athletes 24-25t
    attentiveness of 4
    learning styles of 4-6
    player positioning on bench 215-216
    roles and positions of 54-55f
playoffs in season plan 28
Poirier, Huskey 98
positional guidelines 54-55f
power play
    advanced skills for 162-164
    breakout patterns for 171f-175f
    drills for practicing power play
        breakouts 177f-179
    mental elements of 161-162
    neutral zone regrouping on 179f-
        181f
    offensive zone play on 181-190
power play formations and options
    breakouts and regroups 189-190
    face-offs and the power play 186-
        188f
    5 v 3 power plays 188-192
    4 v 3 power plays 192f-193f
    general introduction to 182-183
    offensive zone options for 5 v 3

power play 190-192
 1-3-1 power play 184*f*-185*f*
 overload 185-186*f*
 summary on 193-194
 umbrella formation 183*f*-184*f*
practices
 conditioning and 33-34
 cool-down period 31, 32
 drills 31-32
 high-tempo 32-33
 planning 29-31
 warm-up 31
pregame speeches 22
pressure to win 9
prime scoring area 40*f*, 51
principle of support 39, 41
principle of time and space 39, 40-41
puck
 dump-ins 112-115
 goalie's focus on 44
puck movement, rapid 98, 182
puck protection
 and close support 145-146
 and retrieval 164
puck protection drills
 chairman of the boards drill 147*f*
 cycles vs. 1, 2, or 3 defenders
  (three pucks) 149
 get off the wall game 147*f*
 3 v 3 low with two point players
  149
 three zones puck protection 146
 2 v 0 cycling 148*f*
purpose of team 9-10

Q

quarterback and point of attack 182
quick up drill 102*f*

R

rapid puck movement principle 98,
 182
recruitment of players 35-38
resources 221-222
role modeling 8
Roosevelt, Franklin 7
Ross, Rusty 19-20

S

Sakic, Joe 133
schedule, game 25-26
school mission/philosophy 10-13
scoring area, prime 40*f*, 51
scoring goals
 best practice for 127-128
 goal-scoring drills 132*f*-141*f*

in practice 129-130
 shooter's illusion 128
 tactics for 129
scouting 220
screens, deflections, and rebounds
 164
scrimmaging 32. *See also* drills and
 practices
season plan
 athlete assessment 24-25*t*
 example of 28
 goals 26-27
 schedule of games 25-26
 start of season 27
shooter's illusion 128
shooting drills for defensemen
 point shot and backdoor shooting
  drill 143*f*
 snap shot two-step drill 142*f*
 snap shot two-step drill under
  pressure 142*f*-143
 trapped puck two steps off wall
  and shoot 144*f*
 walking the line drill series 143*f*-
  144*f*
short-term goals 26-27
6 v 5 face-offs 210-211*f*
special teams play
 advanced skills for 162-164
 breakout patterns for power play
  171*f*-175*f*
 breakouts and regroups 168
 drills for practicing power play
  breakouts 177*f*-179
 4 v 4 situations 205-210
 6 v 5 face-offs 210-211*f*
 mental elements of power play
  161-162
 neutral zone regrouping on power
  play 179*f*-181*f*
 offensive concepts 164-168
 offensive zone play on power play
  181-190
 penalty killing 194-205
 power play formations and
  options 182-194
 scoring on initial entry 176*f*
 speed and timing 168-169
speeches, pregame 22
steering and angling
 drills 117, 118*f*
 as forechecking skills 115-117
Stenlund, Vern 227*f*-228
stretching the defense 167-168

support, principle of 39, 41, 165
swing tandem forecheck 198*f*
Sydor, Darryl 167

T

tandem forechecking 197-198
teaching
 coaching and 3-4
 moments 6
 players' attention and 4
 preparation for 4
 styles 4-6
team-building experiences 27
team play principles
 control of time and space 39, 40-
  41
 support concept 39, 41, 165
technician, coach as 8
three zones puck protection 146
time and space, principle of 39, 40-41
time limit of power plays 162
training camp protocol 28
trapping forechecks 122-124*f*, 198-
  200*f*
trapping 2 v 3 drill 85*f*
traps, defined 122
turn-up shooting drill 100*f*
Twist, Peter 34
2-1-2 defensive zone coverage
 fundamentals 52-54

U

umbrella formation 183*f*-184*f*

V

videos/resources 222
videotaped games 219-220

W

walkouts or wraparounds 135*f*
Walsh, Shawn 202, 216
warm-up phase of practice 31
weight room workouts 28
wings/high forwards
 breakout drills for 70*f*-72*f*
 Mohawk turns by 69, 70
 responsibilities of 55, 69
 teaching points for 69-70
winning
 goal-setting and 20-21
 importance of 10
 pressure to win 9

Z

Zelepukin, Valeri 161

ABOUT THE AUTHORS

Red Gendron, Vern Stenlund, and Bob O'Connor.

Over the past 20 years **Dennis "Red" Gendron** has coached hockey at nearly every level—with consistently great results. As a high school coach he was twice named Coach of the Year for high school hockey in Vermont and led his team to four state championships; as an assistant coach at the University of Maine, he steered his players to an NCAA championship; and as an assistant coach with the New Jersey Devils, he helped guide the team all the way to a 1995 Stanley Cup. He has also coached the Albany River Rats, a minor professional team, and the US National Junior Team, a national select team that competes internationally. He is presently a professional scout for the Devils.

Through the years, Gendron has attended countless hockey symposiums as both participant and presenter at venues all over North America and in Europe. In addition to his coaching experiences, he is known as one of the finest hockey clinicians in the world. He has spent most of the last 20 summers working with players from the earliest stages of their development to those who compete at the most accomplished levels. He previously served as USA Hockey's New England Director of Coaching Education, and he has been very active as a Huron Hockey School Instructor.

Gendron has a master's degree in education administration from the University of Maine at Orono. He lives in Clifton Park, New York, with his wife Janet. In his free time he enjoys playing golf, coaching softball, and reading.

K. Vern Stenlund is a leading hockey instructor who played professionally and has coached at all levels. He is also a consultant to the Huron Hockey School and has assisted in establishing satellite clinics in the United States and Canada.

227

Maximize players' speed and power

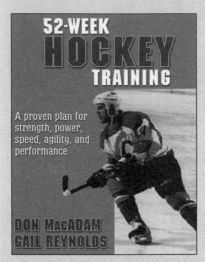

Anyone can play ice hockey by learning to perform the skills of the game...but you can only play at your peak performance if you get in shape. *52-Week Hockey Training* covers the essentials of hockey fitness and divides the year-round training plan into four primary phases: preseason, in-season, postseason, and off-season. Each season reflects a change in priorities, goals, and emphases as the hockey year progresses and provides detailed workouts to allow you to get in shape—and stay in shape—for top-level hockey.

2001 • Approx 200 pages • ISBN 0-7360-4204-0

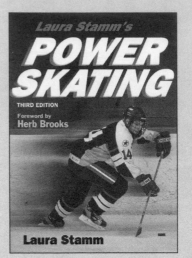

Develop explosive acceleration to get to the puck and goal with an extra burst of speed! Internationally acclaimed skating coach Laura Stamm has taught thousands of amateur and pro players how to get an edge by moving more efficiently on the ice. Now in its third edition, *Laura Stamm's Power Skating* introduces additional coverage of the topics most important to today's hockey coaches and players as well as the critical components to explosive skating. Let *Laura Stamm's Power Skating* give you the edge on the ice!

2001 • 240 pages • ISBN 0-7360-3735-7

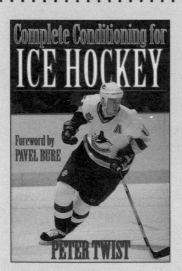

Maximize your training with NHL strength and conditioning coach Peter Twist. Packed with 125 on- and off-ice training exercises and drills, *Complete Conditioning for Ice Hockey* provides you with the tools you need to improve flexibility, endurance, strength, and agility. Get in rock-hard hockey shape to perform at your best!

1997 • 256 pages • ISBN 0-87322-887-1

High-Performance Skating for Hockey provides the very best instruction by one of the world's top skating instructors, Steve Cady. From essential fundamentals to advanced techniques, learn and master every key skating move to gain the confidence, control, and speed you need to excel on the ice.

To complement the book, the *High-Performance Skating for Hockey* video will challenge you to further develop and refine your skating skills to make every split-second on the ice count.

1998 • 200 pages • ISBN 0-88011-773-7
1998 • 53-minute videotape • ISBN 0-88011-821-0
PAL ISBN 0-88011-827-X

To place your order, U.S. customers call
TOLL FREE 1-800-747-4457

Customers outside the U.S. should place orders using the appropriate telephone number/address shown in the front of this book.

HUMAN KINETICS
The Premier Publisher for Sports & Fitness
P.O. Box 5076, Champaign, IL 61825-5076
www.HumanKinetics.com

Sharpen skills to improve performance

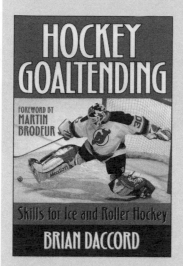

A sure-fire guide to reaching your potential in the net, *Hockey Goaltending* provides a well-illustrated and comprehensive look at mastering the unique skills and challenges faced by goaltenders. Accompanying 135 photos and illustrations is detailed instruction on the fundamental skills required to play goal, strategies for dealing with every shooting situation, and complete off-ice conditioning programs.

1998 • 200 pages • ISBN 0-88011-791-5

In hockey, the team that moves the puck more effectively usually comes out on top. Whether you're attacking the net, passing through the neutral zone, or looking for quick transitions on turnovers, sharp passing and receiving skills can carry your team to victory. *Hockey Drills for Passing & Receiving* provides expert instruction for moving the puck with speed and precision for a winning offensive attack.

1999 • 216 pages • ISBN 0-7360-0004-6

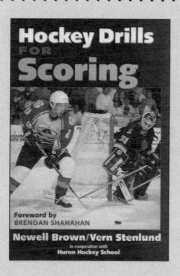

Make every shot count and become a more potent offensive threat by practicing these 70 scoring drills, many of which can be performed on ice or pavement. *Hockey Drills for Scoring* provides every tip you need for quick, creative, and accurate shotmaking. Through a sequence of competitive and challenging drills, you'll improve shooting technique and learn special ways to light up the scoreboard.

1997 • 216 pages • ISBN 0-88011-736-2

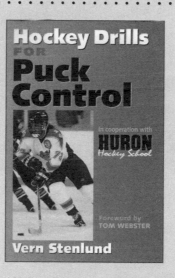

Hockey is a game of speed and strength, but it's also a contest of skill and precision. Teams that control the puck also control the game and score more goals. *Hockey Drills for Puck Control* presents 70 challenging drills— from fundamental to advanced and from solo practices to game situations—to help you better control the puck and help your team put more points on the scoreboard.

1996 • 192 pages • ISBN 0-87322-998-3

To place your order, U.S. customers call

TOLL FREE 1-800-747-4457

Customers outside the U.S. should place orders using the appropriate telephone number/address shown in the front of this book.

HUMAN KINETICS
The Premier Publisher for Sports & Fitness
P.O. Box 5076, Champaign, IL 61825-5076
www.HumanKinetics.com

You'll find
other outstanding
coaching resources at

www.HumanKinetics.com

In the U.S. call

1-800-747-4457

Australia.. 08 8277 1555
Canada 1-800-465-7301
Europe..+44 (0) 113 255 5665
New Zealand.....................................0064 9 448 1207

 HUMAN KINETICS
The Premier Publisher for Sports & Fitness
P.O. Box 5076 • Champaign, IL 61825-5076 USA